Cycle Babble

**James Randerson
and Peter Walker**

For the Guardian Bike Blog community

Cycle Babble

BLOGGERS ON BIKING

James Randerson and Peter Walker

guardianbooks

Acknowledgements

A huge thank you to the community of readers who have offered their thoughts, wit and criticism on the Guardian's Bike Blog since it started in June 2009. It is your enthusiasm and (mostly) good-natured debate that makes the Bike Blog one of the most vibrant and informative places on the Guardian website. Thanks also to everyone who has written for the blog or done interviews for the Bike Podcast. Sorry to those whose work we were not able to include.

None of this would have happened without the hard work of a huge number of people: Adam Vaughan, Jessica Aldred, Shiona Tregaskis, Felicity Carus, Damian Carrington, Sarah Phillips, Sean Clarke, Francesca Panetta, Janine Gibson, Nell Boase, Tom Happold and Ian Katz. We also needed lots of help creating this book, not least from our publisher Lisa Darnell, as well as Christine Ottery, Arwa Aburawa and Kristen Harrison. We have also received invaluable support from the London Cycling Campaign, the CTC and PC James Aveling and PC Mike Notley of London's City police.

Contents

Introduction
ZOE WILLIAMS

This is the litmus test of any mode of transport: what kind of person does it turn you into? Do you become a neurotic or a lionheart? Aggressive or co-operative? Are you friendly or do you turn into an idiot?

Flying makes people impatient, and drivers have a lot in common but can't get on; the more they have in common, the more poisonous they are to one another, like fighting dogs.

Trains are a mixed bag; some people are nice on them; most people are drunk. On these terms, which are the only ones that matter, cycling rules.

Cycling is the king of A to B. Because whatever our differences, we love one another. We smile and haloo; we overtake with grace; we cede passage grudge-free; we have a sense of community, even a Blitz spirit, and not just because we might be about to get run over.

We revel in our differences, which are plenty: Lycra mankini or tweed trousers tucked into your sock? Traffic lights – a suggestion or an order? Racer or hybrid, helmet or commando, freewheel or fixie? Nothing sours the bond.

If I saw David Cameron cycling past me, I would probably smile at him. I mean, look, I hope I wouldn't. I just don't know if I'd be able to help myself.

This unshakeable warmth makes it a pleasure to listen to one another's advice and stories and curiosities, even if they are nuts. I am, of course, referring to Matt Seaton, and his smart safety tips, like "take a tow in the slipstream of a bus". It's like English Jackass.

I love to read blogs about journeys that I know I don't have the fitness or the time or the knackers for. I love reading about Shimano racing shoes, or padded-arse cycling shorts, and all the equipment that probably even Bradley Wiggins doesn't really need. I love reading about the genitals of the Polish Cycling team, in their unflattering national colour (which, since you ask, is red). I love it when a Sheffield cyclist posts a terse remark calling everybody who doesn't live in Sheffield a pussy.

There are pleasures in this anthology that many of us will never know first hand – the excitement of a naked ride, described with respectful reserve by Matthew Sparkes. "Neil, who was painted bright green from head to toe, told me that for him it was a mixture of an environmental protest and a celebration of the human body." Or Ben Thomas's night cycle poetry, which smoked out all the other riders who like it best when they can't see where they're going.

Besides the naturists and environmentalists and the Tour de France riders, and the many awesome acts performed on two wheels, there are practical tips that I could read all day (my particular favourite, this from OxfordBiker: "Those red rubber bands discarded by posties are great for holding in your jeans at the ankle, emergency light fittings, stopping locks bouncing around etc"). It was actually from the Guardian Bike Blog that I learnt you could solve your D-lock storage issues by just shoving it down the back of your trousers. But from some angles this is not unlike cycling naked.

Drama is conflict, of course; it can't all be "aren't we cool, and don't we all love one another?" There is a lot of fighting, with drivers, with councils, with road surfaces, with the limits of your physical strength, with the laws of the physical universe.

There are obscure details and observations. My brother-in-law fell off his bike the other day and got a scab so huge it looked like a falafel stuck to his knee.

That's the thing with cycle lore: you read it, and you just want to join in. You'll use anything. You can't help yourself.

Chapter 1

Tales from trail and tarmac

If your daily commute involves a bus, train or car, I slightly doubt that you begin every journey with a faint but perceptible sense of anticipation. Weariness, boredom, anomie, impatience, yes; but thrill as to the potential for incident and adventure, I doubt. Unless perhaps you are some kind of performance artist bus rider.

But if you use a bike to get around, then I believe that every time you swing your leg over the saddle, your heart lifts a little at a moment pregnant with possibility.

For one thing, there is the choice that confronts you: which route shall I take this morning? Will it be the high-octane challenge of the main roads, where I must assert my right to occupy my space, and dodge and weave the buses and taxis and trucks, vans and cars? Or will I take the scenic route, on quiet back streets where I can slow to read the blue plaque on the town house commemorating some eminent Victorian physician or obscure Edwardian poet, or look up to notice a detail of Arts and Crafts masonry, or an urban kestrel hovering above the roof of a block of flats?

To set out on a bike is always to travel with the expectation of an encounter. We are not bound by the rules of public transport of politely pretending that our fellow passengers are invisible and that whatever temporary association binds us is purely a coincidence of direction and certainly not to be mistaken as a justification for social intercourse. Nor are we prisoners of the myth of invisibility of the private motorist, who feels impregnable in his (usually his) sound-system asociality, but is, in reality, a goldfish trapped in a bowl and a figure of pity and derision.

On a bike, stopped at a light, tourists ask us directions – because we know the topography of cities better than town planners, police officers and civil engineers. Better, even, than GoogleEarth, because we know contours and gradients too – we feel them in our legs.

We have words with the taxi driver who cut us up. We get short shrift from the cabbie, but sympathy from the rider behind who saw it all. And every few weeks, I run into someone I know. We ride the next mile together, annoying drivers by riding two abreast while we chat. A happy accident, this brief convergence of busy lives. Occasionally, I meet a friend for coffee where our morning commuting routes intersect.

But riding a bike is only incidentally social. Often, its finest hours are those spent alone, in that rare and desirable commodity of private communion with oneself: uncluttered by routine thought, just open to experience. It's a gusty day, a sunny day; the leaves are turning, the blossom is coming out; a cold wind puts a ruddy burn on our cheeks, a summer breeze dries our perspiration. We experience the seasons, feel the weather in its fine detail of temperature, pressure, humidity, Beaufort scale, sun strength. Our senses are engaged, yet our minds set free to wander.

I envy the round-the-world trippers, the cyclist explorers of continents. When I read about their expeditions and exploits, I always think to myself "One day, one day…" – even though I know I probably never will. But I don't honestly feel the poorer, because I do have my bike adventures. Every day.

Matt Seaton

Matt Seaton has written three books about cycling: *Two Wheels, On Your Bike* and *The Escape Artist*. He is also a regular contributor to *Rouleur* magazine.

A moonlit bike ride to remember

JAMES RANDERSON

What I love most is its sheer random pointlessness. You meet at a pub in east London, jump on your bike with a bunch of equally certifiable folk and cycle to a place that once rivalled the capital as a teeming medieval port, but has been mostly consumed by the advancing sea. Oh yes, and you cycle pretty much non-stop through the night.

This is the Dunwich Dynamo, a legendary, annual 116-mile summer bike ride to the eponymous Suffolk coastal town that attracts around 1,000 people riding a sometimes weird and wonderful variety of two- (and occasionally three-) wheeled steeds. There is no official start time. There is little to guide you save for a list of instructions and the crowd. There is no prize for getting there first. And there is no magic safety car to sweep up those whose body or bike has given up.

Legend has it that the first Dynamo was a spur of the moment decision to ride to the beach by a group of cycle couriers buoyed up by a few pints on a Friday after work. It still retains that anarchic, underground feel, but Southwark Cyclists, who organise the event, have made it accessible to anyone.

This year was my first Dynamo and despite a few half-hearted weekend rides to top up my bike-to-work fitness I felt woefully under-prepared. The longest I had ever cycled was London to Brighton – more hilly than the Dynamo route, but only around half the distance. And crucially, I didn't do that while my body was expecting to be comfortably tucked up in bed.

Surprisingly, it wasn't the missed sleep that felt hard though. Somehow, constant physical exercise and regular high carbohydrate snacks (a tip from some Dynamo veterans) fooled my body into thinking that being on a bike at 3am was normal. Much harder was the sheer physical and mental exhaustion of spending more than 12 hours in the saddle – and a dodgy knee meant that I did the last 30 miles pedalling practically with one leg only.

But even now, the memory of the pain is receding. I'm left with a lump-in-the-throat recollection of a very special weekend and a sensory experience that no motorist could understand.

There were the mates who stopped to help me fix my puncture. The lady floating above the crowd on her penny farthing. The bemused looks from staggering Essex clubbers. The lovely family on deckchairs outside their home in the Suffolk countryside who cheered us on and toasted us with their beers. The feeling of the summer's heat trapped under trees in the countryside while the night cool clung to dips and troughs in the landscape. The heady trill of an early morning skylark as the sun began to touch the clouds ahead in the east. And the wonderful cleansing dip in the sea – that was my prize at the finish.

COMMENTS

jeffd Yes, brilliant. Haven't cycled that far for many years

Highlights:

- Realising about 30 miles out that I would definitely make it, almost euphoric as a result. Even a six-mile detour didn't dent that feeling.
- Welcome on Dunwich beach from wife, daughter and grandchild armed with bottle of Speckled Hen. Never, but never, has a beer tasted so good.
- Sleep in the car. So deep, so peaceful.
- Sense of community.
- Lack of four-wheeled vehicles.

Lowlights:

- Pale into insignificance but the morning rain didn't help

HelenPidd Loved it!

Highlights:

- Watching a trail of flickering lights head into the distance as the sun set over Essex.

- Roast chicken sandwiches at Needham Lake as the sun came up.

- That banner outside a random house in Suffolk welcoming the Tour de Dunwich, asking whether "Maggot" was going to make it.

- The man holding the sign saying "ALLEZ!".

- Swimming in the sea.

- The first cup of tea in Dunwich.

Lowlights:

- Burnt eyelids after beach snooze

- Rain that started as soon as we got out of the sea and continued for two hours while we were already at our coldest and wettest.

The Étape du Tour: the agony and the agony

ADAM FRANTZIS

After a fitful few hours' sleep in the optimistically named Premiere Classe hotel, we are woken by a 4.30am alarm. Trying to eat as much porridge as I can keep down, I assemble my bike and slap on suncream in the pitch dark as riders fertilise the nearby park. And so the day I've spent the past six months training for begins.

I'm hoping the hours spent slogging up Highgate Hill in north London over and over again will be enough for me to finish the ordeal before the "broom wagon" sweeps me up and I have to face the ignominy of reaching the finish line by coach. At least the £1,400 charity money I've raised for Médecins Sans Frontières is safe; my self-esteem is another matter.

The Étape du Tour is the annual opportunity for amateur riders to tackle a Tour de France mountain stage with closed roads, support cars and feeding stations. Four days before the pros whizz through the Pyrenees, 10,000 deranged and dehydrated amateurs from around the world wheeze their way over the same course, taking in over 110 miles and three huge climbs totalling 3,600m. As if completing the course wasn't enough of a challenge, we need to average around 11mph or the broom wagon brings your day to an end.

This year's event includes the infamous Col du Tourmalet – 2,115m of pure pain, equivalent to cycling up Highgate Hill 30 times.

The other 9,999 Tour de France wannabees are mostly male 40-somethings sporting the latest kit, but there are a sprinkling of women and some wiry old men on vintage steel-framed steeds.

At the other end of the spectrum there are those on the latest carbon nanotube-framed dream machines, probably £2m worth of bikes all lined up in a row. Not the time for bike envy.

The clock hits 7am and the first riders are off. After an hour of a steady paced spin through the foothills – overtaking my pal Andy – I approached Marie-Blanque, the first, and some say the harshest, of the three Pyrenean climbs with a gradient that keeps on giving from 2 to 12% over its 10km. People were already walking.

I'd tackled this one before in training, so I was pacing myself well, keeping my heart rate down and congratulating myself on my decision to go for a triple chainset rather than manning up with a compact. But I ended up walking the last kilometre anyway, due to the numbers of riders packing the road. Some were relieved, others irate. I was having a flashback to Ditchling Beacon on the London to Brighton bike ride.

While eating a ham and cheese roll prepared by one of my soigneurs (my mum) in the queue for the Col, I bumped into the legendary Ron "Étape" who was one of the first Brits to ride the event and who has now tackled it more than a dozen times. Nice to see a familiar face – but still no sign of Andy.

By this stage the peloton had by thinned out after a climb through shaded woods, and with the amazing views as we reached the summit's feeding station I was actually starting to enjoy the ride despite feeling exhausted. People had now sussed out how best to replenish supplies at the feeding stations – leave bike, run in, grab food, return to bike. This made for something of a steeplechase over bikes to get to the tables strewn with fruit, cake and weird tubes of French branded energy gels, which I don't recommend. Still no sign of Andy.

After the great, long descent at speeds of 47mph to Argeles-Gazost, the next three hours were possibly the hardest in my life. The Tour riders get to climb the Tourmalet twice. Once was enough for me. The official climb took me 2 hours and 10 minutes (double what the fastest Étape rider managed) but before that there are several hundred meters of hurting as you head up the valley.

The temperature was over 35C, with very little shade, but we had sunshine; amazing views; friendly crowds cheering us on; kids lining up by the roadside to high-five you, and people cooling us down with garden hoses and bottles filled from ice-cold roadside springs.

Then there were the diehard Tour fans camped on the roadside for a week to see the pros go by. Fully kitted out with sound systems blaring out questionable Euro-rock, BBQs and spray paint to tag the road with the names of their favoured riders.

But it was still hell. By the time I finished the climb after just over 10 hours in the saddle, I was shaking and close to blubbing. As if that wasn't bad enough, I then noticed a text from Andy saying he was waiting for me and had finished 45 minutes earlier.

Would I do it again? Probably not. Should you? Maybe, but hopefully not all of you. There's way too many people already, and the mountain passes would need widening.

In the end, only 6,888 riders completed the course so that broom wagon must have been pretty full. As the official Étape website says: "A lot of participants were eliminated during the Tourmalet climbing, most of them were not enough prepared and trained." Take note if you plan to do it.

COMMENTS

pancakealley I watched it a couple of years ago, and it was quite spectacular! The image that stuck in my mind were all those grown men wrapped in silver foil blankets, shaking and crying, as they'd suffered from hypothermia coming down from the Tourmalet. Totally nuts, but respect.

shanklymad I did the Étape this year and I thought it was harder than anything I've done in the UK – those mountains just go on and on. Tourmalet was like something out of Dante's Inferno, people lying on the road, weaving all over the place. There were lots of guys walking up with £5,000 bikes (and shaved legs!). Still, a great event – wonderful organisation, marvellous scenery and a good esprit de corps.

badboy8 Having done the Étape this year I totally get the emotional outpouring at the end. I had to take myself off to a quiet corner of the Tourmalet to "get something out of my eye" once I'd crossed the line. In fact I feel myself welling just thinking about it.

The ghostly pleasures of night cycling

BEN THOMAS

Every time I ride my bike off-road at night, I get the strangest feeling. Travelling along in a little circle of light that stretches a few metres in front, there's a sense of passing silently and unseen, like a ghost, through something huge.

The mile through the woods on my longer route home is not one of the busiest sections of the National Cycle Network. I've never seen anyone else there after about 7pm. But that doesn't fully account for the complete isolation of that short black stretch of path.

Here in the still dark, quiet seems quieter, fast faster, and strangeness stranger. There are one-tonne concrete blocks on the wider sections, dropped there to stop cars attempting to find a way through, and on top of one is what looks like a dead bird, red-brown and skeletal, perhaps left by a farmer with a shotgun. Maybe a decomposing signal to crows that might venture into those fields. In the mornings I never gave it a second thought, but one night I had to slow down for a closer look. It wasn't a bird after all, but the sheared-off front of a frame and forks, slowly rusting away. Score one for the birds. The ride felt a little uneasier after that.

In the dark the bike, hundreds of components flying in close formation (its tyres, for now, unpunctured by blackthorn twigs) becomes a creature and lines from American poet Robert Frost always come to mind:

> The woods are lovely, dark and deep,
>
> But I have promises to keep,
>
> And miles to go before I sleep,
>
> And miles to go before I sleep.

A puncture or some other problem would mean a very long walk (assuming I still could walk) and a very long wait for a taxi driver who might not agree to ferry me home. Even if the iron horse keeps cantering smoothly along, I've still a little way to go before I cross into the county where my children are asleep. I won't be home for a while.

But there is a pleasure here that I'll remember all the coming week, simply toiling away through the forest in my little cocoon of light.

COMMENTS

hrababble Night cycling deserves a quiet street, or in this case path. Just watch out for those deer – a chum of mine was night cycling and along trotted a deer keeping time with his ride. The deer then dashed into the undergrowth only to come hurtling out a second later sending said friend flying and slightly concussing the deer in the process. The collision and landing also managed to shatter his elbow. He's not so keen on deer now.

Wowbagger Riding on a clear night is just perfect. Last year, a few of us did a solstice ride from Glastonbury Tor, where we watched the sun set, to Stonehenge, where we were in time for sunrise. Sadly it was a bit cloudy in the morning. Highlights of the ride? I was knocked off by a badger. And we braved the Challenger tanks which were practising their manoeuvres on the Larkhill artillery range.

Drspeedy I love riding at night for the enhanced sense of smell. Even in the winter, there are pools of scent from plants or the black frosty earth smell of open fields.

Idiot-grin fun in the dirt

PETER WALKER

The temperature is hovering fractionally below zero, the iron-hard grass is topped with frozen snow, and I'm about to go cycling. But what really worries me isn't the conditions, it's the bike.

Rather than tackling a treacherous off-road course with the familiar mountain bike aids of thick tyres, front suspension and powerful disc brakes, I'm sitting atop a skittish road frame with drop bars. The tyres might be knobbly but they still look alarmingly skinny to me. "This is the first time you've tried cyclocross, in these conditions?" the man next to me on the start-line asks, looking genuinely concerned. "Good luck. You'll need it."

Cyclocross is one of those niche sports that inspires undying passion among its fans but gets barely a flicker of recognition or interest from the wider public. Ask someone vaguely cycle-savvy and they might say, "Isn't that what they used to do before mountain biking?"

Devised more than 100 years ago mainly as a way for road riders to keep fit in the off season, cyclocross is a winter-only sport in which racers repeatedly lap a compact off-road circuit built around sharp turns, steep slopes and man-made obstacles such as wooden barriers or raised earth humps.

Some obstacles are sufficiently tricky that riders have to dismount, hoist the bike on to a shoulder and break into a sprint. So while the bikes aren't quite the same as their road-race cousins – for example they have different frame angles, more powerful cantilever brakes and thicker tyres – the emphasis remains on light weight.

The upstart newcomer of mountain biking might now be far bigger but cyclocross hasn't gone away. In fact it's currently more popular than it has been for decades, helped by the general increase in the popularity of cycling and the sport's relative cheapness, at least compared to mountain biking.

Which takes me back to this freezing Saturday morning in December. I'm at Herne Hill stadium in south London, which apart from the famous 1948 Olympics-vintage riding track also has a cyclocross course which snakes through the centre of the circuit and through the surrounding grassland.

For other riders it's round 11 of the London Cyclocross League, but for me it's my first ever go at the sport, although I've done a lot of mountain biking. My nervousness isn't helped by the icy conditions, or the fact that Ben from Condor Cycles, which are sponsoring the event, has lent me his own rather flash bike. He claims to be confident in my ability but looks undeniably nervous.

In the end, though, it is absolute, fantastic, idiot-grin fun. It's a huge challenge – with such thin tyres, riding lines have to be chosen precisely, while the constant turns and climbs require flat-out aerobic effort. But the endless laps of the same course mean even tortoises like me still feel fully part of the race, and you quickly get embroiled in individual battles with those of a similar standard.

Today, the weather even adds to the fun as you dodge the tumbling riders ahead. Even with the frozen snow and occasional sheet ice I only come off once. That, to my shame, happens when I pass the official race photographer on a bend and concentrate on looking suitably heroic rather than my racing line.

I won't be competing for prizes for a while, coming a lowly 84th out of 111 riders. But I'd love to try it again. There's just one potential obstacle: I'd have to buy yet another bike.

COMMENTS

Rangakoo That looks like damn good fun, especially with the ice/snow. All we have here is dust and rocks!

7moon This is going to sound silly. But cyclocross is BIG in Belgium (where I happen to live). Thousands of fans go to support their hero's at races and throughout the winter season we have live coverage of cyclocross races on national TV. Last year there was even a reality TV show about a cyclocross team. I kid you not.

mroli Looks like such great fun (apart from the cleaning of the bike afterwards)…

London to Manchester at 10mph

PETER ROBINS

Some time after midnight on a midsummer day around the start of the last century, the chief leader-writer of the then-Manchester Guardian mounted his bicycle outside the city's

Royal Exchange and set off for London. He thought he should get to know his country. And to give his knowledge "a backbone, something central, columnar and sturdy", he wanted a thorough memory of at least "one great trunk road".

"A push-bicycle was the thing," he wrote, decades later. "You certainly see most when you walk, but you cannot walk to London in a day, and one unbroken day's view of the whole stretch of road was the object. By car the thing would be easy, but then travel by car is only semi-travel, verging on the demi-semi-travel that you get in trains. You must feel a road with your muscles, as well as see it, before even your eyes can get a full sense of it."

C. E. Montague was 19 hours in the saddle, stopping for breakfast in Derby, lunch in Market Harborough and, as he contemplated giving up, "such a high-tea as makes history" in Newport Pagnell.

He reached Mayfair at 11pm. The England he saw must have seemed lost even by 1924, when he recalled the experience in a book called The Right Place. His great road is not tarred, and all the other traffic seems to be pedalling, horse-drawn or on foot:

"Riding forth from Derby, I breasted a powerful inward current of clerks. Outside this system of concentric suction the broad Vale of Trent was all in a hum. The air had been quiet as a nun before; now the multifarious buzz of grasshoppers, flies, bees and the rest was swelling insistently towards the dry roar of Dog-day noons.

"From each small town the rakish little carts of butchers were radiating lightly on their quest for orders; young housewives, not without baskets, were closing behind them the garden gates of trim villas and cycling away to the day's shopping in Shardlow or Loughborough. About Leicester the outward tide of butchers seemed to have paused, turned and set inward."

I'm going to pause here for a moment, too, to imagine grasshoppers being the most piercing noise on a national trunk road.

But even if the clerks are now protected by four-door saloons, and the butchers' carts have evolved into Tesco lorries, Montague is still right about the capacity of cycling to teach you a landscape.

If you want to feel the difference between Sheffield and Nottingham, between south Yorks and north Notts, try a stretch of national cycle route six. (I should warn you that the time I tried this, it also taught me not to go into a forest with just commuter lights: part of the trail had been ripped out to discourage motorbikes).

If you need a precise sense of the difference between north-west and north-east London, head out for Oxford and for Cambridge, comparing the Grand Union Canal with the Lea Navigation.

For these purposes, a winding leisure route, however picturesque, can be counterproductive. It's too hard to sense exactly where you are; at least, it is if your sense of direction is as bad as mine. The ideal is a straight-ish, formerly major road from which later developments have removed the scarier traffic. From the Oxford ride, the single-carriageway section of the A40 would be a fine example.

Which brings me to the other point of this blogpost. Ever since I read Montague's account of his journey, a couple of years ago, I've harboured a vague and unwise desire to retrace his tyre tracks. (This would be a good place to insert your choice of sharp remark about how much modern Guardian staff need to get to know their country).

I don't have Montague's fitness and determination – he was a mountaineer, and a man who volunteered to fight in the first world war at the age of 47, though he had to dye his hair and dissemble about his age before he could find a recruiting officer to accept him. But I've done shorter long rides, 80 miles or so, without too much difficulty. My current excuse is that I don't have his peaceful route.

Montague's great trunk road, "from London to Manchester, running through St Albans, Woburn, Northampton, Leicester, Derby and Buxton", looks to have been what is now the A6. This now finishes at Luton, but according to its Wikipedia entry, used to join up with the A1.

Probably best, for quiet cycling, that it no longer does. Stretches of the A6 look sleepy enough to fit my ideal; others really, really don't. Some midsummer night, I swear, I'll work out the necessary detours – perhaps you could help me do it – and set out for Manchester.

COMMENTS

orchidsoroysters I don't know that route but cycling on main roads is no fun. I spent a busy day on the A34 once and wouldn't repeat it.

If you can, travel by side roads/minor roads, but sometimes you can't win. One of the busiest roads I ever cycled on was in the Peak District, Buxton to somewhere. It seemed like a country road until the tea-time rush hour traffic appeared.

OakenGrove Sounds like a thoroughly uninspiring route. What exactly do you think you're going to see, riding through the desolate wasteland that is the Midlands? Boy racers? Off-licences? A pathetic post-industrial-but-not-quite-managing-anything-else-particularly-well economy? Hmmm…

If you actually want to ride somewhere pleasant, go further north, and stay up there.

Wishfort Make sure you have the right clothes for the trip – thick tweeds, a good cardigan and a nice cap, none of this fancy Lyrcra stuff. An oilskin is permissible if it is a trifle damp. Solid leather brogues as well. And a proper bicycle with as many gears as were allowed in those days.

No energy bars or performance drinks – a bottle of water and a couple of meat paste sandwiches should do the trick. And remember to take your pipe for a relaxing smoke when you stop to admire the view.

When the road wins

BEN THOMAS

A conversation overheard recently between two cyclists in Toronto:

"Watch out for the tramlines in the roadway."

"OK."

"Keep your eye on them. You're not used to them being there."

"Sure."

"Watch out. They'll throw you off."

"Sure. AAAAARGH!"

Until you've had control of your bike wrested from you by a groove in the ground, it's difficult to appreciate what a violently unpleasant experience it is. Once you know, you get the jitters when any linear obstacle comes close.

"Cross it at a good big angle," says your head. "Don't go near the bastard!" says your heart. So you compromise, try to cross it at five degrees, and it chucks you right off again.

That's one hazard. But what's sent you flying? Share your stories.

COMMENTS

louliddiard Earlier this week I was filtering through traffic when a woman flung open the door of her parked car right in front of me. No time to brake – me sprawled awkwardly in the road, narrowly avoiding my leg being crushed under the wheels of a passing car. I, of course, started my angry tirade of swearing until I realised I was outside a school and she had been dropping her kids off. Doesn't excuse the car-dooring but I did feel bad when I saw her kids in the back seat listening to my choicest swear words.

Theox I rode into the back of a bus at 23-ish mph. I was merging into a left hand lane and looking over my shoulder when the bus stopped. I wrote off the bike and my helmet but did absolutely no damage to the bus whatsoever. In fact the driver didn't notice and drove off. Very embarrassing.

JourneyMan4 Managed to completely stack it when accelerating from a red light in front of London Zoo. There were many, many children around. Their laughter still haunts me at night.

Flyswot Euston Road, about two years ago, cycling along the bus lane at a fair lick, probably 20+ mph when a white van (actually it was blue, but you get the picture) pulled across me from the lane to my right, without warning, to get into a side street. My evasive manoeuvre wasn't quite enough to avoid him, and the nearside rear corner clipped my front wheel, turning it 90 degrees and shooting me over the handlebars. The bike landed in the middle of the bus lane, I landed on my back and facing the way I had come.

From my reclined position, I got to spend what seemed like an eternity locked in eye contact with the driver of the double decker that had also been doing 20+ mph about 10 metres behind as it skidded towards me, collected my bike and finally stopped with its front bumper hovering above my knee. I'm not ashamed to admit that a little bit of wee came out.

Total damage: bent handlebars, a broken pedal, and slightly soiled underpants.

Plataea In Belgium if there is an accident between a car and a bike it is automatically assumed to be the fault of the car driver. This comprehensively cuts the crap in terms of not taking account of cyclists. There are still daft drivers – but generally it is not bad compared to the idiocy that I read here. God help the driver that tries to piss off after an accident. Also many of the police are cyclists and thus know what the score is.

Mmmmf About 15+ years ago, coming round the inside of that hideous corner from Parliament Square into Whitehall. Came up the inside of a bus which had slowed down in traffic, accelerating hard. Just as I neared the front some tw*t appeared running across the road in front of the bus, from the far side.

It was either hit him or bale off the side of the bike onto the pavement. Without thinking about it, I did the decent thing and hit the kerb. As I looked up, from my spread-eagled state, to see him running up the steps into the Treasury I realised it was Michael Portillo, then a junior minister. The really galling thing is that the f**ker didn't even look to see what had happened.

To this day my biggest single regret is that I didn't batter him, full tilt.

Naynaynay I've just bought a bike to cycle to work on. I'm beginning to regret it after reading this lot.

nebbish Could you run a Bike Blog article that doesn't make me want to take the bus, please?

When you couldn't give a 4X about riding politely

STUART MILLAR

Cycling etiquette, from the correct way to pass a lorry (see page 100) to the proper behaviour on a towpath (see page 70), is perhaps the most revisited theme on the Guardian's Bike Blog. It's certainly the one guaranteed to provoke the feistiest comments.

So I'm going out on a limb here and suggest that not all of us want to be polite and proper all the time when we ride our bikes. Sometimes we just want to put the power down and charge, using any means at our disposal to get past the rider in front and beat them to the line, and if that involves elbows or cutting them up, so be it. Obviously not a great idea during the morning commute, but the good news is that there is a two-wheeled sport that not only allows such behaviour but positively encourages it: 4X mountain bike racing.

The concept of 4X – as in "four-cross" – is simple. Four riders race shoulder-to-shoulder down a track littered with big jumps, drops, step-ups, step-downs and banked corners (called berms). When the start gate drops, it's a battle to apply the power down the straight and make it into the first bend ahead of the rest. Then it's just a matter of keeping the bike wheel-side down while fending off the chasing pack to the finish line. Imagine BMX racing but bigger, meaner and a lot gnarlier.

In the UK, 4X racing is booming. The National Points Series (NPS) is the biggest in Europe. And the success of the NPS means there are great tracks across the country for anyone who wants to give it a go, including South West Extreme and ukbikepark in the West Country, Chicksands in the south-east and Dalby forest in the north-east.

The beauty of these tracks is that you don't have to be a World Cup racer to enjoy them. Nor do you have to sign up to a formal race series like the NPS. All you need are a few mates (three ideally) and the competitive urge to ride your bike faster than them that you've probably had since the stabilisers first came off.

You don't even need much specialist gear, though a full-face or dirt jump helmet is a must, and elbow and knee pads are a wise investment. But any decent mountain bike with front suspension will do the job. Just lower the seat right down, push to the top of the start ramp and go.

COMMENT

Mmmmmf Waahay! Enough of the ethical living for once; cut to the bike porn – that's more like it!

Facing the Osijco moment

BEN THOMAS

Osijco is not a town in Baja California or a Japanese import/export company, but the term for a crisis moment that afflicts all cyclists at some time. Osijco is when you realise you should really turn back, or at least stop and sort something out, but a little voice says, "Oh Sod It, Just Carry On" – hence Osijco. Something somewhere rattling itself off the bike? Got a slow-ish puncture? Gear changes sounding like somebody shaking a cutlery drawer? Oh sod it, just carry on.

The Osijco moment can come on the way to work or on a transcontinental trip. The rhythm of the pedals and the wheels is the same – and the fact that every second you've gone a little bit further away from where you're thinking about turning back to.

In Douglas Whitehead's interesting series about his bike ride to Amritsar, he offers a few tips to would-be distance riders. One is: "Cycling with a rucksack is a sure route to back pain and misery".

Well, duh (as they say in Tajikistan). Has anyone ever really set off on a giga-ride with a large rucksack and not turned back before the end of their street? Yes, they probably have. In fact I can imagine doing it myself. On Acacia Avenue, it would have been easy to sort out the problem, and slightly annoying rather than painful. By the time I reached Nepal, however, my back would have become an open weeping sore from top to bottom and my thoracic vertibrae would have fused. I'd have had hundreds of Osijco moments en route, but each time it would have been more difficult to stop and turn round.

Ojisco moments don't have to build up to a peak of heroic stupidity. They are mostly fairly mundane, but still potentially hazardous.

When I started using clipless pedals, for example, I found the idea incredibly dangerous. But probably it would actually be pretty easy to twist my feet out – otherwise clipless pedals would be illegal or something. So I fitted them on my bike ready for the ride home and cycled round an empty car park a couple of times to try them. Yes, it was fairly easy to get my feet out. Would I be able to do it in traffic when a light turned red? Yes … probably. Osijco. At the first set of lights, I dropped as though poleaxed and lay thrashing around in the road.

I'm assuming these things happen to other people too. Please reassure me.

COMMENTS

thechief15 I generally work on the basis that if it's something with the drive train or rear brake it can wait until I arrive. Front brake, wheels/tyres/tubes however need taking care of at the time.

nocod I once fixed a seriously balding tyre with Sellotape for a few weeks, replacing it every three days, or when the added-on layers wouldn't get through the forks. One day at a set of traffic lights the inner tube escaped, ballooning up in seconds to the size of a football till it exploded, tearing the tyre and itself in half. Bemused by this and holding two strips of rubber I looked up to see to see four vehicles failing to go through a green light for their drivers laughing. Happy days.

sk8dancer Ah, the clipless slow motion fall.

I fitted clipless on my mate Pete's bike and we went for a long ride. I was looking forward to the inevitable moment when he would end up clipped in and on the road (I had two of these when I first went clipless).

We rode 20 miles with no mishaps and I was gutted until we reached a zebra crossing, surrounded by yummy mummy buggies, loads of kids and a busload of passengers. We stopped to let them across and it happened. Poor Pete grasped desperately onto the rail near the pavement as he went down slowly, to the rapturous cheer from myself and the masses.

Time for an end to charity bike rides?

MATT SEATON

One of the first bike rides of any distance I did – from London to Oxford, about 50 miles – was a fundraiser, for the Nicaragua Solidarity Campaign. That probably tells you how long ago it was: nearly 25 years. While Oliver North was busy backchannelling millions from arms sales to Iran to fund the Contras, we raised a few hundred quid to aid Daniel Ortega's beleaguered Sandinista government. My Sandino T-shirt long since fell apart, went in the rag bin, and probably saw its last service cleaning a bike.

But I'm grateful for the experience of that and a few similar rides I did in my early 20s, which proved an essential transition from being a daily commuter to a more aspiring sort of cyclist. It was a journey that eventually took me, via club cycling and amateur racing, to some of my most treasured cycling memories – from the Chiltern Hills to Alpe d'Huez.

So this blog is going to seem all the more churlish and hypocritical. Yet I feel compelled to ask: are there now too many charity bike rides? And aren't you just a weeny bit sick of them?

Perhaps they still perform the same valuable function of giving relatively inexperienced riders an entirely new and enlarged perspective on cycling and what it could be for them. But I believe the world has turned: when I was getting into cycling, we were, like the Sandinistas, a plucky but imperilled few; there were no sportives or Sky rides. Today, the choices are broad and varied, way beyond the scope of my twentysomething imagination.

Yet, almost literally, you can't move for charity bike rides. I don't get it: why should anyone make a donation to charity because you've ridden 50 or 60 miles across some nice countryside? Given four or five or six hours, virtually anyone can cover the distance. It simply isn't a physical achievement worth recording; it is, so to speak, a walk in the park.

I am all for raising money for charity – and I'd always happily make a donation to a cause championed by someone willing to swim the Channel, walk to Antarctica, run (as Eddie Izzard did) 30 marathons in nearly as many days, or some similar slightly insane feat. But I balk at being required to be impressed by something that many of us do most weekends anyway. For me, it would be like asking someone to sponsor me for going on a cycle touring holiday. Why would you?

If I'm introduced as a certified bikenut at a party (strangely, it happens), I often get asked: "Oh, have you done the London-to-Brighton ride?" To which my answer is, no, I've never done it – because it means sharing the road with 30,000 other cyclists and no one can even ride up Ditchling Beacon (the big hill behind Brighton, and the best bit) because of all the folk pushing their bikes. OK, so that's a tad snobby, but I do ride to Brighton (and back) at least a couple of times a year, sometimes solo, sometimes with friends. It's glorious, and even if it leaves your legs weary, it still beats charity fatigue, any day.

We should be honest with ourselves: cycling is a pleasure and a privilege, so why not own it as such? The only person you need to impress or satisfy with your cycling exploits and excursions is yourself. Just ride and be happy, without the guilt trip.

COMMENTS

BarryMcC Well, my dad dropped down dead four years ago of an undiagnosed heart condition. He'd popped out of the house for something. We never had a chance to speak to him again. Being a keen mountain biker I was over the moon to find that the British Heart Foundation was doing the London-to-south-coast again this year.

Well, after reading this article, I feel like scum now. Thanks for that.

stevehynd Why do you need to be impressed by someone's actions to donate to charity?

elyob I agree that if you can easily cycle 60 miles and do so on a weekend, it's a bit of a cheat to ask people to sponsor you. That's why I upped my challenge to Lands End to John O'Groats.

Personally I do still take part in the rides, but feel that the money I donate as part of the participation cost is my own contribution. I don't ask friends and family to sponsor me for this.

Now, can we get onto the subject of jumping out of airplanes for charity, or taking cheap cycling holidays down the Nile with a minimum £2,000 sponsorship?

TonySweeney People ask for sponsorship for challenging, difficult, arduous things. Most people who do charity bike rides aren't regular cyclists, aren't fit enough to do the ride and return with tales of how hard it was, probably because it was, for them, and partly to justify their sponsor money.

All of this tells people – both those doing the rides and those they talk to and who sponsor them – that cycling is hard work.

We need to get more people on their bikes. The way to do it is for cyclists to tell everyone how great riding the bike is. Not for charity bike rides to spread the myth that it has to be hard work.

sazza42 This article upsets me on two levels. As a very casual cyclist, it just confirms the awful snobbery of 'proper' cyclists. Why can't cycling be more like running which is so inclusive and supportive now that anyone can compete and not be looked down on?

On the fundraising side of things – have you any idea how hard it is to raise money? I think a lot of people think that charities should keep quiet and out of sight and the money will just come in anyway. The basic principle of fundraising is that if you don't ask, you don't get.

Chapter 2

Law and theft

This chapter deals with some of the hottest topics on the Guardian's Bike Blog – issues that we come back to time and again because they always spark vigorous and passionate debate in the comment thread. Is cycling on the pavement and running red lights (admit it, most of us have done it) really as bad as the Clarkson-esque mouth-frothers would have us believe? Why do police seem to turn a blind eye to motorists who misuse advanced stop lines at traffic lights? And is it legal, let alone safe, to cycle without any brakes?

The chapter brings the perspectives of police and ex-thief together, while getting to bottom of the surprisingly thorny question of whether bike boxes at junctions have any legal value whatsoever.

One thing that gets the bike blog community up in arms to a man and woman though is the perennial issue of bike theft. Most of us have felt that cascade of emotions from confusion to disbelief to powerless rage that comes with a stolen bike. Here we ask an ex-thief why he used to do it and pull together tips from the London Cycling Campaign and readers on how to avoid losing your beloved 2-wheeled steed. And on the question of what to do with bike thieves, the bike blog's normally mild-mannered crowd is of virtually one voice – hanging is too good for them.

James Randerson

Cycling without brakes means breaking the law

MATTHEW SPARKES

The odd emergency stop is an inescapable fact of life for the cyclist, which is why it seems odd to me that there are thousands of riders in the UK merrily cruising along without brakes. And they are breaking the law.

There are BMXs, often fitted with a freewheel and stopped with a trainer to the tyre, the braver subsection of fixed-gear riders and those whose bike is badly maintained to the point where there are no working brakes to speak of.

The most common, and probably the fastest, are brakeless fixed-gear ("fixie") riders. At least their fixed wheel can act as a rear brake, if they resist the rotation of the pedals.

They often claim that riding brakeless provides a heightened sense of awareness and demands a great deal of foresight and affinity with traffic, which they suggest is enough to keep them safe.

I've ridden fixed for several years and while lots of people I ride with do go brakeless, I have a front calliper. I may not reach for that lever often, but I'm glad of it when I do.

Lots of people argue that a skilled brakeless rider can stop faster than an inexperienced commuter with brakes, which I've always found rather disingenuous. Others claim that adding a brake in any scenario will improve the likelihood of a safe outcome should the worst happen.

But arguments over safety aside, the fact is that brakeless riders are strictly breaking the law in the UK.

Chris Juden is technical officer at the national cyclists' organisation CTC, and an expert on what is legal and illegal when it comes to cycling. He explained that there are two relevant chunks of legislation; one which sets out what can be legally sold as a new bicycle, and the other that mandates what a bicycle needs to be legal on the road.

The second one, or Pedal Cycle Construction and Use Regulations 1983, says you need two brakes: one on the rear wheel and one on the front. A fixed wheel counts as a rear brake, but you still need a calliper on the front.

"A front brake is necessary on a bicycle," he said. "If you're trying to stop a bicycle, or any vehicle, as quickly as you can there will be hardly any weight on the back wheel."

"If you're slowing down gradually the back wheel's fine, but if you're slowing down in an emergency forget about the back brake.

"It takes a great deal of skill to brake with a fixed wheel like that but some people can do that," added Mr Juden. "A skilled rider with a front brake will stop in half the distance. You need a front brake to be safe."

The Berlin police tend to agree. They have been busily confiscating any bicycles they see without two brakes, and in Australia it was recently announced that manufacturers could face fines of up to A\$1.1m (£630,000) for supplying fixies new.

In the US the law varies from state to state, but in most places it says you need to have brakes fitted which allow you to skid on a dry pavement. That would suggest that just a fixed wheel would be enough, as long as the rider can learn to skid.

There have been instances of people being charged anyway, because of the vague wording, leading some advocacy groups to fight for explicit wording to allow fixed gears without brakes.

I asked the Metropolitan Police for their views and they told me that although technically illegal, brakeless riders were "not an issue that our traffic branch have come across".

However, they went on to say that if a rider was caught then they would be summonsed to court rather than being issued with a fixed penalty notice, as you might get for jumping a red light.

What the outcome would be then is unclear, as there's no record at all of it happening. Considering the Met's response it seems unlikely that anyone will find out soon, either. I've certainly never heard of anyone being pulled over for having no front brake.

The real problem for brakeless riders in the UK could come after an accident. If your bike is not legally roadworthy then any insurance you have could be invalidated, and you could possibly be left open to legal action by any injured parties.

COMMENTS

Cowspassage Unfortunately, some people reckon their bikes look a lot cooler without unsightly brakes, levers and cables. They are willing to increase their chances of death for this vanity.

Trois "Lots of people argue that a skilled brakeless rider can stop faster than an inexperienced commuter with brakes."

Maybe so, but when do you decide that you personally are "skilled"? Lots of studies of drivers have shown that people routinely over-estimate their own abilities. I am sure the same psychology applies to us cyclists.

BarryMcC The vast proportion of braking efficiency comes from the front. This is why cars have the bias set to the front, and a motorcyclist (as I believe) will favour the front brake.

This is because when you travel forward the weight of the bike+rider is behind the front wheel. When you apply the front brake, the front tyre wants to dig into the ground – seen as 'brake dive' on MTB's/etc. This downward force on the tyre imparts even more friction into the tyre+road. Therefore, you stop quickly.

afrobabe dang this is a haven of smug righteousness....

Riding brakeless may not be strictly legal, but it is cool, and therefore will continue whether most of the opinionated on here like it or not.

SatelliteOne "Lots of people argue that a skilled brakeless rider can stop faster than an inexperienced commuter with brakes."

Some people reckon that they're better drivers when they're pissed than most people sober, it doesn't mean that they're right.

iainl Hopefully Darwin will sort this little piece of stupidity out before they harm anyone else.

Bikes are a must-have for modern civil disobedience

PETER WALKER

When the location of this year's Climate Camp protest was finally revealed on Wednesday, the first activists to arrive were a select group in rented vans, tasked with setting up tripods and fencing off a section of the land at Blackheath, south-east London.

But shortly afterwards, the first influx of protesters taking part in the "swoop" on the site from a series of meeting points around the capital was a contingent of around 150 people, all riding bicycles. They – with me in tow – had spent about 90 minutes pedalling en masse around central London, awaiting word on where the camp would be.

It's a fair bet these days that whenever there is an environmentally based protest, particularly in an urban area, a gang of cyclists will be involved somewhere or other. In fact, bikes are becoming a must-have element of all sorts of modern civil disobedience.

Many of these bike-based actions are making a point about transport and cycling issues: Critical Mass, the group celebration of taking over a city's streets with bikes is a good example, and is held regularly in dozens of places around the world

There are exceptions: last year activists from one Indian political party staged a bike rally to protest, somewhat counterintuitively, against a rise in fuel prices. And there is the long-established, if still baffling to some, practice of naked bike rides.

So what is it that makes the bicycle and the demonstration such good companions? To me, there are two factors at play.

Firstly, if you're in a group, there is something undeniably liberating about riding around a city surrounded by cyclists. I've never been on a Critical Mass ride, so going to Blackheath was a strange sensation – no longer a vulnerable solo rider lined up against the massed metal forces of the motorised traffic, I was part of an entity too big to ignore or shove unthinkingly into the kerb.

Second, if you're a solo campaigner in an urban environment then the bike is the mode of transport most guaranteed to get you to your protest on time and – perhaps more important still – give you the best chance of slipping away from pursuing authorities. When I worked for another news organisation in Beijing I'd regularly pedal to meetings or protests, nipping down narrow lanes to shake off the unmarked police cars, which routinely trail foreign journalists in China.

There is, of course, a catch for protesters: the police – at least in parts of the UK – have noticed this and now send officers out on bikes of their own. Some of the police riders look noticeably fitter and keener than they once did. Perhaps it's just a matter of time before we see Bullitt-style car chases around our cities – but this time on bikes.

COMMENT

BalbKubrox Oh dear: and I'd just thought that I was getting to work every day and going out for a breath of fresh air at weekends. Now I find that I'm part of a worldwide insurrectionary movement dedicated to overthrowing globalised capitalism as we know it.

Why I was foolish to mock police bike training

PETER WALKER

I'm walking through the 1960s housing estate when a policeman, cycling furiously, overtakes. In a single elegant move he rear-wheel skids his bike to halt, drops the bike and approaches, arm held out: "Just a second, sir." I take an instinctive step back – straight on to the front wheel of another police bike. A burly arm pulls me backwards across the handlebars. Helpless, my collar is well and truly felt.

This is, luckily, a training exercise, but if the officers involved – PCs James Aveling and Mike Notley – had been minded to take me in for questioning you could understand why.

About three weeks ago I wrote what was, in retrospect, a slightly foolish post for this blog. Why, I wondered, did police in Northampton need 10 hours of training before they were allowed out on a bike? How hard could it be? A number of readers put me right. "The 10 hour training is NOT about learning to ride a bike, it is about using the bike as a Policing Tool," wrote secretcyclist, a police cycle patrol instructor, "It teaches such matters as low speed riding skills to deal safely with negotiating crowded areas (what is the slowest you can safely ride your bike?), obstacle riding (down steps, up steps, pothole doging, safe emergency braking) and using the bike as a means of protection or defence."

Soon afterwards, London's City police, the only force in the UK with a full-time, dedicated cycling squad, got in touch. Their training course wasn't 10 hours, but four days. Would I care to try a condensed version?

And so it was, earlier this week, that I was wheeling my mountain bike through Snow Hill police station, headquarters of the force's cycle team. I feared the worst, but Aveling, a bike patrol officer for nine years and now head instructor, could hardly have been nicer.

We began with a ride through the streets, Aveling and Notley, a new recruit to the patrol, following behind and noting my mistakes. Despite years of commuting experience it seems I made several, not least glancing carelessly behind me using peripheral vision rather than twisting round for a proper look. Aveling even gently rebuked me for using the middle of a narrow cycle lane. I should have been on its far edge, nearer the middle of the road.

Aveling also classes my failure to wear a reflective fluorescent vest a "mistake" – in fact my biggest – something we agree to differ about.

I'm given a taster of some of the many skills cycling police are expected to master. To start, there's a lot of fiddly riding in tight circles around cones to perfect low-speed handling skills.

More fun is going up and down stairs. Descending is fairly straightforward to anyone who's been mountain biking – weight to the back, bum over the rear wheel – but going up is less intuitive. "It's easy," Aveling tells me. "Get some momentum going, stand up in the saddle and stop pedalling. Don't try and lift the wheels, just hit the first step straight on – treat it like it was a normal slope." It works – the bike bumps itself up the stairs as I cling on.

This is simple stuff for Aveling, who can chase a wrongdoer more or less anywhere. At 6ft 3in and 15 stone he is essentially your urban criminal's worst nightmare. Recently he pursued a pair of miscreants down a flight of steps into a Tube station. "They gave up when they saw I'd followed them," he says. "One of them told me, 'You're a nutter.'"

He and Notley then show me their method for tackling fugitives. With all the skidding about it's a bit like The Sweeney but with a mountain bike instead of a Ford Granada. Aveling demonstrates the various ways to deal with potentially violent ne'er do wells. The most dramatic involves propelling the bike forwards into them, handlebars first. This would hurt, given the weight of equipment the bikes carry in panniers.

Away from the excitement, Aveling stresses how difficult it can be when such training is mocked.

He points to the case of a police community support officer with no training who was killed by a skip truck on his first day of bike patrol in Wigan in 2007. "Police drivers get weeks of training, so do motorcyclists," says Aveling. "Why should the cyclists be different?"

COMMENTS

steford I'm all for the anyone, including the police, using bikes but when those police on bikes only seem to target cyclists (I saw some young children being rebuked yesterday in Shepherd's Bush for riding on the pavement) it makes you want to see them back in cars being able to effectively follow and stop drivers and deal with driving offences.

InebriatEd Fantastic article. I was rather ashamed at the way the papers attacked the cycling manual.

Why do police target red-light jumpers?

PETER WALKER

Why do police devote time to ticketing cyclists who jump red lights? The obvious answer is: because they're breaking the law. But of course it's more complex than that.

Every police force has to prioritise. Given, some cyclists ask, that of the 600 or so pedestrians killed in the UK each year, about one on average is struck by a bike, why bother? Why not devote the resources to real traffic dangers like light-jumping cars and trucks?

I got a chance to put this to the police force at the very front line of urban cycling in the UK. London's City police are known for being particularly active in targeting cyclists. In fact, many London riders see the force as decidedly anti-bike, a curious paradox given that it has the country's only dedicated cycling police unit.

"I don't think we're anti-cyclist. A couple of years ago we could perhaps have been accused of that, but things have changed," said Superintendent Lorraine Cussen of Snow Hill police station.

Why, then, do I see so many City officers pulling over cyclists? The main answer, it seems, is public demand.

Police forces are now obliged by central government to tackle issues flagged up by local communities. In the City, this tends to bring complaints about rough sleepers and law-flouting cyclists.

"When we ask the community what they want us to do, cycling comes up again and again," Cussen says. "It's the same in other police areas – when people are asked what they're most concerned about it's often anti-social behaviour rather than more serious crimes."

Recent statistics from these demand-led operations show that officers also pull over miscreant drivers (pedestrians who sprint suicidally into traffic are not breaking any laws, so can only be warned). But this doesn't mean they're less worried about the red light-allergic cyclists.

PC James Aveling, a City bike patrol officer for nine years, argues that it's a bigger problem than the accident statistics suggest. For one thing, he says, there is no legal obligation to report collisions between bikes and pedestrians, so many never reach the statistics books. He and his colleagues also deal with more and more angry confrontations between cyclists and pedestrians.

With more than 800 officers and just over one square mile of streets to patrol, the force can make a real difference, he says: "We're never going to stop it completely, but we want to try and improve behaviour. There's what we call the lemming effect – if one cyclist crosses on a red, others tend to follow. If it's a courier doing it they maybe know what they're doing, but lots of others simply don't."

Aveling also filled me in on another great cyclist mystery: why do police sometimes seem lax on drivers and motorcyclists who stray into bike lanes and bike-only advance stop zones (ASZs)?

The bike lane question is simple: if it is bounded by a dotted line rather than a continuous one then it is purely advisory, meaning it has no legal status. "Some councils paint the lanes green," Aveling adds. "That doesn't mean anything either."

As for the ASZs, the issue is decidedly murky: they are usually bounded by a continuous white line except for a small gap on the kerb-side edge, which is the only legal way to enter them. Even as a cyclist you're officially committing an offence if you enter the ASZ from the centre or right, I'm told.

Booking cars which enter the zone is tricky, Aveling says, as it's not illegal if they stop in one if a light turns red as they're part-way in. Officers thus have to watch a driver creep in on an already red light. There are also rumours that some officers see the penalty for the infringement – six points on the licence, the same as you'd get for sailing all the way through the red light – as somewhat dispoportionate.

More generally, Aveling is sceptical about ASZs, believing they suit experienced cyclists but not beginners, who might be better off sitting behind waiting traffic rather than pushing through.

He's far too polite to say so, but I get the distinct impression that overall, he's not too impressed with a lot of the cycling infrastructure on UK roads. That makes two of us.

COMMENTS

AlexandreDumbass I spend a lot of time cycling on roads and there is nothing more annoying than waiting at a red light and someone else on a bike comes cruising past, stops briefly to look left and right and then crosses the junction.

I can see why drivers and pedestrians get so annoyed by cyclists because so many of them seem to think the road laws don't apply to them. Unfortunately there is little or no hope of catching people doing this unless there happens to be a police officer watching at the time.

thechief15 The penalty for pulling into an ASZ isn't disproportionate at all. When there is an advanced stop zone the stop line for motorised traffic is the first line, cross the first line and from an official stand point you have passed through a red light. This is surely also a failing by the police to do their job, they are paid to uphold the law, not to decide if the penalties for transgression are correct.

murraw Considering the sheer volume of traffic, pedestrian and other offences that the police COMPLETELY IGNORE – including the at-times blatant misuse of advance stopping zones, cars sprawling into the cycle lane, pedestrians not obeying the walk/don't walk signals – I think it's a bit rough to target cyclists proceeding carefully through empty intersections when they're just trying not to lose their momentum. Especially when the lights are on a four-way stop.

Fedger A red light is a red light, all cyclists should stop at them. Everyone should respect the rules of the road, it'll help with cyclist PR and stop people getting squished. Seems pretty simple to me.

Is driving into a bike zone actually illegal?

JAMES RANDERSON

A couple of days ago I blogged about my encounter with an Addison Lee minicab driver who drove into the protected bike zone at a red traffic light.

This happens frustratingly frequently and is clearly contrary to the Highway Code. (Point 178 states: "Motorists, including motorcyclists, MUST stop at the first white line reached if the lights are amber or red".) But is it actually illegal? And if so what penalties do drivers face?

When I started looking into this, the answer turned out to be surprisingly contradictory. Peter Walker touched on this in a previous blog in which he asked the police why they apparently turn a blind eye to the offence:

Booking cars which enter the zone is tricky, [PC James] Aveling says, as it's not illegal if they stop in one if a light turns red as they're part-way in. Officers thus have to watch a driver creep in on an already red light. There are also rumours that some officers see the penalty for the infringement – six points on the licence, the same as you'd get for sailing all the way through the red light – as somewhat disproportionate.

So the offence comes under failure to stop at a red light.

Not so, says bike blog reader Nick Lane:

Cycle stop boxes are NOT legally enforceable, no points of fines can be levied against a vehicle entering or using one. Therefore they are NOT illegal.

In 2004 I had a lengthy correspondence with a chief inspector of road policy policing in which I queried why officers were not fining or awarding penalty points to motorists who compromised [advanced stop line] boxes. His reply on each occasion was emphatic – it is not an offence and therefore they cannot take action. He advised that I should not interpret the Highway Code as a set of laws attached to which were penalties, but rather as a set of guidelines.

Can that really be true? What is the point of saying in the Highway Code that drivers "MUST" not do something if there is no sanction for transgression? If that is correct, it's no wonder so many people do it.

The preface to the Highway Code suggests that the chief inspector is wrong. It states:

> *Many of the rules in the code are legal requirements, and if you disobey these rules you are committing a criminal offence. You may be fined, given penalty points on your licence or be disqualified from driving. In the most serious cases you may be sent to prison. Such rules are identified by the use of the words 'MUST/MUST NOT'.*

For chapter and verse on the subject I called the Association of Chief Police Officers (ACPO) (they ought to know, right?). After a day on the case, the press officer got back to me to say that nobody at ACPO knew the answer. She suggested I contact the Department for Transport (DfT). So I did.

At last some clarity. The DfT said that driving into a bike zone when the lights are red is an offence. It carries a £60 penalty and three points on your driving licence (maximum £1,000 fine if it goes to court). Police have some discretion over which bit of the Road Traffic Act to use, but most likely it will fall under "Failure to comply with a traffic sign or road marking".

So driving into a bike zone when the lights are red is illegal. Although there is apparently a great deal of confusion among the police themselves. One thing is for sure. Booking drivers for this offence is not a priority.

COMMENTS

prjfortyfive If a car is over the first line and then the light goes red it must stop in the green area, so if you see a car in the green area don't berate it unless you saw it roll over the first line.

mswa I think there's an element of drivers not being used to them yet. For most people on the roads they weren't part of their driver education.

DamianCarrington This is a massive bugbear for me. I usually tell the driver they shouldn't be there – most act surprised. I have also stopped several times to talk to the police who were booking other cyclists for jumping red lights and riding on the pavement (fair cop). They say: "we are not here [today] to book people for driving into the AS box". Have you ever? "er, no".

MsOwl On my route home, in Norwich, some numpty has spray painted a big white car in the bike zone box next to the painted bike.

snowfreak2 Recent anecdote – I was on my scooter pulled up at a traffic light. A cyclist deliberately pulled up right in the middle of the AS – to make a point – there by causing a delay to ALL road users when pulling away from the lights.

Monchberter Pulling up in the middle of the ASL is perfectly acceptable and safer for the cyclist. It's called 'taking the lane' and prevents other road users making potentially dangerous overtaking maneuvers. I'm a qualified cycling instructor and this is the accepted and correct way to safeguard yourself and other road users, hence why I teach it.

Antisocial cycling is annoying – but not harmful

DEBRA ROLFE

Campaigns coordinator of CTC, the UK's national cycling organisation

Why do those of us who venture out on two wheels run the risk of being called Lycra louts or being compared to the evil overlord of a galactic empire? Take MP David Curry, who once said "the only time I have been knocked down in my life was by a cyclist going like a bat out of hell ... dressed like Darth Vader, as they all do!" Sadly, however, the idea that cyclists are a threat to civilisation seems to show no sign of abating.

Much of the concern with antisocial cycling focuses on jumping red lights and riding on the pavement. Both are illegal and have the potential to cause great annoyance to others, but do they actually cause harm?

There is no evidence that cyclists who jump red lights are particularly dangerous to anyone, including themselves. From 2001–5, only 2% of pedestrian injuries in London were the result of cyclists jumping red lights. During that same period, 55% of pedestrian injuries in London were the result of motorists jumping red lights. Jumping red lights is illegal for both cyclists and motorists, but it is much more likely to cause harm when motorists do it.

Cyclists should be where they belong – on the road. Cycling on the pavement is annoying, but it's not as dangerous as you might think. In the past 10 years, not a single pedestrian in London has been killed by a cyclist on the pavement – yet 54 pedestrians have been killed by motorists driving on the pavement.

Compared to other forms of illegal and antisocial behaviour, antisocial cycling is not particularly harmful. Of course, the rare instances when bad cycling causes injury and even death are tragic and should be investigated by the police. However, we need to put it in perspective: it is very rare, and that is why it hits the headlines when it happens.

Cyclists just aren't that much of a problem. Much illegal cycling is the result of ignorance and fear of cycling on hostile roads, rather than malice. I'd like to see all cyclists offered cycle training and cyclists who break the law required to undergo it.

For those who are about to shout "cyclists ought to be tested and licensed!", please understand that this would create a spectacular level of bureaucracy, not least of which would be delivering a theory test to a three year old. This would put people off cycling – and our society would miss out on the benefits that cycling provides to our health, environment, economy and quality of life.

There are millions of cyclists out there, and only one Darth Vader. Just like motorists, some are nice and some are nasty, and even the nasty cyclists are fairly harmless. Instead of getting apoplectic about the perceived dangers of bad cycling, let's focus on changing what killed 2,538 people on UK roads last year – bad driving.

COMMENTS

Lordgall If a cyclist is too scared to ride in the road (where they legally should be) then perhaps they shouldn't be riding at all?

EMnut I think the problems of traffic speeding out of control, and jumping red lights is by far the greater problem than cyclists on pavements. I am a cyclist and a pedestrian, and do get irked by kids hoofing down the pavement narrowly missing pensioners etc. But then a quick walk up to the main road junction and I can understand why they are forced to do this.

Kazbah Many of my town's cycle paths are actually ON THE PAVEMENT, and almost all end abruptly.

Will anything stop the bike thieves?

JUDITH SOAL

My bike was stolen yesterday. Again. It was locked up (£99.99 mega-security lock) outside my home at about 4pm and when I came out about two hours later it was gone.

It's my third bike theft in about two years. The one stolen yesterday was recovered by police once before in a pre-dawn raid on a known bike dealer's house. I'm not holding my breath this will happen again. I've also had my saddle stolen a few times, and once my bike was stripped outside a yoga class, leaving me with a frame, two wheels and little else.

Cycle theft has always been bad, but it really feels like it's getting worse. Apparently, insurers have seen a 25% rise in claims over the past year.

Belinda Scott, of Condor Cycles, calls it a surge. "There's a real plague going on at the moment," she said. "And it's not just people being careless. We had a guy the other day who'd just bought his bicycle from us, he locked it up with two locks at London Bridge and left it for 15 minutes and it was taken." So that's the two locks theory gone then.

My bicycle was an expensive one, bought through the cycle-to-work scheme that I've just finished paying off. I'm thinking of downgrading next time in the hope that I'll stop attracting so much attention from thieves. Will that help?

Other advice seems to be to paint it pink, cover it in black tape, or hire a 24-hour bike-minder. Anyone tried this? Or anything else that works?

COMMENTS

Brant I live in Amsterdam and bike theft is the only prolific crime we have here – how to stop it happening, impossible, if someone wants to steal your bike, they'll steal it. But you can lessen the liklihood by always locking your bike to something, never leave it overnight, and of course don't have quick-release saddle or wheels. I'm on my 4th bike in 3 years.

Larski The best deterrent is allegedly a basket. Even bike thieves need to keep up their street cred apparently.

grahma As an experienced bike-loss victim, I can honestly say that the only way not to get your bike nicked is to have a crap bike. I have just that at the moment and it refuses to go anywhere – much to my great disappointment!

How to stop your bike being stolen

MIKE CAVENETT

Communications Officer at the London Cycling Campaign

There are good reasons why the London Cycling Campaign recently launched its Beat the Thief campaign. In recent years, bike theft has grown to pandemic proportions, with the Metropolitan police's own figures showing bike theft increasing 75% per year in the worst areas.

A doubling in the number of London cyclists over the past decade, along with the introduction of the Cycle to Work tax scheme (giving some employees as much as 50% off a new bike up to the value of £1,000), has meant there are simply more good bikes out there to be pinched.

In a recent survey, 80% of respondents reported having at least one bike taken – and one in six said they had recognised a stolen bike for sale on the internet. The evidence suggests this is a problem that has got out of hand.

In London alone, an estimated 80,000 bicycles are stolen every year, with a total value as high as £30m. Some of the thefts are opportunist crimes but there are also knowledgeable and efficient gangs in operation: it's not unusual to hear about vans pulling up outside suburban train stations or City offices, with thieves liberating the 10 or 15 most valuable bicycles (and motorbikes in some cases) before startled onlookers have even reached for a phone.

Bike theft has also been identified as a route into more serious crime for young people because the pickings are rich, while convictions are low considering the number of crimes.

Most frustrating for Londoners is seeing the plundered wares brazenly sold on the internet and at street markets. A trip down Brick Lane market looking for your own stolen property has become a sad part of London bike culture.

And you don't have to wear a deerstalker to pick out the dodgy "bargains" on Gumtree. Cyclist Amelia Coulam, who saw her bike for sale on the site after it was stolen, said: "I was so angry, because this person was selling at least 20 bikes under various names."

Some are quick to blame the police, who have been accused of treating bike theft as trivial. But the police are not always in control of their own priorities, so lobbyists have to focus on changing politicians' attitudes to ensure cycle theft becomes a law enforcement priority.

Surely bike theft is equally frustrating for politicians? Yes, cycling budgets are tiny compared with spend on roads and public transport, but millions of pounds of taxpayers' money is still spent encouraging this non-polluting, congestion-busting, health-boosting mode of transport.

How discouraging then to discover that (according to a French study) one in four victims doesn't replace their stolen bike – because of frustration or lack of funds – and that two-thirds of London cyclists report using their bike less often because of the risk of theft.

So what can be done? Well, the Dutch had an overwhelming problem with bike theft but halved it during a decade of concerted efforts from national and regional government, law enforcement agencies, manufacturers, internet sellers and bike shops. They standardised bike numbering and encouraged bike sellers to sign up to a code of practice that encourages buyers to choose honest sellers and not buy stolen goods unwittingly.

London Cycling Campaign has for a long time been calling for a specialist bike-theft police squad to make life tougher for thieves. And internet sites must work with the police to make selling stolen bikes much more difficult. Consistently strong policing of street markets and a Dutch-style bike shop code of practice would make a difference too.

Longer term, the UK needs more secure cycle parking. Employers who provide car spaces should be compelled to provide secure bike spaces too (you can fit at least 10 bikes into the space for one car), and every UK city needs secure parking in city centres, at transport hubs and around residential developments.

A central repository for stolen bikes in each city, like the vast facility in Amsterdam, would help reunite owners with bikes, many of which are never returned to their owner because the individual cannot be traced.

The good news is that persistent lobbying by campaigners seems to be having some effect. Recently, Gumtree has shown a willingness to address the problem; the police are making the right noises; and Transport for London has been asking cyclists what more can be done.

Ignoring bike theft for years has created a serious problem: now it will take years of effective policing and policymaking to fix it.

COMMENTS

henitysweet It shouldn't be a case of buy a bike you don't like because theives won't like it either!

If the police have identified bike theft as a gateway into heavier crimes then surely harsher punishments and more time spent investigating bike theft would stop or reduce the more serious crimes.

lucy2902 Buyers need to be responsible too. If it looks too good to be true – it probably is.

A bike thief speaks

FREDERIKA WHITEHEAD

Omar Aziz started stealing bikes when he was 17 and carried on until he finally weaned himself off crack cocaine at the age of 29. Now he wants to make amends. He is volunteering in his local area.

Aziz stole a lot of bikes to feed his habit: "When I sell one thing I go and buy my drugs, smoke it, when it finishes, I have to go and get more. I nick another bike," he said.

The easiest pickings were bikes secured with cheap locks. "Some people think they don't have enough money and they buy thin locks, and I used to go and just push the bike and pull it and the lock will break."

Today Aziz locks his own bike up with two thick chains, through both wheels and the frame. Thieves can get through thick chains with the right equipment but it takes a lot of time and heavy cutting equipment. But even that didn't always deter him. On at least one occasion, having eyed-up a bike, Aziz first stole tools before going back for the bike.

CCTV it seems, is also no deterrent. "Even if there is cameras they don't care. For me the best place to leave your bike is a place where there are people around."

But even the busiest streets empty out eventually, so if Aziz really wanted a particular bike he would damage a tyre so the owner would leave it in the rack for longer. "Someone, if they find their tyre punctured they should take their bike with them, right at that minute because someone has done it on purpose to come and take it after."

Owners of bikes costing more than a few hundred quid should always take them indoors. Whenever Aziz's crack dealer got wind of an expensive bike locked up in the area he would send Aziz out to fetch it. Thieves also watch where expensive bike are regularly parked. For anyone with outdoor parking, he recommends riding a cheaper bike.

Aziz himself also chose to steal the more expensive bikes just to ride them as far as the sale point, regardless of the fact that he was rarely paid more than £20–30 for any bike he stole – the price of a few rocks of crack cocaine. "I used to steal the £800 bike when I need the rock and sell it for £20 pounds. Sometimes I was very desperate."

"I take them to pubs, coffee shops, kebab shops. People buy them and know that I'm a crack head and they say he's a crack head, give him a tenner, give him 20 and they sell it."

In London, Aziz found stolen bikes were particularly easy to sell. "There is a really slight chance of you getting caught when you are nicking bikes. You just crack it, get on it, gone. When they nick bikes they paint them … you don't even know it's your bike. [In London] no one is going to know, they are not going to stop you…You can steal from north London and go to west London and you're alright."

Aziz says he feels bad about the things he did while he was an addict. "I know its bad, you know. That's why I'm doing voluntary work to give something back. I feel bad you know. I didn't do it just to keep it for myself. I done it to feed my habit."

Two weeks ago Aziz had his own bike stolen while he was buying cigarettes from his local shop. He started to call the police but decided to catch the thief himself instead. "I left it outside the shop for 10 seconds just to buy cigarettes. I come back out and my bike is gone."

"I felt very very very very angry when my bike got stolen. If I'd caught the man who stole it that minute. I don't know what I could have done, honestly. But I caught him a week later and he said to me he bought it for £2.50. But then I said what goes around comes around."

It took Aziz just days to find his stolen bike. "For me it's been stressful. Honestly. He was on crack. I could see it in his face that he was in a bad way and I felt sorry. I thought what am I going to do to him. But people can't help it. They see your bike and … you give them any chance and they will take it. It's not safe, it's not safe at all. Everywhere you go lock your bike."

Note: Omar Aziz is not the ex-bike thief's real name and he was not paid for speaking to the Guardian

COMMENTS

Deebles You wouldn't get people nicking bikes if other people didn't buy stolen bikes. I've sworn off buying secondhand full stop after having two bikes nicked and one smashed to pieces by thieves that couldn't get through the lock (they'd managed to cut partway through though, making that useless as well).

Barnbybran back in a sec...

goes outside to bring brand new bike in

Oakengrove Considering how easy it is to store bikes compared to cars, and how easy it is to boost a bike compared to a car, I think it would be good for more employers to provide secure indoor storage for their employees.

CharlesDarwin If you have a nice bike, paint it (and all the parts) some ugly colour. A £5 can of Hammerite will protect your investment. I did a brand new £600 Marin in brown and yellow 25 years ago, and I still own the bike.

Bait bikes: entrapment or a way to beat the thieves?

FREDERIKA WHITEHEAD

If you're a cyclist then you'll surely agree: bike theft is a scourge, and any method the police use to combat it is to be welcomed.

Any method? There is a technique shown to dramatically reduce cycle theft levels, and yet it remains hugely controversial – bait bikes.

This tactic, also known as decoy or tracker bikes, sees police leaving badly locked, or even unlocked, bicycles in vulnerable locations. They are fitted with hidden GPS devices, letting officers trace them to the thieves, or better still to a lock-up or warehouse used by gangs to store lots of stolen bikes.

Police forces around the country are to deploy bait bikes after a series of successful pilot schemes throughout 2008 and 2009, with London's mayor, Boris Johnson, also approving the tactic for the capital earlier this month.

The pilot schemes seemed to show bait bikes are a significant deterrent. Bikes thefts dropped by 45% at Cambridge rail station when British Transport Police tested the method. Even in the UK's bike theft capital, London, rates dropped by around a third in one local trial.

The argument in favour was summed up by Jenny Jones, one of two Greens in the London Assembly:

There are two main deterrents to cycling: road safety and theft. Gangs of young kids often steal the bikes and pass them on to criminals who store them in lock ups and garages before selling them. The advantage of using bait bikes is that it enables you to track the stolen bike back to the organised gang lock up, rather than just arresting the young bike thieves... You've got to get the gangs. You've got to find out where they keep the bikes.

The contrasting view can be summed up in one word: entrapment. Critics argue that particularly when bait bikes are left unlocked they are an open incentive to commit crime, most notably to drug addicts or the young and impulsive.

A drugs treatment adviser to the Home Office, speaking anonymously, described it as "lazy policing", adding, "There is so much else they can do to prevent bike theft that doesn't involve leaving temptation in the way of drug addicts that we have spent months helping to get clean."

Linda Oliver, from Bristol's early intervention service, which helps local young people, said:

"In many countries, this practice would be classified as entrapment and would be illegal, the courts would view this as luring people into crime."

Others can fall foul of bait bikes. One Cambridge University student recounted leaving a local nightclub after a few drinks and thinking it would be a good idea to "borrow" an unlocked cycle he spotted nearby. Even though police let him off with a warning, he was perturbed by the tactic:

> I think that this is a honeypot trap of the most wasteful kind, and should not be a method of catching the gangs of bike thieves that doubtless exist – it's striking at the bottom rung of the ladder, and this always proves ineffective.

Would you be happy to see bait bikes used in your neighbourhood?

COMMENTS

howardmarch What's wrong with "lazy policing" if it works?

cycleloopy I am all for it, particulary if it leads police to the bast*?d who nicked my bike.

What is the difference between taking an unlocked bike and shop lifting? Both are wrong, immoral and and in both cases the thief knows that they are taking an item that does not belong to them. Would anybody consider security guards in shops as an entrapment to catch shoplifters?

Of course not; nobody has any excuse for STEALING.

nonogame i think technically it is entrapment but i am of the mind that bike thieves should be beheaded…with sharpened rusty spoons so i don't really care.

Three times Olympic gold medal winner Sir Chris Hoy on how to train to be a champion

INTERVIEW BY SEAN INGLE

Sean Ingle: Can you suggest a workout for beginner cyclists as well as experts?

Sir Chris Hoy: In terms of my training I do a lot of stuff like looking at acceleration; how to start; your top end speed; and the ability to hold onto that speed when you feel the lactic acid kick in. I would say that the toughest thing that we do, or the one that causes the most pain, is sessions on a static bike in the lab or the gym. I go flat out for 30 seconds and then have a minute's break where I peddle gently or stop. I do that four times in a row and then have half an hours break or easy peddling and do it again. It doesn't sound like much, it's only 4 minutes of effort in total but if you do it hard enough and at the right intensity you're on your knees in complete agony at the end of it. It's so effective at training the body to deal with lactic acid and that's the one thing that slows you down because once the lactic acid builds up, you're in pain and your muscles don't work anymore and that's when you slow down.

We don't recommend that you do that from the beginning but it's about writing a little programme for yourself. That could just be something small, say your ride to work is 5 miles, you could add an extra mile to your route and try to get there in the same time, or it could be that you just set yourself a time to beat. Find out what your fastest time to work and fastest time back from work is and try to improve it. It sounds dead simple but it's all about making small incremental improvements. If you go and make drastic changes then the next day you'll be so sore that you'll be put off it so it's better for you to do small amounts. It is also better for your health too.

SI: Do you cycle for fun when you're not racing and if so what bike do you use?

CH: Yes I do. I think it's important to cycle for fun as well as training otherwise I'd just associate it with pain. Riding for fun on country lanes reminds me why I took it up in the first place – what it's all about. I also plan to get to mountain biking when I finish my cycling career because I just love that, there is nothing better than getting up to the hills away from everything with the peace and quiet, where you can enjoy just being active.

SI: Are there any particular routes that you are fond of?

CH: I guess the ones that mean the most to me are the Pentland Hills in Edinburgh, I used to go there in my teens and it's amazing that so close to a major city you can feel that faraway from it all. There are also great parts in the Lake District, in Wales – just numerous places that you can get off road and away from all the traffic and make the most of mountain biking.

SI: What hopes do you have for London 2012? What legacy will it leave for cycling?

CH: From a track cycling perspective we're getting this amazing facility and we've already seen what the Manchester velodrome has done for British cycling. So to have another centre where we can reach out to a wider audience, to have more school kids come down and try it out is just going to double our chances of having future champions ten or twenty years down the line. It's just very exciting because until 1994 there was no indoor velodrome in Britain and we were fighting a losing battle trying to compete against the top nations. Now we have one in Newport, we're going to get one in London and one's going to be built in Glasgow for the 2014 Commonwealth Games so it's a great state of affairs. It's a very exciting time which will bring more people into the sport and that in itself will hopefully set up a great legacy and continue the trend that Britain is the top cycling nation in the world.

This is an abridged version of an interview that appeared on the Guardian's bike podcast. You can hear the unedited interview at gu.com/p/28yjg

Chapter 3

My daily ride

Beware. This chapter may make you feel seriously inadequate.
It certainly did me.

First, there is Michael the cycle courier who rides between
50 and 100 miles a day ferrying stuff around London that
has to be there "right goddam now". Then there's the Norfolk
paramedic cycle response unit who ride up to 35 miles a day
carrying 50 kilos of medical kit – and when they get there they
have to save people's lives.

Bike Blog regular Matthew Sparkes nonchalantly describes his
50-mile-a-day commute and his conversion to spaghetti fetishist
just to fuel the journey. Even Stuart Jeffries' embarrassing, yet
strangely impressive, canal episode puts my 25 minute daily
pootle to the Guardian offices to shame.

But I shouldn't feel put down. Nay, I refuse to.

If reading the wisdom of the Bike Blog fraternity has taught me
anything it is this – take pride in your own version of bike heaven
and other cyclists will respect you – even love you – for it.

Whatever your daily cycle experience, be it Lycra-clad urban
warfare or beaming, tweedy, sit-up-and-beg ambling bliss, you
are living. I mean really living – air in your lungs; sweat on your
brow; and time for your brain to unwind or create. As Michael
puts it, "Your worst day on a bike will be better than your best
day in an office."

There is one niggling worry though. Will the joy be quite the
same if everyone joined us? If all the drivers took to two wheels
there would be no subversive pleasure in weaving between the

traffic – because there wouldn't be any. No more knowing nods from others in the fraternity. Non-cyclists would not look at you with a mixture of respect and concern for your mental health just for braving the weather and the traffic twice a day. In short, that special feeling (oh let's admit it, smugness) would be gone, and with it some of the magic – wouldn't it?

Banish that thought my friends. Don't try to hog the loveliness. Go forth and tell everyone you know. Let them feel it too. Just don't mention Stuart's canal incident.

James Randerson

The life and hard times of a London courier

MICHAEL (INTERVIEW BY MATTHEW SPARKES)

Michael has been a cycle courier in London for eight years, come rain or shine

When I first moved to London I saw these guys hanging around with bikes and radios. I asked a friend about them and he explained that they were couriers. I couldn't believe you could get paid to ride a bike; I knew it was what I wanted to do. I got my first bike when I was five and I've ridden ever since. I cycle everywhere, inside and outside work: I can't imagine not having a bike.

Most people are friendly towards us, but there are bad apples. We all have stories about cabbies and bus drivers, but my pet peeve is pedestrians who cross without looking, then say, "I didn't see you". I've been hit from behind by a car, and I've had a pedestrian walk out in front of me.

The distance we cover varies. On a slow day about 50 miles, but when we're busy it can reach 100. We generally work from nine to six, with a 30-minute lunch break if we have time. We mostly carry small envelopes, clothing samples and A4 files. Most of our work is for the press, media companies and legal firms. We used to do a lot for banks but not so much now.

As you can imagine, digital took a lot of business away from the industry. The amount of work has been falling steadily for the last five years, and I only earn about 60% of what I did eight years ago.

Like most couriers I get paid per package, not per hour; that's why we're always in a hurry. The pay depends on who you work for and how good you are, but is generally between £200 and £600 per week.

Yes, some of us are reckless, but they tend to be the ones that are new to the business. People who see us ride may think we're dangerous; too quick and taking big chances, but they don't take into account the amount of riding a courier does. We spend so much time on our bikes that it gives you a high level of control. The last thing we want is to get hurt, because if we don't work we don't earn. Some of us wear helmets, some don't. No courier would look down on you for wearing one, but security rules in some buildings mean you have to check it in and out, which is a waste of time.

We carry an Xda palmtop which our jobs are sent on, plus a radio and a mobile phone. Thick plastic bags to protect the packages on rainy days are vital too. I've got a Dolan and a Raleigh fixed gear for work, an unknown brand fixed gear for outside of work and a Cannondale Scalpel mountain bike.

I honestly enjoy riding for work, but like everything there are days when it's no fun – especially when it's raining. Courier work doesn't stop if it rains. You just have to grit your teeth and get on with it. Believe me, a day of continual rain is very unpleasant.

But I always remember something another courier told me: "Your worst day on a bike will be better than your best day in an office." He was right, I couldn't imagine being locked in a box all day. Not seeing the sun or feeling the wind on my skin would be a nightmare.

COMMENTS

aftertherain I'm envious. It is true that inner city sleet beats sitting in the office any day.

nickmead I worked as a cycle courier for six months when I first moved to London about 12 years ago.

Was a great way to get to know the back routes around the City and I was super-fit doing around 80 miles a day, although I did get knocked off five or six times (mostly by drivers trying to turn left over the top of me). In the evening I would have a shower and the water running down the plug hole would be black from the accumulated grime of a day soaking up exhaust fumes.

PeterWalker Michael is making me feel all nostalgic.

Before I was a journalist I was a courier for a couple of years in London and then for another 18 months or so in Sydney. I entered the trade as an unsporty novice who'd barely cycled since childhood – the entry-level Raleigh MTB I began on was widely if gently mocked by other couriers. I left a cycling nut with a level of fitness I know full well I'll never be able to match in my life.

It's perhaps sometimes an easy job to over-romanticise, and in my day, certainly, lots of courier firms treated riders appallingly. But there was a great feeling of camaraderie.

And the funny thing was, the office wags who'd go, 'Nice weather out there?' when you'd arrive with a package dripping with rain would always be mysteriously quiet when the sun shone.

loverlover After 12 years, I handed in my radio last week. I loved my job for about seven of those. For someone in their 20s, with few, if any, responsibilities beyond finding a good party, and who loves riding, it truly is the best job in the world. The camaraderie of the courier scene is second to none, as is the buzz of having five or six packages in your bag that have to be at their destinations right goddamn now. There are days when you wonder why you bother, but even on The Day It Rained Hard All Day Long or The Day I Rode Down Euston Road With A Blizzard In My Face, I'd rather have been doing that than being in an office of any type.

That said, it has no long-term prospects at all. Any more than about three years and the job becomes a roundabout with no exit – the longer you're in it, the harder it gets to get out. It took me two years of moaning to actually do anything about extricating myself and a further three to achieve it. I'll miss the riding, but there are many things I won't:

Ludicrous security arrangements. Security guards in general. Stuck-up, dismissive receptionists (particularly fashion and PR ones) who think they matter any more than you do – I'll take a dismissive attitude from someone in authority, but a phone-answering coffee maker? Please. The knowledge that you are utterly expendable to the company you work for, and whose office staff's wages you're out there earning. Sitting empty in a doorway in winter freezing for an hour. Idiot pedestrians. Idiot bus drivers. Paying for the privilege of having a radio. Paying for an XDA that is just as vital for the company as it is for you. Earning as little as 40 quid for nine hours riding that could conceivably end up with you dead under a bus.

But when it's good, when the work's flowing and the sun's out and the wheels are turning, it's like nothing else. When I thought about what I wanted to do otherwise, I thought about what I like doing – being out and about in the best city in the world, having a natter, being my own man. That's why by this time next week, I'll be a black cab driver. I've consciously gone for an old Fairway cab, with the petrol cap that's known as the "courier handle". Grab a hold, my brothers!

The paramedic cyclist – saving lives through pedal power

CARL SMITH (INTERVIEW BY MATTHEW SPARKES)

Founded the Cycle Response Unit in Kings Lynn, Norfolk, adding bike paramedics to the ambulance service and shaving 999 response times by minutes

We can do anywhere between 25 and 35 miles in a 12-hour shift, and the bike weighs 50kg when fully loaded. So, considering we may have to resuscitate someone as soon as we arrive on scene, we need a very high level of fitness.

We carry a wide range of equipment on specialised mountain bikes. Most of it is the same as a traditional ambulance carries, but smaller. We have a defibrillator the size of the palm of your hand, rather than the big one carried on ambulances, and the oxygen and entonox cylinders are miniature too. We treat about 60% of patients at the scene, allowing ambulances to attend to the patients who really need transporting.

We're based in the borough council CCTV control room, and a lot of the time we're well on the way while the 999 call is still being made. It's well understood that from the time you go into cardiac arrest, your chances of survival drop by about 10% every minute until a defibrillator gets to you. Having a highly trained medic on a bike offers the patient the most appropriate care, which is not always taking people straight to hospital.

The Cycle Response Unit can be sent to any 999 call. We've attended child births, cardiac arrests, road traffic collisions, assaults, overdoses and strokes, to mention just a few. If someone needs to be taken to hospital, we call an ambulance, but sometimes we can tell them not to hurry – which reduces the chance of an accident.

When it's raining, we get wet. Riders do sometimes call me and have a little moan when it rains, but I remind them about the days when it's sunny and they're out there in their shorts – when all the other crews are stuck in a hot ambulance.

The team enjoy it; they're out there, keeping fit, and doing a job they love.

Prior to joining the ambulance service I'd done a few different jobs, from bus driver to undertaker, and I'm still a retained firefighter.

Unfortunately, assaults on NHS staff are on the increase, with drink and drugs being a major factor. Thankfully, CCTV is watching our every move. One thing that sadly wasn't caught was when my colleague Paul was trying to impress some children in the local park, skidded and fell off the bike.

COMMENTS

hhazzahh Cool. Great idea. Nice job. In Norfolk. Not sure about the Highlands.

ArnoG But the question on everyone's lips: Do they have to go "nee naah, nee naah" as they ride around?

Fwoggie That is some fitness, to cycle between 25 and 35 miles with 50kg of kit. I cycle 14 miles every day to/from work with 10kg of kit and consider that a good work out, this is something else. I wish them all the best for the winter season; the frost isn't too bad, it's the ridiculous winds you sometimes get.

I'm missing my bike commute, and it's making me grumpy

VICTORIA HAZAEL

Works at CTC, a national organisation representing cyclists in the UK

For the past month, I've not been cycling to work. I've been getting in a warm, dry, cosy car instead. I thought it would be a treat, a break from pedalling along wet and cold roads in some of the worst weather of the year – but how wrong I was. The result of driving to work is I'm grumpy and getting even more unfit by the day.

The reason I'm not cycling is because I'm house-sitting for friends and need a car to get back to take the dog out at lunchtime. In the morning, I've been moving sloth-like from the cocoon of my duvet to the snug warmth of the car.

I then sit and drive just under five miles to work, only moving to change gear – I do not break into a sweat and my heart only races through stress, not exertion. When I arrive at work, I park close to the front door, so if I'm lucky I take maybe two or three gulps of fresh air and I'm inside. It's no way to start the day.

I'm not alone in finding it difficult to get started without my dose of fresh air and exercise before work: most teachers will tell you that children who walk or cycle to school are more alert and ready to learn than those who arrive by car. Research completed more than 10 years ago also shows that children who exercise have better concentration and are less disruptive, so maybe this explains why I'm feeling so sluggish not cycling.

Cycling to work has other benefits too: according to a study in the Netherlands published in 2009, employees who regularly cycle to work take on average one day less sick leave every year compared with those who do not cycle to work. Add to that the fact that regular cyclists typically enjoy a level of fitness equivalent to someone 10 years younger.

What's more, cycling to work decreases the risk of dying by approximately 40%, plus all the other health benefits: the reduced risk of developing diseases such as diabetes, high blood pressure, colon and breast cancer. Looking at those stats, driving to work must be a death wish.

Logically, driving is the easy option: it should be the stress-free, easy way to get to work, but let me tell you it is not. Just a few days into my month of driving, I begin to get more and more annoyed by the traffic jams and school run mums and dads clogging the roads.

As the cyclists sail past my window while I'm stuck in a queue, I envy them and can see why drivers on my route get annoyed with me when I'm on my bike – it's not just because I get in the way, it's also because I'm always moving and making progress.

I also thought that by driving, I might get a bit of a lie-in, but that's not happened yet, as I have to have a little flexibility in my journey time just in case there is yet another jam. This means I leave at exactly the same time as when I cycle, so I'm not saving any time and, on top of it all, I'm paying for the privilege by burning expensive petrol.

Before you start thinking I'm an exercise nut, let me set the record straight: I'm not the kind of girl who cycles 40 miles in a headwind dressed head to toe in Lycra just for fun.

You see, the truth is I don't really like exercise – my default mode is to avoid it if I can. This month, without cycling, I've done no real exercise: I feel guilty then try to go to the gym, but riding a stationary bike feels pointless, as there is no incentive for me to climb an imaginary hill. The result is I slack off and take it easier than I would if I was on a real road; and going to the gym costs me two things I can't afford: time and money.

I'll be back on my bike tomorrow, because my friends are back from their holiday. Not cycling has made me realise I ride because it's easier, cheaper and I get a bit of exercise without having to make a big effort. Cycling puts me in a good mood, so I'm better equipped to face a day at work.

I don't drink coffee, but usually I don't need to – it's the wind in my hair and, especially at this time of year, the rain and sleet on my face that really wake me up.

COMMENTS

thereverent You really remember how much fun it is when you stop for a while. The fun is the underrated bit of cycle commuting. It's not any fun being in a car/bus/tube/train even if you are warm and can read or play on an iPhone.

eyup What a great post. Thank you. I wish more people knew just how true everything you wrote is. And do you notice that the more you do it the more energy you have?

Ormur I agree with everything. For a few weeks now I have not been able to cycle to work every day but am coming in by car. Driving to work is stressful and annoying. Dealing with road rage is not the best way to start the day Cant wait to start my regular commuting on my bike again.

Dwese I began cycling the 12-mile round trip to work as a money-saving effort at the end of the summer 2009. I usually average two to three colds a winter (I work in a public building with lots of schoolchildren). This past winter not a thing. Healthy as a horse!

A bike commuter's shower – in a bottle

HELEN PIDD

Of all the excuses for not cycling to work a lack of showers is perhaps the most rational. No one wants to tramp into the office looking as if they've had a sauna with their clothes on. But now a Texan firm has come up with a solution; a "shower in a bottle" that promises to get even the sweatiest commuter clean with no need for running water.

But is it what the xenophobic might call a "French shower"? An expensive version of dousing yourself with Lynx instead of having a wash? Or spraying your clothes with Febreze?

To test Rocket Shower, I slipped into a toilet cubicle after cycling on a hot day. Feeling slightly weird, I took off my dirty clothes, sprayed myself all over with Rocket Shower, waited a few seconds and then dried off with the technical hand towel in the "jet pack" (£19.99 from Fitsense.co.uk). It contains witch hazel to cleanse, alcohol to help sweat evaporate and kill bacteria, peppermint to cool the skin and grapefruit oil – to stop you smelling like an alcoholic.

To my surprise it worked rather well. I felt cool, dry and confident enough to head to a packed co-worker's leaving party where no one seemed to wrinkle their nose in disgust.

Result – the only downer is that now you'll need a new excuse for getting the bus.

How do you cope in a workplace with no showers? Share your tips below.

COMMENTS

gunduzs As a confirmed lazy bastard and man who has a somewhat lackadaisical attitude to hygiene (I fully maintain that bathing every day is a stupid and unnecessary eccentricity) this little gig really appeals to me. Top invention.

slippedstitch I really don't see the need for such a product, and I'd be interested in the sources and environmental impact of its materials. If your office doesn't have a shower, it might still have a disabled loo with its own private sink behind a closed door. If your office doesn't, your local Starbucks probably does. Take a change of clothes, a bar of soap, a flannel and a small towel. Strip. Wash smellier bits. Put fresh clothes on. Fold cycling wear away in bag, place flannel and towel somewhere discrete to dry. Done. Unless it is a seriously hot day and/ or you really work up a sweat on your cycle, you should be fine.

nietzsche39 Wear a breathable top. Change it for a fresh top when you get to work. Is it that difficult?

apiaryist As a resident of Austin, Texas, I'd like to point out that it's been 38 degrees every day for the last month. If I didn't have a shower at work, it would not be possible to commute on a bike.

TheFarrago I use unscented babywipes. You can buy "cleansing wipes" but they're the same thing except a lot more expensive.

Bike swap: A hybrid for a Brompton

BEN THOMAS AND JAMES RANDERSON

Dear James,

I'd quite like to ride a folding bike, you said. OK, I said, but I hope you haven't got a hybrid to offer me in return.

I had always feared that I was irrationally and snobbishly anti-hybrid, particularly regarding its "commuter" incarnation. After this swap, I'm more comfortable about my bigotry.

It's quite light, it's quite responsive, its gears work (mine don't) and it's got some nice bits bolted on. But in the end I just can't see the point of making a commuter hybrid and then trying to make it as fast as possible, which I think Specialized have done – most notably with the slim rims and tyres, which wouldn't be out of place on a racing frame; and the feel of the ride, which is pretty firm (despite carbon-fibre seatpost and forks).

If you're going to blast your way across town on a light bike with 27cm wheels and a nice taut frame, why not do it on … a road bike? You may like the fact that your riding position is more upright on a hybrid – but then, how odd to have all this speed-generating machinery below you and to sit like an Edwardian gentleman, in a tootling-along posture. I've nothing against tootling, but you can do it in more comfort (and dare I say it, style) if your bike isn't yearning for you to lean forward a bit so you can use your legs more efficiently.

If you absolutely must sit all tall and proud and erect while trying to go fast, don't buy a hybrid – get your local bike shop to put flat bars on a road bike. (But not the ones Specialized have used on this bike, they're about two feet wide. Not ideal for making your way through the perma-jam up to the advanced stop line.)

Another thing. I've got to say it: Specialized. It now belongs firmly on the Cool Brands list – that is, big brands that everyone knows are cool. Can big brands be cool? Anyway, if everyone knows something's cool, it's not. (It's also a lot more tempting for thieves.)

Happy cycling,

Ben

Dear Ben,

Thanks for at least entertaining the notion that my bike might be cool. But I'm afraid I won't be taking any style tips from a man who rides a two-wheeled folding pogo stick. After tottering dangerously around the streets of London on your contraption, survival was far closer to the front of my mind than fashion.

My friend who works in a bike shop (and is admittedly a bit of a bike snob like you) reckons that there are only three types of people who ride Bromptons – attractive women, men in suits and weird men.

I haven't seen you dressed up for work recently …

No sir, I found that riding your Brompton was more likely to elicit the derision of gangs of kids on their way to school than coy jealous glances as my sleek lines glided past. The ride was like bouncing along on a space-hopper attached by a pole – such is the irritating, energy-sapping suspension.

It was exciting though, I'll give you that. Riding this it transformed me instantly into a super-powerful giant. All my body movements were exaggerated with often near-fatal consequences. As I took a hand off the handlebars to signal ahead of a junction, the sudden upset to the bike's equilibrium sent me veering dangerously towards a parked car or oncoming traffic. So I was reduced to the slow, timid and stand-offish cyclist I used to be. At least cars don't push me around on my "Frankenstein" machine.

By the way sir, the feeling of uncomfortable vulnerability is not helped by the lack of much acceleration or real speed. At least you had the grace to admit your gears don't work, but when you handed the thing to me, your description of the top two as "cruising gears" was rather wide of the mark. I suppose you meant that the frequent skipping means it is not advisable to stand up in the saddle. Don't worry, I didn't.

But what of the Brompton's trump card you ask – the foldability? Well it's a useful trick I'll grant you that, although it has a habit of performing it when you don't want it to – but more of that next time …

Good luck on the cycle home,

James

Dear James,

OK, so you had trouble riding my Brompton. But you're wrong to imply it's dangerous. The Brompton is horrible to ride if you take any pleasure in cycling, you said – wobbly, clumsy, unstable…

Folks, the Brompton may take you a little while to get used to it, perhaps longer if you're not very good at balancing. But once you do, small wheels become the opposite of clumsy. They're not right for long-distance touring or racing, but – with someone competent at the top of the stem – they're perfect for town riding.

And you think it's slow. Well sir, I don't agree: perhaps we need to set up some kind of contest.

Most importantly, though, you need to stop worrying about what schoolchildren might think of you.

OK James, don't get a folder – if you hardly ever need to fold it, I'll admit you'd have to be a bit of an enthusiast to buy a Brompton as your only bike.

But the next time you do get a bike, be a bit weirder. Learn to love the feeling of unorthodoxy that the Brompton stirred in your uneasy breast. Get kinky, man. Stop wearing a suit to the office. Find out about the smaller bike-makers that are excellent and truly cool, in this country alone, not to mention the rest of Europe and further afield. Take a look at the bikes created by some of the wonderful nutters on Critical Mass rides.

Many people love their Specialized Sirruses (Sirri?), and I'm the last person to tell someone they shouldn't love their bike. If it was the only bike in the world, I'd use a Sirrus over any other kind of wheeled transport, too. But only if.

A hybrid is a bike that you end up with if you walk into an average bike shop with £600 to spend and not much idea of where (or even if) you want to ride. Give it half an hour's thought and you could end up with something homegrown, unusual or amazing instead.

The Specialised Sirrus Elite tries to tick all the boxes – comfort, speed, coolness, sensibleness. But just like with cars, you can't have it all. It's a Vauxhall Calibra on two wheels.

Yours sincerely

Ben

Dear Ben,

You have stirred the wrath of Sirrus-lovers everywhere, so watch out on your route home. I don't fancy your chances of out-running us.

With hindsight I think I was a little unfair in expecting your two-wheeled bouncy-castle to operate as a bike (or at least as something that will take you comfortably from A to B). Because it does have the major engineering compromise built-in of being able to fold up – which I admit is a spectacular trick.

Maybe I didn't have long enough on it to get into the handling, but after your helpful tutorial, folding it up at least turned out to be not as difficult as I had feared. And its bendability proved very useful. I went to a party after work one evening and it was quite refreshing not to have to find a suitable lamp-post and wonder whether my bike would still be locked to it when I came out.

But sir, your Brompton does have an annoying habit of folding up when you don't want it to – for example, when going over kerbs or carrying it up the stairs to my flat. You did provide me with some classy frayed bungees to avoid this, but I felt it would be better to experience the bike in its intended state.

I'm struggling to know how to respond to the Calibra jibe. You say my middle-of-the-road Sirrus tries to do comfort, speed, coolness and sensibleness all in one, but fails. It may not be the fastest, most comfortable, coolest or most sensible bicycle – but at least it comes close. To use a different analogy, your bike is like an ace-high poker hand – one great card (the ace of foldability) but let down by the rest. And it costs a couple of hundred quid more than my Sirrus.

But I reckon it might be time to bury the hatchet. If huge armies of commuters begin streaming out of railway stations across the land clutching Bromptoms that will whisk them to their workplaces I will be a very happy man. Just so long as I am not one of them.

Yours sincerely,

James

COMMENTS

SarahLindon I have some sympathy for both riders. I moved to the suburbs about a year ago and switched from a Dawes Super Galaxy tourer to a Brompton-plus-train for my commute. The transition felt very strange. The Brompton is indeed a bumpy ride, I have to pedal away busily to keep moving – no elegant gliding – and I feel less able to claim my space on the road. On the other hand, I am cultivating my tootling talents, as I sense tootling is probably a saner approach in cities than my old urge toward ever greater speed.

phreakdown Oh no! I'm just about to order my Brompton for trips to London so I don't have to ride the bus with nutters, and as a spare bike for when friends visit, etc. I'm a little worried. Almost very worried… Am I now a "weird man"?

Mmmmf I'll admit to a love / hate relationship with the Bromp but, at the end of the day, I ride it because it's what the train operating companies will let me take on board in the rush hour. I'm fittish, but I'm not up to riding from Sussex to Clerkenwell daily. Even 20" wheel folders won't fit between the seat backs, so if I had a nice quicker folder like a Mezzo or an Airnimal I'd have to leave it at the end of the carriage and risk getting it nicked. It also wouldn't fit under my desk at work.

I might look like a weird bloke but then I am quite a weird bloke deep down, so I might as well run with it.

CaptainBlunder If there is anything guaranteed to get me into a flying eruption of pointless cycling fury it is being overtaken by a folding bike. There I am, minding my own business, daydreaming away, when along comes someone pumping their legs on a foldie, burning rubber in my face. The sheer implausibility and impudence of it first stuns me and then kicks me into action. I. Won't. Be. Beaten. By. A. Folding. Bike. goes my brain and I am now forced into a pointless race against a person who doesn't know they're racing. At least I usually win.

BalbKubrox Why all this one-eyed zealotry? Different types of bike serve different purposes, and I'd be a fool if I complained because my tin opener won't open the front door as well.

Don't stray from that towpath

STUART JEFFRIES

Have you ever cycled into the canal while commuting to work? You really ought to try – it's most refreshing. I did it earlier this week and, as I told the kind people who helped me out, I regret nothing. Or nothing very much.

This is what happened. I was cycling along the towpath of the Regent's Canal near King's Cross in north London thinking happy thoughts. I'd just read a news story about how women are getting more and more beautiful while men remain as pathetically cavemanny as ever. How lovely to be a heterosexual man in this day and age, I thought. Then I saw ahead of me an oncoming cyclist, and between him and me a couple strolling towards him.

The woman stepped sharply to the left towards the canal to avoid the cyclist. I swerved sharply to the left to avoid her and suddenly my visual field was full of grey/brown water coming to me very fast.

Then time slowed down and a series of questions went through my mind. Could I fall in such a way that the bike stayed on the towpath? Could I get my watch out of my pocket and hurl it on to the path before I went under? Could I reach my mobile, film the event and produce a multimedia audiovisual package that would really show my bosses that I'm not just a dinosaur of print journalism? Disappointingly, the answer to all three questions was no.

I stood up in the canal, thinking that the water wasn't as cold as I'd feared. I wondered how much swan poo was in the water and if it was toxic. I was quite pleased I hadn't landed on a supermarket trolley or the remains of another cyclist. The water came up to my chest and I had quite a nice chat with Laura and Jamie as they leaned with concerned looks down on me from the towpath. They looked so well dressed and dry that I felt at a bit of a social disadvantage. We did that very British dance: They were incredibly apologetic and self-abasing, I poo-pooed their apologies, saying it was entirely my fault. I'm not sure what happened to the oncoming cyclist.

They helped me pull the bike out of the water. My saddlebag was soaked, but amazingly some of the contents wrapped in a plastic bag – including my book and sandwiches which I later ate – were bone dry.

I climbed out of the canal smelling of my new fragrance, eau de Grand Union, and began wringing out my T-shirt when my colleague Hannah walked by pristine and stylish in a summer dress. In the circumstances, it was very kind of her to talk to me at all. She suggested I must be concussed and should walk the few yards to work and have a cup of tea. Instead I pulled on a reasonably dry cagoule (classy), cycled home, chucked my damp clothes in the washing machine, showered, dabbed my grazed shins with Dettol, and blow dried my Oyster Card, debit card, phone, and watch.

Then I cycled back to work: I had to get back on my saddle and face down my demons. I retraced my route along the towpath. There are tyre marks swerving across the grass verge of towpath at the point I went into the drink. I stood there for a few moments and whistled the guitar riff from The Good the Bad and the Ugly (where did that come from?).

The only downside of my accident was that my mobile phone doesn't work any more. I'd wanted an upgrade anyway. My bike (fingers crossed) seems to be in good condition.

Of course it was all my fault. The British Waterways code of conduct gives priority to pedestrians over cyclists, which is something that some cyclists don't take seriously enough. Hannah told me that a cyclist had shouted "Move!" at her the other day as they barrelled down the same towpath I cycle along every day. That sort of rudeness is contrary to the British Waterways cycling code which says: "be considerate and courteous to all users. Carry a bell and use it, or say excuse me as you approach all other users."

For the most part any friction between cyclists and pedestrians is the fault of a sizeable minority of the former. That said, for cyclists like me riding on the canal towpath is irresistible: it's a rustic idyll away from the raging roads.

COMMENTS

Chatelaine Next time, why not stop and dismount until the approaching cyclist and pedestrians have passed by? That way, you'll be a fixed obstacle that they have to negotiate, and none of you will have to second-guess each other's movements.

Glad it only took a few dabs of Dettol to fix you!

ChrisByrne Seems you were going a bit too fast for the conditions. I've seen other cyclists racing along a towpath on the Union Canal in Edinburgh and passing pedestrians at speed. Not only is it not safe but it misses the whole point of using a towpath on a canal. Why not slow down a bit and enjoy the ride?

Mmmmf Good lord; you come across some pious prigs whilst out blogging – the bloke made an honest mistake and owned up to it. Fair enough. A genuinely bad cyclist would just have baled into the pedestrians (and I can guarantee you 90% of motorists would choose to hit a pedestrian rather than, say, a wall – I've seen it happen).

chevron2000 HA! I, too, have cycled into the canal. On my new bike when I had just started cycling again after a good 10-year moratorium.

I was overtaking a chap who hadn't heard my bell and walked into me, knocking me very slowly into the brackish depths. I can report that the water between Broadway Market and Angel is slightly deeper, reaching just to my neck.

I cycled home after my unsuspecting assailant kindly pulled me out. A couple of passers-by said: "What have you done?" As though there was another major water source nearby.

The children of London Fields primary school crowded around the playground fence to shout, "Oh my days, what is dat?"

nobodyisinnocent Highly overrated cycle route. Crap road surface, smelly tramps, idiot joggers with iPods and sometimes pitbulls running alongside them.

A Tour de Norfolk commute is rough without the right fuel

MATTHEW SPARKES

Until recently, I worked six miles from home. Commuting by bike was simple, carefree and I barely broke a sweat.

A month ago I transferred to an office 25 miles away, and getting to my desk has suddenly become a serious business. Each day is a fresh stage in my own, private Tour de Norfolk.

Problems emerged that just weren't an issue on a short, urban commute; the roads are so remote that a fully charged mobile and decent toolkit are vital, as is one day a week on the train for rest and shirt/boxer short replenishment.

But by far the biggest issue is food. Even on my longest rides, I'd never given much thought to nutrition, but to ride 50 miles a day takes forethought. And quantity.

Swallowing a huge bowl of pasta the night before helps – it's what proper athletes call carbohydrate loading – but it's not easy. Sometimes it can feel like you're the sole contestant in some torturous spaghetti-eating competition. That's the main problem with burning a couple of thousand extra calories a day: you have to eat them all.

This sounds fun at first, but the novelty quickly wears off. If you don't eat enough of the right foods, at the right time, then getting to work is a serious slog. This means planning evening meals, and making-do at work for the return leg.

I've toyed with snacks on the bike, which help reduce the need to plan supper so anally, but this also comes with problems. After an hour of riding, eating on the go can be painful and tedious.

I turned to specialised gels and bars from the cycling shop for a while; all sciencey and crammed into lurid tubes and sachets. I found they worked well, were small and easy to carry, but cost a fortune. Do the maths and it soon becomes ludicrous.

Individual gels are around £2 each, and most manufacturers recommend you eat one per 20 minutes of riding. So, a 110 minute ride, 10 times a week, will cost £110. Even buying in bulk, this is no option.

After a couple of weeks I decided that the best course was to make my own. Having done some research online, I'd found hundreds of slightly varying recipes for energy bars. I decided to make one up.

I compiled a list of good sources of slow-release energy, and another list of things I could eat regularly without getting bored. The union of the two went into the recipe, which was based around a basic flapjack.

They worked out much cheaper, with around £4 of ingredients making 20-30 snack-sized bars. It takes some time, but a batch will last a week of commuting, and can be easily kept in the fridge.

Overall, they worked just as well as the hi-tech gels, but eating them is still hard work on occasion. Eating, like riding, can become a chore if you're forced into it. It's far better when you're free to do it as and when you please.

And there's the biggest lesson to be learned from a long commute; when it stops being fun, stop. When you wake up and find yourself craving a ride, start again.

COMMENTS

stuffedolive Oh come on! 50 miles a day at touring pace – which is what this is – does not require loads of specialist food – gels and energy bars my perineum! It just requires you to eat your normal meals but adding some extra carbs in too, like an extra couple of slices of bread with each meal or an extra dollop of pasta. There's no way you should be wasting money on overhyped 'sports nutrition'.

PeterWalker That 20-minutes-per-gel formula sounds far too frequent for a commute. I'd guess that was calculated for a race, and not an intake you'd want every day.

ChrisByrne My grandad used to cycle 25 miles each way to work for the best part of 20 years, well into his 60s. I don't think they had gel bars back in the 1950s. I'm pretty sure he was fuelled by porridge plus a packed lunch which he took with him.

LordLucan When I were a lad, got up at half past 3, bowl of gruel, cycled 45 miles to work, did 12 hour shift down pit with only half a sandwich and a pot of tea, cycled 62 miles home just to make it hard for meself, ate tea then off to the club for 12 pints of best. Beer boy, that's what you need, more beer!

John Snow explains how cycling gave him his big break in journalism

INTERVIEW BY MATT WELLS

Matt Wells: What bike do you ride?

Jon Snow: I guess you'd call it a cross breed, it's a ridgeback. It's not a mountain bike and its not a road bike either.

MW: But this isn't your regular bike is it?

JS: Well, it is at the moment because I had my regular bike nicked. A very beautiful bike it was too, hand built by Condor with a titanium frame. In fact the insurance company has paid up so I will be getting another one.

MW: You've been riding your bike to work for some time now, haven't you?

JS: Almost embarrassingly long now. I have been riding to work for 40 years.

MW: Why?

JS: Well I guess because it's efficient, more than anything else. Fundamentally, I know how long it will take to get there and back and more importantly as a reporter in London, I know how long it will take me to get anywhere. And almost invariably it is faster than anything else.

MW: They take about cycling tribes, do you belong to any one?

JS: No, I talk about cycling genres and I probably belong to the least discussed genre which is the jobbing cyclist.

MW: What does that involve?

JS: Well, a jobbing cyclist is someone who in the end cycles to live rather than to recreate and I am someone who simply rides for functional reasons. The other great thing about cycling is that of course, one of the spin-offs is that it keeps you fit. I mean for a guy of 62, I can still go like a train. The other thing of course is the environment.

MW: Does that make you feel superior to your colleagues...

JS: Well, I feel elevated.

MW: So, what's your typical day like?

JS: Well, I get in at around 9.30, I have a meeting with the editor and then you start your slog. That might involve cycling down to Whitehall and going to a briefing or something.

MW: How many times will you use your bike in a week?

JS: Oh my goodness, in the day at least half a dozen times.

MW: Now, I've noticed that down in Whitehall and the Westminster area it's quite difficult to lock up your bike because they won't let you.

JS: You know I obtained a parliamentary pass solely so I would be able to lock my bike – I mean I rarely ever go in there for anything worthwhile. The only place that they are seriously deferential about it all is Downing Street. If I go there, I'm allowed to take my bike in through the Thatcher memorial gates and I can leave it unlocked leaning against the wall.

MW: Is that a special Snow privilege?

JS: Yes, it's a special Snow privilege. "Ah, Mr Paxman, come on in!" That's what I get.

MW: Do you find that cycling helps you think and prepare for work?

JS: Yes, yes it's fantastic.

MW: And have you ever found that it gives you a journalistic advantage?

JS: Oh 100%. All the time, I wouldn't be where I am without my bike. I mean the fact is I got spotted while a reporter on LBC radio during the period when the IRA was bombing us across London in 1974–5 and ITN offered me a job on the strength of the fact that I always seemed to the scene of the bomb first. Well, the fact of the matter is that as soon as the blast went off, the old police tapes would go up and no one would be able to get in. The traffic would back-up and there would be taxis full of hacks trying to get there. I'd go steaming down the outside and if you took the tapes fast enough they couldn't stop you getting in anyway. The police have got too much to do to chuck you out and you'd be able to do the broadcast from the site.

MW: Can I ask you a little bit about your campaigning – you're president of CTC which is the UK's national cycling organisation. What do you think of the perennial cycling campaign issues, for example what's your view on cycle lanes?

JS: I'm not in tune with CTC when it comes to that. They do not necessarily support separated cycle ways but I do. I think that Europe has shown us that separated cycles ways – in towns anyway – are pretty essential. I'd like to ban all parking on the left-hand side of the road and every left-hand side of every road should be a cycle lane but I know that won't happen I'm afraid.

MW: We have a number of cycling politicians now, in London we famously have a cycling mayor in Boris Johnson.

JS: Still a minority to be honest. Boris, in a sense, is represented as doubly eccentric through his bicycle.

MW: In your experience, has it made any difference for you as a cyclist to have a cycling mayor?

JS: No, I don't think it has actually, in fact as much was done by Ken Livingstone for cycling as has been done by Boris and as far as I know he never went on a bike.

MW: Do you think that having a cycling Prime Minister in David Cameron will make a difference to cycling policy?

JS: No, I don't think it will. I think to be honest the only thing that will make a difference is major volume and I think the volume is getting better. The recession is also particularly good for cycling. I mean it's an amazing thing but cyclist shops are doing better than ever – people are definitely leaving their cars and taking up bikes.

This is an abridged version of an interview that appeared on the Guardian's bike podcast. You can hear the unedited interview at gu.com/p/2f9vv

Chapter 4

Women on bikes

First things first: just because this chapter is dedicated to ladies and bicycling should in no way imply that the rest of the book is for blokes. Most cycling experiences covered elsewhere are universal, whether it's the fear of being flattened by a bin truck or the excruciating embarrassment of saddle sore. But there are some problems only female riders face, be it the logistics of pedalling while pregnant or the difficulties of retaining one's modesty while cycling in a summer dress.

I've never subscribed to any of the Mars/Venus claptrap, but I must concede that women behave quite differently to men on two wheels. We're less masochistic in our gear usage, for starters: if I need to get in bottom gear to climb a hill, I'll do it without a thought, while many men of my acquaintance take a perverse pride in never going down onto the "granny" ring if anyone else is looking.

But a more worrying gender trait is the tendency for women to cycle more meekly, hugging the kerb as if to apologise for having the cheek to take up space on the road. Anna Leach describes why what might initially seem courteous behaviour is actually suicidal madness. Cower in the gutter and cars are less likely to see you and are way more likely to squeeze past you at close proximity. Not just that, but you're far more susceptible to punctures caused by the glass and other debris that tends to end up being swept to the side of the street. The flipside is that some research has shown that drivers actually give *more* space to women cyclists – or at least cyclists with flowing, ladylike locks.

A big issue for the modern two-wheeled woman is receiving the wrong sort of attention, however. Rare is the lady cyclist who hasn't endured comments of the "Lucky saddle!" or "I wish you we riding me, love" variety. A dismaying number of women have even had their bottoms patted as they struggled up a hill. Dawn Foster once had her top pulled down as she waited for the lights to change. A number of blogs have discussed the best way to deal with this behaviour. One commenter suggested the problem would be best solved by simply banning men from the roads. Foster decided to get even by documenting sexist encounters in her personal blog, 101Wankers, and plotting crime hotspots on a Google Map. A post about her endeavours generated one of the liveliest debates in Guardian Bike Blog history.

Chauvinistic nonsense is not confined to the world of the everyday cyclist, alas, as I discovered when the Tour of Britain advertised for attractive women to kiss riders at the end of each stage. Do podium girls belong in modern cycling? I asked. As ever, the readers had a lot to say.

Helen Pidd

Helen Pidd is the author of Bicycle: Love Your Bike: The Complete Guide to Everyday Cycling

Cycling while pregnant helps prepare you for childbirth

SAM HADDAD

Editor of Cooler, a sport and style title for young women

When I first emailed colleagues to let them know I was pregnant among the congratulations and "That'll cause a dip in the Smirnoff share price"-type chortle came this unexpected note from our receptionist, "You're not still cycling to work are you? Is that safe?"

The truth was I didn't know. As an avid cyclist, with a firm belief that riding to and from work makes my commute not just bearable but actually quite pleasurable, it was one of the first things I'd Googled after the positive test. Yet the advice was conflicting. Everyone agreed on the physical and psychological benefits of moderate, low-impact exercise during a low-risk pregnancy, and the NHS advises women to "keep up your normal daily physical activity or exercise for as long as you feel comfortable". But it also warns against cycling "because there's a risk of falling". A sentiment echoed by parenting sites, such as the National Childbirth Trust and BabyCentre, the latter warning against all but riding an exercise bike as "even if you're an experienced cyclist, there's a danger you'll fall or be knocked off your bike."

Really? Granted some accidents will be tragically unavoidable, but isn't that the case when you cross a road or get into your car?

Thankfully the CTC – the national cyclists' organisation – was on hand with positive advice and useful tips from raising your handlebars and fitting lower gears to the more spirited "cut down on those off-road descents and don't race-train in a pack". They also tell you to consult your doctor first, which I did. She saw no reason why I shouldn't cycle as long as I took it easy and listened to my body. At three months in, my body was feeling good, with the only sniff of morning sickness coming on the rare mornings when I took the train and bus to work, which also doubled my journey time.

As you'd expect things are more enlightened on the continent. I met a Dutch lady on holiday and asked if she was planning to cycle through her third pregnancy. Her incredulous reply was, "Of course, how else would I get around?" And as Mikael Colville-Andersen of the Copenhagen-based bike blog Cycle Chic says: "Cycling is virtually prescribed for pregnant women in Denmark." He even devotes a post to beautiful pregnant cyclists in all their glory. On a thread on the CTC Facebook page Merlijn Janssens illustrates the different mentality in the UK: "When pregnant with my first one nobody in the Netherlands questioned [me] cycling, here everybody looks at you like you are committing a deadly sin."

I'm now a week shy of seven months pregnant and still merrily, if not a little more breathlessly, cycling my 15-mile round commute to work. I feel really good and my doctor is impressed by how "mobile" I am for this stage of my pregnancy. I'm still riding my much-loved single speed, though I've mentally tuned into the fact I will probably have to switch to a more upright Dutch-style bike for the final stretch, as even the smallest inclines are getting ever tougher. Or I may have to stop cycling altogether, who knows. I'm keeping an open mind about it.

Over the last month even the baggiest of my husband's t-shirts have ceased to hide my ever-expanding bump, which has led to me getting more than my fair share of funny looks from strangers, ranging from the quizzical double takes to downright disapproval. Last week a taxi driver hollered, "You shouldn't be on your bike in your condition love!" after I barked at him for dangerously cutting me up in a bus lane. And a friend stopped me in the street to the other day to say, complete with worried face, "Promise me you'll stop cycling soon". As if the mere act of me cycling was mortally wounding her.

But I've drawn comfort from the advice of fellow cyclists who rode until late in their pregnancy, such as Sarah Buck, formerly a designer at bike fashion brand Cyclodelic. She was a bike courier for 10 years and never considered not cycling while pregnant. "No one dared tell me not to cycle or they'd have been in trouble. But I felt so comfortable on the bike it was never going to be an issue for me. I was cycling from Camberwell to Hackney, an hour and a half of light-impact exercise a day and really do think it benefited my body and mind. I had a really healthy pregnancy, and as you're not putting weight on your legs, it's actually easier than walking."

Josie Dew, author of seven cycle travel books and vice-president of the CTC cycled 10–15 miles daily throughout both her pregnancies including the actual days she went into labour. "I recommend cycling while pregnant (that is if your body is already used to a daily pounding of pedals) and then cycling up a 1:4 hill on your due date. Seems to get things moving along nicely and at quite a pace, too."

"I'm 44 so at first the doctors were a bit panicky about my age but then they realised I was quite fit from all the cycling I do. It was quite hard going by the end, like being really unfit, but it made me feel happy and keeping active is key….And my midwife thinks being a cyclist definitely helped my stamina during birth. If you're used to being tired and pushing yourself through 10 more mountain passes, it helps you handle the pain of childbirth."

Here's hoping she's right.

COMMENTS

wheeledweenie Pregnant women seem to be fair game when it comes to being bossed around by strangers and I know my friends with children get sick of it. Surely it's up to the individual woman as to whether they want to cycle or not? If there's no medical reason not to and it makes you feel good then good for you!

LadyPage Of course you should be careful during pregnancy because you have the responsibility of another life to think of – but that doesn't mean you have to sit at home wrapped up in blankets. In both my pregancies I climbed ladders and did DIY and exercised – but personally I wouldn't ride a bike when pregnant because I don't trust all road users to be vigilant and the potential for just one awkward fall is high and could be utterly devastating.

chinebee I cycled every day until I was about 7 and a half months pregnant, even though I had to field a lot of similar negative comments from people who thought pregnant women should "look after themselves" by staying at home and taking it easy. I'm convinced the daily cycle helped keep me energetic, fit and healthy throughout my pregnancy.

Cycling while pregnant: the verdict

SAM HADDAD

A few months back I wrote about my experience of cycling while seven months pregnant and now, as three-month old Herbie kips in the next room (perhaps dreaming of his first bike?), I thought you might like to know how it all went.

While I'd said I was keeping an open mind about cycling right until the point of lift off, I hadn't really imagined that I would do it. And certainly not given the heatwave we had at the start of summer, when the mercury seemed to nestle in the high 20s for weeks on end. Yet that's exactly what I ended up doing. In fact I had a very enjoyable ride up the hill home from yoga the night before I went into labour, overtaking a bemused middle-aged commuter in the process.

At eight months, even my bike-loving husband was tentatively asking when I might call it a day, or at the very least switch to the upright Dutch-style bike I'd bought for the latter stages of pregnancy in place of my single speed. I did often wonder, "Might this be my last week? Is it going to get too difficult? Will I get all wobbly?" but perhaps because I was going at such a glacial pace it never seemed to be an issue and the only times I felt faint or uncomfortable in the heat were on the rare days that I squished my ever-expanding belly into a sweaty tube carriage.

Two weeks out, I finished work so stopped my 15-mile cross-London commute but kept riding shorter local trips, in part for the endorphin hit but also because cycling was so much easier than waddling down the street. Not that I was really waddling, as aside from my sizable bump I'd managed to keep in surprisingly ok shape. As I sat with other pregnant women with similar due dates to mine, comparing their myriad ailments, from insomnia and varicose veins, to backache and breathlessness, I was almost embarrassed by how good I felt.

I'd deliberately take stairs slowly as they huffed and puffed beside me and sheepishly lock my bike up around the corner at antenatal classes. Once, I was busted and was quick to pretend I'd cycled two minutes down the road rather than the 15-minute jaunt I'd actually done.

The pros of keeping your weight down in pregnancy have recently been well-documented and though I have no science to back my specific case up I firmly believe staying fit with all that cycling (and yoga towards the end) led me to have a relatively straight-forward, and if not enjoyable then certainly endurable, birth. Especially compared to all the horror birth stories I'd heard other mums bandy about. My labour took just nine hours, which is pretty quick for a first child, and I relied on my leg strength a lot throughout and especially during the – for want of a better expression – pushing phase.

The cycle travel author Josie Dew had compared childbirth to taking on mountain passes and told me: "Cycling helps you push through the pain barriers of labour." I'm sure tackling tough peaks on a four-day charity ride in Cornwall last summer helped me mentally. And once Herbie was born I did feel the kind of dizzy euphoria you might associate with having done Ditchling Beacon on the South Downs, albeit 80 times in a row.

I appreciate there could be no link between the pregnancy and birth I had and the regular cycling. I could just have been lucky. Herbie is a happy, healthy and, for now at least, chilled-out little boy, so I feel extremely fortunate as it is. The only mild downer, which I appreciate isn't really a downer in the scheme of things, is how little I've been able to cycle since he was born. I can safely say I was in better shape when I had him than I am now!

Quite soon after the birth my bright blue steed had started to call my name across the front room (I never did switch to the Dutch-style bike). But my doctor suggested I might like to wait three weeks before taking it out for a spin. When I did it, I felt like a kid again and I still do on the two or so, painfully short, rides I try to fit in on a weekly basis. Commuting by bike is pretty much the only thing I miss about working, especially when my husband rides off into the kind of crisp blue mornings we've been having recently. I don't just miss the buzz of riding, I miss it being something I do everyday, rather than have to squeeze in.

But I don't want to wish this time away, as I know before long I'll be back riding to work with a child seat either enhancing or ruining the look of my bike, depending on your take. Until then I've invested in a turbo trainer so I can put the miles in while Herbie bats at his playmat. Let's hope he likes bikes.

COMMENTS

anewstart for sure, he'll love 'em.

Katali Well done, you. Hope you manage to get a few more rides done soon, and that the three of you enjoy many years of cycling!

Gipfeli I rode my bike until the day before I gave birth to my son. I got some funny looks but with a few adaptions anything is possible. Due to my bump I was forced to lower my seat so that I could sidle off the bike rather than the traditional dismount.

PhineasPPhagBrake There is a bike rack outside the maternity clinic near where I live. Whenever I go past it always conjures up the image of heavily pregnant women cycling to the clinic, giving birth and then cycling home – OK, maybe this is a little too far fetched

How to cycle in a summer dress

GWLADYS FOUCHÉ

My skirt gently fluttered as I cycled to work this morning, the sun was shining, the temperature sizzling. I felt I was in a François Truffaut film. But then the wind caught my skirt, it flew upwards, and little was left for the imagination for passers-by. Not very classy.

I love cycling in a summer dress but it has its embarrassing pitfalls. Keeping your modesty is a bit of a challenge when your dress progressively recedes up your thighs.

I could keep a hand on my skirt, but then rapid braking is out of the question. And no one cares about looking good when your brains are splattered all over the pavement.

My ride is a women's hybrid, with its middle bar slightly lower than on a man's. But I still have to contort myself like a snake to get on to it. Riding a man's bike is out of the question because, if I wore a tight-fitted dress, I will never be able to get in place.

Perhaps the solution is to ditch the sports bike and buy an old-fashioned sit up and beg model. Or perhaps I should convince a Paul Newman-lookalike to ferry me around town like he does Katharine Ross in Butch Cassidy and the Sundance Kid. Now that would be a fun ride.

How is it that some women manage to look effortlessly stylist? Any tips?

COMMENTS

MsMisplaced Some lovely bloomers?

I have a Pashley and dresses wafting where they shouldn't is still a problem. Pencil skirts and fabulous 50s/60s wiggle dresses are where I'm at now – though they would probably make it quite difficult to clamber onto a hybrid.

PDanTic Sit on your skirt. Trust me. It sounds like it'll be awkward/impossible/ridiculous-looking, but there are some very artful ways you can arrange even the floatiest of skirts so that they'll go nowhere.

Short, tight skirts on the other hand I've never managed to reconcile with cycling. They ride up and up and up, and there's only so much thigh you can show with any decency. Heck, there's only so much thigh before it turns into something else at the top...

Iouliddiard I have the exact same issue all the time but after a few embarrassing gusts of wind I have a solution. I keep a safety pin pinned into the hem of my dresses, when it's time to get on my bike I pin the front of the dress to the back, between my knees and create my shorts/dress hybrid. It's the only way I've found to keep my dignity and a good summer cycling wardrobe!

beastGP I hear HRM the Queen has small lead weights (or similar) sewn into the hems of her skirts to prevent any jetway incidents of national embarrassment. Something similar should work fairly well?

Ethelberga I wear three-quarter length cycling shorts underneath floaty dresses. They look like leggings, too, so I don't feel silly when I get off the bike.

Grakken Personally I enjoy the fact that wearing a skirt allows the air to circulate a bit. I don't think many people have seen my pants, and to be honest I don't really care. But then again, I do wear quite big pants.

Lysander Just had a brainwave! How about constructing a pair of large bicycle-clips that are worn around the thigh rather than the ankle? Easy to put-on and remove; they'd stop the skirt wafting up any higher than mid-thigh. Available in sizes from 'Kiera Knightly' up to 'HGV'.

Why do I have to endure such unwanted attention on my bike

JESSICA REED

Forget modesty: it's about catcalling. Unlike Gwladys (see previous blog), I quickly gave up on the idea of biking with a skirt on. A pity really, because the thought of commuting to work wearing light and fluttering fabrics is especially appealing during summer time. But from now on, I'm all about ugly Lycra capri pants.

My admission of defeat isn't about wanting to keep my poise: looking silly isn't too much of a problem if I am in the midst of a strenuous physical exercise. What made me give up dresses was the never-ending catcalls hurled my way day in, day out. No matter that I was just commuting to work at 8.30am looking dishevelled, or biking through the park on a Sunday afternoon looking nice: if biking on my own, unwelcome remarks were de circonstance. I have heard it all: from builders demanding that I "flash my boobs, love" and older men asking if I had panties on, to teenagers making furtive kissing sounds supposed to suggest appreciation. I even once encountered a pedestrian who, having spotted me cycling from afar in a deserted street, stopped in the middle of a crossroads only to bend down with a huge grin, trying to catch a glimpse of my knickers.

At first, politely ignoring lurid comments while avoiding eye contact with the offenders seemed like a good solution. But such unwanted attention quickly became tiring, if not unsettling. After a few months of weekly (if not daily, during summer months) street harassment, I decided to resort to a more aggressive tactic and ditched my much-loved Dutch bike, bought myself a hybrid, and started dressing head-to-toe in black Lycra. And wouldn't you know? The catcalling ceased immediately, except for that recent time when I had the incredible audacity to go on a bike ride wearing shorts. But does it really have to come to that? Should women have to police their own clothes, rather than men watch their behaviour?

I would love to hear about how female cyclists deal with catcalling. Do you say something back, or do you just shrug and keep on going?

COMMENTS

ladylady I've yet to ditch the skirt but I cycle equipped with an ultimate deterrent to male attention (unwanted and wanted).

Not the helmet but a toddler. I thought the seat on its own would work but it has to have a child in it.

possetpot Ah, the joys of being old and invisible.

Helenajulia After a particularly harrowing cat call incident, when a couple of male drivers followed me as I cycled down an alleyway while yelling "Lucky bike" etc, I threw my bike to the ground and burst into tears. The men were devastated: "Sorry, love, we didn't mean any offence." While not a strategy I'd necessarily advocate, it did seem to have an effect.

Lizka I have battled with this exact issue since I started cycling in London, but I refuse to give up my beautiful Pashley and start wearing Lycra. Dilemma!

No. No dilemma any more. I have an excellent solution.

It works best in those situations where you're sat at a red light receiving unwanted attention. No matter what bike you ride, or how you dress, here's what you need to do:

1) Be brave. You'll pull this off better the more confidence and bravado you chuck into it.

2) Upon hearing the offending jibe, turn and face your victim. Look him right in the eye. Look unimpressed but not angry. At this moment, you should arrange your face somewhere near deadpan.

3) Scrutinise your victim's appearance. However much of it you can see. If he's on foot, look him up and down. If he's in a car, examine the car (let's face it, it's probably crappy). Let him see that you are judging him.

4) Laugh. Not like a maniac, like someone who couldn't be more amused by such a pathetic individual deigning to be so bold as to utter a single syllable to you, most superior and lovely cyclist.

5) Cycle away feeling better, and knowing you've brought his macho bravado crashing down. Ohhhh yeaaah.

catmum Ideally, all men would be banned from the roads. This would solve more than one problem.

How I expose sexist idiots online

DAWN FOSTER

Blogger at 101wankers.com

I believe the only way you can really know a city is by bike. But the one thing that spoils matters, and it seems to thrive whenever I'm on my bike, is the abuse I receive from pedestrians and motorists alike.

The sight of me whizzing away on two wheels seemed to increase some people's boldness to the point where they'd shout insults they'd never dare express to people who would have the time to stop and challenge them.

As I zoomed from work to home and back again, I'd often let such insults fester in my head. I wondered – why had they chosen to shout them at me?

Whenever I mentioned these incidents, I met with disparate responses. Men would usually imply I was exaggerating, that I was oversensitive and incorrectly ascribing all comments shouted in public to myself.

My female friends would be indignant, explain that such incidents were commonplace, happened more often than not and be annoyed that men could be so convinced that this kind of thing didn't happen.

One evening, after struggling up a particularly steep hill in Greenwich, I was angry and aggrieved that an athletic feat met with only sexist comments – "Come on love, put some back into it!" and "I hope you put as much effort into the bedroom!".

I ranted about it to some friends in a nearby pub. They asked if I noticed whether comments and altercations were concentrated in certain areas. I wasn't sure, but finding out seemed like an interesting experiment. The following day I started cataloguing the comments I experienced, and recording them on Google Maps.

What I found was interesting. Firstly, the opportunity to write about the abuse hurled at me dispersed my anger. I was able to retaliate in a calmer, more amusing way. People found my responses to these idiotic comments funny. I made my peace with the idiots by exposing them.

Secondly, hundreds of women wrote me emails, responded to my blog and spoke to me on Twitter to tell me they'd had identical experiences. They didn't tell me of every incident – they were too numerous – but they told me about their worst ones.

I told people about the time a pedestrian pulled my top down at a traffic light; they told me of people spitting at them and throwing building braces at them as they drove by. A dozen women told me they'd had their backsides slapped by drivers and passengers. I'd opened the flood gates by daring to speak out and say that enough was enough.

What surprised me was that far more men than women contacted me. They said they'd had no idea of the level of abuse women received, and that when they mentioned my site to female cyclists they opened a Pandora's Box of untapped resentment towards the sexist abuse they'd experienced over the years.

Male correspondents were appalled and ashamed of how much grief their friends had experienced, and apologised for something they'd personally had no part in.

The experience of writing the blog has changed me. Before, I felt cowed by taunts and one-liners, now I think "what an excellent blog post".

I enjoy responding on the blog, my readers adore it, and I hope some of the abusive drivers and pedestrians realise they are being cordially mocked throughout the internet.

COMMENTS

marmot99 From a male cyclist's perspective , we also see a lot of abuse but it takes the form of violence and aggression rather than humiliation and denigration. So the form of the abuse varies by the sex of the rider, but the abuse is constant. So the question is what can we do to 'normalize' cycling and remove the outsider status of people who choose to ride bicycles.

My preferred solution? Get cycling recognised as a religion so that abusing cyclists becomes illegal.

Pidd I reckon I get "lucky saddle!" around once a fortnight. More if I'm not wearing a helmet. Less if I'm wearing a cagoule. I tend to react with my most withering look.

Bluefish59 I ride around York all the time, and given that Yorkshire is often perceived as the birthplace of the unreconstructed male, I get very little sexist abuse. Mind you the high viz jacket and matching cycle clips may have something to do with it. Abusers up here fall into 2 categories: Bus drivers and taxi drivers. Seems like London is the birthplace of unreconstructed wankers...

Applespider Only abusive comment I've ever had was from a bloke screaming at me to use hand signals (despite the fact I was going straight on in the right lane) so I did give him a hand signal... with one finger :-)

geofarce I got a backside slap from a car full of teenagers but the muppets did it on a stretch of road with roadworks so I caught up a couple of minutes later and gave the top of the car a flat hand slap. It makes a hell of a noise if you are in the car but does no damage. I then left them for dust.

dawnhfoster Hello! Interesting comments. I tend not to remonstrate with abusers, though when I lived in Coventry, I was particularly exasperated one day when a motorist leaned over to say: "You can ride my bike, if you want" with a wink. "Do you have a bike?" I asked. He looked sheepish, and admitted he didn't. I may have laughed.

From the catwalks to the bike lane

ANNA GLOWINSKI

Founder of women's cycle clothing brand Ana Nichoola

Women's cycle wear is receiving a lot of press, with new fashion brands popping up and trusted cycling brands bringing out inspired women's ranges. The change is centred on image. I am sure that bike brands Assos and Gore have made leaps and bounds in technology, but the fastest movement is the fusion of function with form. Bicycles are becoming works of art, race teams compete for the hottest kit and commuter fashion has turned the streets into a catwalk.

There are always the moaners to bring the excitement down a peg or two, though. You know the type: the "real cyclists" who look down on this supposedly self-indulgent desire for beauty; or the lot who have ridden the same bike since they were born and swear you don't need anything other than plastic bags on your feet and an old tent over your head when it's wet.

When the sustainable transport charity Sustrans launched its Bike Belles site, complete with fashion pages, every cycling forum you could chance upon had "real cyclists" pulling it apart. Yet it didn't take much searching to find discussions by the same people about the lack of nice female cycle clothing.

I race bicycles, and I have been lucky enough to pick up sponsorship with Mule Bar, who have created a women's team. We are all super-competitive, but in the grand scheme of things, not that fast. Our sponsor consciously picked women with a "healthy" attitude to racing: at team meetings we will discuss a training plan, and maybe some bike parts, and then bike colours, and inevitably we will move on to whether a white skinsuit will show off cellulite, or what is the best mascara if you know you're going to sweat.

The team's love of the sport as well as fashion is a reflection of the changes that are happening in racing cycling. Rachel Atherton and Shanaze Reade, two of the world's fastest female downhillers and BMXers respectively, are snapped up for fashion shoots, further glamourising their sports. And it's not a bad thing. Look at Victoria Pendleton – wearing mascara in a race doesn't make her go any slower.

That's just the tip of it. Cycling is not only a physical sport, it is also transport: at some point, you have to arrive and I won't be turning up to a bar wearing two Tesco Bags for Life.

Sometimes feeling that you look good is fundamental to your confidence: for example, in a job interview. Of course, cycling throws all sorts of practical considerations at you: you need your skin to breathe, to be covered if it rains, to be visible at day and night. But it is increasingly possible to add a little feminine touch to your outfit, without sacrificing the fundamentals.

There is something good happening in cycling, with more women taking to it and looking better doing it. It is exciting and it is important. With the bicycle fashion industry having grown so quickly, and bicycle photography becoming highly competitive, I can't wait to see the rise of the next cycling-inspired art form, and the role of women within that.

COMMENT

MissScarlet Hear, hear! Why shouldn't we want to look good when we cycle?

It would be lovely to cycle to meet friends and then go on home – in an outfit I don't feel ashamed to be seen in. If that doesn't make me a 'proper cyclist', I'm comfortable with that!

What's stopping teenage girls from cycling?

SARAH PHILLIPS

Teenage girls don't ride bikes. Or so says the Darlington Media Group, who have set about trying to rectify the problem with a campaign to get young women cycling.

Several years ago, the National Children's Bureau published research that revealed that on average, boys cycle 138 miles a year and girls only 24 miles. This still rings true. Christie Rae, 16, from Newcastle told me: "I do have a bike, but I don't really use it. Only sometimes in the summer when my friends and I cycle round to see each other. I don't know many girls that do, actually."

Darlington's project began with the production of a documentary called Beauty and the Bike, chronicling a trip made by a group of teenage girls to Bremen in Germany, where they met their cycling-loving peers and found out about the joys of the open road. It all sounds slightly twee, but addresses the important issue that girls tend to get to a certain age and it's no longer the done thing to get about by bike.

I have every admiration for such attempts to get women enjoying the numerous benefits of cycling, but what is frustrating is the focus on appearance that is often so integral to these sorts of schemes. Aside from the title, BATB, which incidentally has been used for a similar scheme in the past, Darlington's site makes it clear they are keen to address the important issue of remaining fashionable while cycling. But as I recall, it was an overprotective mother that stopped me from spending too much time around the bike sheds in my teenage years, rather than any personal concerns over the way I looked.

Another offender is the site Bike Belles (www.bikebelles.org.uk), run by the otherwise excellent charity Sustrans, which encourages women of all ages to take up cycling. One helpful section dedicated to beauty tips provides such gems as: "Use waterproof mascara when it's raining on your bike, and take a powder compact for a quick refresher on arrival." Admittedly, I write as someone who occasionally arrives at the office sporting a minor oil slick on my face, but I sincerely doubt that women are so image conscious that this is what is stopping them.

Aside from fashion tips, the beauty bikers and belles both voice concerns over the lack of decent cycle lanes and safety issues that make our roads a wholly unappealing prospect. Those two are serious issues that would put inexperienced riders off, and are much more worthy of a campaign to get people, regardless of gender, on their bikes.

COMMENTS

sverdlovsk I'm more convinced by the safety argument than the 'looking good' argument. In Holland you certainly see all sexes and ages cycling around the place. Largely because they have excellent cycle lanes. Build the infrastructure and I'm sure more female cyclists will follow.

Skitten As a teenage girl in the '80s, living in a village, I used to cycle often.

As a grown woman, with a bike, and a desire to cycle to work, I can't, because the only road I can take to work is incredibly fast and dangerous and doesn't have a bicycle lane.

poefaced I used to cycle all the time as a teenager. I do it less so now and that partly is because of vanity. I like to think it's the "acceptable" kind though, I have to be smart for work and can't always face the hassle of bringing in all the kit required to fix me after a long cycle.

Boredstupid The only thing you need to point out to get teenage girls to cycle is what an improvement it will make on their butt. Surely this is as important to them as make up?

Why are female cyclists so vulnerable to lorries?

ANNA LEACH

As I cycle home I'm conscious of an ominous rumble behind me. A quick glance over my left shoulder confirms my worst fears: a looming heavy goods vehicle is blocking out the sun.

I don't fancy taking it on with only my helmet and luminous vest as protection, so I veer closer to the kerb so it can overtake. We meet again at traffic lights, and again I shrink towards the edge of the road.

I might think I'm protecting myself, but in fact this is the most dangerous way for a cyclist to interact with a lorry. Some experts believe that behaviour like mine is the reason that far more female cyclists are killed in HGV accidents than men.

This is particularly the case in London, which has the unenviable position of being the epicentre of lorry-related cycling deaths in the UK. Last year, 10 out of 13 fatal cycling accidents in the capital involved women, and eight of them were killed by HGVs, according to the cycling campaign group CTC. This is despite the fact that there are around three times more male cyclists in London than women.

Few cyclists have an understanding of how much lorry drivers can see from their cabs, which were designed for motorway driving rather than London's awkward and elderly street plan.

Every tragic accident is different but certain common themes run through the recent deaths: turning left, roundabouts and women.

But why would gender affect the likelihood of being killed on the roads? Barry Mason, a cycle safety campaigner with Southwark Cyclists, speculates that this is because women are less assertive riders and therefore tend to be less visible. "You see more women cycling very close to the kerb than you do men. They don't take the lane, or overtake lorries on the outside. They sneak up on the inside, which is fatal, literally."

Mason recommends that everyone should have cycling training before taking to their bikes. "Every adult makes errors. A good trainer will iron out all sorts of bad habits." It makes sense, it's a long time since most of us did our cycling proficiency tests at primary school.

There's one simple piece of advice for dealing with lorries: don't be intimidated by them. Mason says: "If you cycle in the gutter they'll treat you accordingly."

COMMENTS

presidentmarcos The authorities could easily save lives just by getting rid of all the stupid ugly railings. They don't need to be there and just encourage motorists to treat the roads like race circuits instead of shared spaces.

DLAF As a new cyclist on the roads (and a woman!) I'm very conscious of HGVs and other long vehicles at junctions – however, I really wish that more experienced and speedy cyclists wouldn't be so impatient, riding up your bum and shouting at you when you wait behind a lorry.

Blaming unassertive cycling is simplistic

ANNA LEACH

Women are slower cyclists, or don't use gears; they lack spatial awareness, think too much about things other than the road in front of them; "men evolved into hunters that need to be aware of their surroundings, while women evolved into homemakers less reliant on their senses".

These were just a few of the comments, some more gender-stereotyped than others, I prompted when I last wrote about this topic (see previous post).

Since then I've spoken to relatives of the women who were killed and learnt that many were experienced and regular cyclists, not shrinking violets either on the road or off it.

Also, of the drivers who were involved in the fatal collisions last year, two were charged with driving offences, one was illegally in the cycle stop box and one was a hit-and-run.

This seems to show there are more factors than the gender of the person riding the bike behind why HGVs represent 5% of the traffic on London's roads, but cause 80% of the fatal collisions with cyclists.

It's worth noting at this point that while this is, of course, a national issue, the high number of recent such incidents in the capital make it a useful place to learn lessons.

One such potential lesson is this: as well as making cyclists more aware, how can we make HGVs safer to share the streets with bikes?

After her daughter, Alex, was killed by a cement mixer while cycling to work at a City law firm in 2000, Cynthia Barlow bought shares in the company that owned the lorry and successfully lobbied them to have state-of-the-art safety equipment fitted.

Cemex lorries now have extra mirrors that dramatically reduce the drivers' blind spots, as well as sensors along the side of that alert them if a cyclist is alongside and an exterior voice warning which say, "Caution, vehicle turning left". The equipment costs £545 per vehicle. Barlow notes:

"At the time my daughter was killed, cement mixers were involved in several fatalities. Since Cemex have fitted the safety equipment there's only been one, where the cyclist was wearing earphones."

The trade association that represents the interests of the transportation industry, the Freight Transport Authority (FTA), has signed up to a programme of pro-cycling initiatives in London led by the city's mayor, Boris Johnson.

However, it does not support the mandatory fitting of this equipment, instead arguing that education of drivers and cyclists is the best way to reduce deaths.

Critics argue that education can only do so much. At the inquest into the death of Meryem Ozekman, a fitness instructor and mother who was killed as she cycled between lessons in April 2009, scaffolding lorry driver Mark Ellis said, "I'm an experienced driver. I'm always checking my mirrors but you can't see all of them all the time."

Amy Aeron-Thomas from the road accident charity RoadPeace says:

"I don't put much faith in education because I think the drivers are under pressure. There's no excuse for any driver to be on the road with a blind spot. They can be designed out. We don't allow blind drivers so why should we allow the equivalent?"

COMMENTS

djcypher Anna points out that a high percentage of the lorry drivers involved in cycle fatalities were charged with criminal offences. How would driver education or cyclist alerting technology have made a difference? These drivers knew that they were doing something illegal but did it anyway.

LeonardHofstadter It amazes me that cyclists are allowed on the same road as other traffic – it is far too dangerous for all concerned. Arguing that car and lorry drivers should be more careful is simply ignoring the issue – no matter how much visibility car & lorry drivers have available to them, accidents will happen.

JasonP Roads are public goods, not a realm exclusively licensed to motorists. Driving is a freedom you enjoy, not a right. Motorists have no economic, historical or moral claim to public roads.

Wanted: top women cyclists (to look pretty)

HELEN PIDD

Happy news for women looking to break into the male dominated world of cycle racing: the Tour of Britain, our island's humble version of the Gallic road race, is looking for a woman to take part.

The bad news is that the chosen lady will not be giving the gents what-for on her bicycle, but looking pretty on the podium, kissing the sweaty cheek of whichever man win's the day's stage.

For the princely sum of £50 per eight-hour day (plus accommodation and expenses), you could become a "presentation hostess" for the eight-day men-only race.

"We've got open minds about who the lucky lady will be, but ideally we'd like to be able to give someone their big break, perhaps an aspiring model or a drama student who is trying to get ahead in their career," said a tour spokesman.

"It's not all glamour and kissing the winning cyclists though, as you'll be the face of The Tour, being shown on the ITV4 highlights and in the hundreds of podium photos that are sent around the world showing the yellow jersey and various other winners."

What is crushingly depressing is that the hostesses (known widely as podium girls and fetishised all over the internet) tend to be top cyclists themselves. The "winner" will join Lauren Bason, who rides for Wolverhampton Wheelers, on the podium. And at this year's Tour de France, Claire Pedrono, cycling champion of Brittany, was given the "honour" or holding up the chalkboard with the information about the riders' times.

Isn't it sad that despite the UK boasting some of the world's finest female cyclists in Nicole Cooke, Victoria Pendleton and Lizzie Armistead, the only visible way for women to get involved in the UK's biggest professional bike race is to give out the prizes?

Alastair Grant, the Tour's commercial manager, doesn't think so. "It's very much part of the history and culture of cycling – for better or worse – that there are presentation hostesses involved in the podium presentations at the end of the stage. Their role is not to stand there and look pretty by any means; they are there to coordinate the activity that goes on. They will be bringing our VIP dignitaries on the stage, handing the trophies to them to hand to the cyclists, they help the riders to put the presentation jerseys on."

COMMENTS

etphonehome Storm in a tea cup. Medal ceremony & pretty girl, what's the problem?

allium Pointless, silly, demeaning nonsense.

Ursi "History and culture" have a lot to answer for.

Olympic gold medalist Rebecca Romero talks about her love-hate relationship with cycling

INTERVIEW BY HELEN PIDD

Helen Pidd: Where do you train at the moment and what are you training for?

Rebecca Romero: I use my local countryside for my long training rides for anything up to five hours and I can fit quite a lot of mileage in. Having had some down time after Beijing I'm building my fitness combining a bit of road racing and deciding over the next year where my race focus is going to lie and my best medal opportunities.

HP: So you're going to be at the London Olympics in some shape or form you hope?

RR: Yeah, but the individual pursuit which I competed in at Beijing was cut from the games. My initial plan was to return to defend my title but now I'm trying out other things, building my fitness and seeing if I can compete at an international level in another discipline. I'd love to see if I was competitive enough to compete in the time trials.

HP: Sometimes I get the impression that elite athletes don't particularly like their sport, they just like winning. Is that true?

RR: That's a tough question, I think for me I've always wanted to win. I've always wanted to be an athlete and go to the Olympic games and so it's the mode that got me there that I feel in love with which was rowing. I fell into cycling.

HP: But it's a lot to do for something that you're not really into.

RR: Well, there are days where you do hate it and you just drag yourself through but there are days when it's really enjoyable.

There also some days when you want to get off your bike and throw it in a ditch – so it's a love/hate relationship really!

HP: Do you every run red lights?

RR: No way, I'm a good cyclist.

HP: Let's talk about what's been happening in the past year. How much of a blow was it when you heard the UCI were binning your events for the Olympics?

RR: Because it was so unexpected, I couldn't believe that they would allow those changes to go through. I didn't lose just one event, I lost two events so I just thought it was the end of my career.

HP: You said yourself that some have benefited from it and now Victoria Pendleton can compete in three events. She seemed to be the one kicking up a fuss after Beijing saying why can't women go for as many medals as the men. Do you ever think that if she hadn't made a fuss you may still have your events?

RR: I do think that but I still support her. I think that Victoria was definitely right to voice her opinions.

HP: Deciding to change sport as you did [Romero was an Olympic rowing medalist before switching to cycling] must take a lot of balls.

RR: I think you ask yourself 'what am I trying to achieve, what am I striving for?' and I wasn't afraid to get stuck into a new sport. I wasn't afraid to say that I wanted to be the best, that I want to win. What I think being an elite athlete is all about is finding the point at which I can do no more. I want to find my breaking point and when I fail then I know I can do no more.

This is an abridged version of an interview that appeared on the Guardian's bike podcast. You can hear the unedited interview at gu.com/p/2h963

Chapter 5

Fighting for road space

I've occasionally pondered the possibility of printing out a sheaf of close-typed A5 sheets to carry in my back pocket every time I cycle. Titled "FAQs for drivers" these would hopefully answer those questions cyclists often face – usually, it has to be said, amid a torrent of fruity language – when confronted by the irate occupant of a vehicle: "Why aren't you riding in the gutter?"; "Why don't you pay road tax?"; "Why don't you have insurance?". Rather than trying to shout above the traffic roar I could politely pass the driver a sheet, suggesting perhaps that, say, item four might enlighten them.

Of course I've never done it, not least because it would make me look like an irritating, self-righteous pedant. But it does illustrate something about cycling in Britain, whether urban or rural: for all the joy it carries you will, inevitably, bump up sooner or later against a gigantic wall of ignorance from other road users.

With only 2% of journeys made on a bike it's perhaps no surprise, but it can still be depressing to realise how most drivers believe cyclists are only allowed on the roads under sufferance. This is shown as much by sheer lack of attention – what cycling organisations called the "Smidsy" ("Sorry mate! I didn't see you") phenomenon – as by aggression.

This is reflected off the roads, too. The transport secretary, Philip Hammond, dismissed the notion he might cycle the short distance from his London flat to his office rather than use a government car by saying it was too dangerous. This was news, presumably, to the hundreds of thousands who ride in the city every day. It's maybe no shock that most cycle lanes look like they were designed by someone whose last bike was a childhood BMX.

Similarly, as Bike Blog readers know only too well, carrying their machine on British trains tends to be, at best, a logistical headache and at worst an utter lottery.

So far, so depressing. But let's not get too gloomy. Apart from the fact that the divisions between the various transport tribes on the roads might not be as complete as we think – see Helen Pidd's piece later in the chapter – things are also gradually changing as more and more people cycle, making bikes an increasingly familiar part of the road landscape.

For now, sadly, we do still face a fight for space. So, just in case you're a non-cycling driver leafing through this book at a friend's house, here's the (brief) answers to my hypothetical questions above: because safety experts, and police, recommend we don't; there's no such thing (see page 122); lots of us do, and it costs mere beans as – unlike your mob – we hardly ever injure or kill anyone.

Peter Walker

What's wrong with a bike lane that's actually big enough to ride in?

CHRIS PECK

Policy Coordinator of the CTC, the UK's National Cyclists' Organisation

A cycle lane recently installed in Poole, Dorset has attracted the ridicule of the tabloids, not least the Daily Mail.

The lane – up part of Constitution Hill – is two metres wide. Of course, the papers probably didn't bother to check that this is CTC and Cycling England's recommended width for cycle lanes.

In fact, the minimum width is supposed to be 1.5m, yet nearly all cycle lanes are well below that, and some are just the width of a bike, others not even that.

The curiosity here is that the papers are complaining that the space for motor vehicles has been squeezed in next to the cycle lane. This makes a change from the normal design of roads, where the cycle lane is normally determined only after the requirements of other road users have been satisfied.

Poole has mostly got this road layout right – and anyway, it's a huge improvement on how the road used to be. As the name suggests, Constitution Hill is an incline, so a full width cycle lane is needed to make up for the differences in speed between toiling cyclists and passing cars.

There is no cycle lane needed on the other side of the road, because cyclists going downhill can more easily keep up with traffic. It looks like – shock horror – this particular lane was designed by people who ride a bike, follow the guidance and know what they are doing. No wonder cycling in south-east Dorset is up 50% in five years.

The Dutch, who know a thing or two about planning for cyclists, recommend a width for cycle lanes of 1.5–2.5m, plus another 0.5m of "critical reaction strip" if the cycle lane passes alongside parked cars. For the most part, cycle lanes in the Netherlands meet this standard.

But one thing the Dutch also do, and one way in which the Poole scheme could have been improved, is to remove the road's central white line altogether. There is, after all, plenty of research to suggest that this approach is perfectly safe and actually may help reduce traffic speeds, and several councils in Britain have already adopted this practice.

Last year, research supported by CTC found that drivers overtook cyclists closer on roads with cycle lanes. This doesn't mean that cycle lanes should never be used, but where they are needed – on busier roads where space is available – they should be wide enough to compensate for people driving slightly closer.

Wider cycle lanes also allow parents to cycle alongside their children or people to sociably cycle two abreast more easily. Again, this a principle behind the Dutch cycle design: you sit beside someone talking to them in a car so if you want to make cycling as attractive as driving you should make sociable cycling possible.

It is amazing that in London the Cycle Superhighways are being built to a design minimum of 1.5 metres wide, yet on some of these routes there are already more than 13,000 cyclists a day, meaning lots of cyclists overtaking other cyclists and the potential for two people to want to cycle next to each other. A measly 1.5m doesn't give the chance to do that – 2m might, but a nice Dutch 2.5m certainly would.

COMMENTS

DNAse I think the Poole cycle lane does serve the purpose of indicating to drivers how much space to give cyclists when overtaking. It shows that they will have to cross the centre line and, as a result, overtaking in the face of oncoming traffic is not acceptable. It shows drivers that they may have to slow down and exercise some patience.

chaz1 It is disappointing (but predictable) that the AA representative attempts to defend the indefensible. The fact is that a broken line on the cycle lane is advisory and car drivers can drive over them. The cycle lane has been purposely designed wide so that drivers are aware of bikes. The AA's solution (and the Daily Mail's) to car drivers' ignorance: get rid of the cycle lane!

EnglishInHolland The Daily Mail reaction to the cycle lane is pretty much what you'd expect. However, I don't understand why even Chris Peck is downplaying what is normal in the Netherlands. Even if you ask for cycle lanes of reasonable width, your expectations are low compared with what is normal for the Dutch. Completely separated cycle paths are far more common than cycle lanes.

It's official: cyclists are not a menace

JAMES RANDERSON

The love and hatred of cycling can bring together strange bedfellows, as demonstrated at a Spectator magazine debate on the subject, chaired by the broadcaster, Andrew Neil. Arguing against the motion that "Cyclists are a menace" were both Ken Livingstone and one of his least favourite journalists, Andrew Gilligan – a man who has referred to the former London mayor as "dishonest" and "arrogant".

As Gilligan put it: "Us agreeing with each other seems about as likely as Imelda Marcos sending her shoes to the menders rather than buying a new pair."

But on the other side too there was a strange alliance, between wild-eyed Daily Mail writer David Thomas and Labour MP Stephen Pound. From Thomas we had the usual joyless speech about "Lycra loonies" and "louts", "driver baiting" and fevered images of lines of poor motorists stuck on country lanes behind plodding cyclists.

"Motorists are an easy target," he lathered, because of their licences and insurance – while cyclists get away with whatever they want. "To a cyclist, a red light is merely a way of bringing a dash of colour to a city street."

Few here will subscribe to Pound's arguments, I suspect, but his entertaining rant was good theatre and at least had a dash of originality. He denounced the headphone-wearing "Lycra-clad velociraptors" who speed around the streets. "Who knows what they are listening to? The Killers certainly. Definitely not the Archers." And he implored reasonable cyclists to turn on the antisocial minority.

On the pro-cycling side of the debate, the arguments were less colourful, but ultimately more convincing (although as a cyclist, I suppose I would say that). Cyclists make up around 2% of the traffic in the London rush hour but they cause just 1% of injuries to pedestrians – almost all of them minor. And of the 204 people killed on London roads last year none was killed by a cyclist. In fact a cyclist has not been responsible for a road death in London for the previous eight years either.

That alone demonstrates cyclists are not the road menace they are sometimes painted as, said Gilligan. "To be a real menace you need more hardware." And he implored the non-cyclists in the crowd: "Instead of hating us, you should join us. You would have nothing to lose but your trains."

Livingstone confided that his special branch officer had advised against cycling. "[He said] I really don't think you should ride a bike because so many people hate you. Someone is bound to run you off the road." But he predicted that once cycling reached a critical mass, a step change would occur in terms of attitudes to cyclists by other road users – as has happened in cities such as Cambridge and Copenhagen.

The proposing side's secret weapon, though, was Baroness Sharples, the octogenarian peer who famously accosted a cyclist with her bag because he'd illegally sped through a pedestrian crossing outside Parliament.

"I didn't hurt him. It was a very small shopping bag and it was very light," she said. Her point was that cyclists who don't follow the rules of the road are frightening to older people and those with limited mobility. She wanted to see more courtesy from everyone.

On the night the audience trounced her side of the debate, voting by 96 to 45 against the motion that "cyclists are a menace". But I suspect few people would argue with what she had to say – particularly if she was carrying a handbag.

COMMENTS

GreyBrother As a daily cyclist I get quietly annoyed with cyclists who ride on pavements, jump red lights and cycle at night without lights. However, this debate is old and tired. It would be far more productive to have a discussion about whether cars are a menace (um…), or taxis (err…) or articulated trucks (hmm…) or buses (uhh…).

The reality is that cycling gets people out of the really menacing vehicles, and the endless debate about cyclists is just a convenient distraction from the real causes of noise, pollution, resource depletion, injury and death.

Leischa On my cycle commute, I see plenty of drivers texting while driving, talking on a mobile while changing lanes and going through an intersection, speeding and generally behaving unpredictably. All of this is much more dangerous than anything cyclists do. The anti-cycling lobby reminds me of smokers: addicts get very defensive about their habit.

knackeredknees We cyclists seem to be fair game to all and sundry at the moment and some of us seem only too happy to condemn other cyclists. I'm getting a bit fed up of these debates – it is perfectly obvious that motor vehicles, whether due to their speed, weight, size and/or incompetence/homicidal tendencies of the driver, are amazingly effective in their ability to kill and maim human beings. Pedestrians and cyclists, due to their very vulnerability, are not.

chaz1 The elephant in the room is the thousands of people each year killed and maimed by motorised vehicles. Compared to that, this debate is trivial.

Copenhagenwoman I have often felt sorry for the British cyclists. Lack of cycle paths, lack of safety, very little bike tolerance. I so much missed cycling when I lived in the UK, but it just seemed too dangerous.

I do admire your polite driving culture compared to many other European countries – giving way to each other, leaving much space between the cars, etc. Many countries could definitely learn a lot from you. However, I think you could learn a lot from other countries when it comes to cycling. I always wondered about the paradox – the polite traffic culture and then this 'dislike' against cyclists. It doesn't make sense.

How would you rule as the UK's cycling tsar?

PETER WALKER

It sounds, on the face of it, as good as any cyclist could hope for:

> *We will develop a National Cycle Plan to promote cycling as a mainstream form of personal transport.*

This comes from the transport section of the grandly-named Building Britain's Future policy document.

These are big words. Unlike – to take the obvious examples – the Netherlands and Denmark, UK governments have never really planned for cycling. Until recently it's been something that was more or less tolerated if it happened, but viewed as a pursuit that all but a handful of enthusiasts grow out of soon enough.

To promote it as a "mainstream" transport choice – that's a very long way from the current situation in Britain where only around 2% of all journeys are taken by bicycle. To give some context, the equivalent figure in the Netherlands in 27%.

The hard bit is how to do it. Well, of course, this is where things get a bit hazy. Other than the chance for an English urban area to win some extra funding by becoming a so-called Sustainable Transport City, the policy document doesn't really contain anything in the way of specifics.

A sceptic would say that this matters little, given that Building Britain's Future is likely to be one of the final policy gasps from Gordon Brown's government – on its way out and thrashing around for any sort of policy initiatives which might, even briefly, arrest the decline.

But there's also an argument that even hearing a British government talk about a national plan to make cycling an everyday transport choice – however vague the methods – is a big step forwards. It's a sign that ministers and civil servants are finally recognising that bikes can play a central role in getting people from place to place, particularly in congested and polluted cities. It's no longer viewed as simply a niche choice for the young, the poor or the faddish.

So where do we go from here?

Let's suppose you were appointed the government's bike tsar tomorrow, with unlimited influence and a huge budget. How would you bring cycling into the mainstream?

Update: To the surprise of few, the National Cycle Plan passed largely unnoticed by cyclists in the 11 months between its launch and Labour leaving office. Those hoping for a pro-cycling voice in government saw the new administration swiftly abolish Cycling England, the quango responsible for encouraging cycling.

COMMENTS

NickInBath What would TsarNickInBath do?

- General tax incentives based on proximity of home and workplace
- Stop building houses on green field sites miles from anywhere
- Build all sorts of houses on brown field sites (with room for bikes, obviously)
- Tax incentives for employers that install showers, lockers and bike parking
- Grants for big-city gyms to install proper bike parking and offer discounts to companies that can't install showers, lockers and bike parks
- Ban driving to school. Boost school buses and bike parking

When can I start? I need a job as it happens.

Polymorph How about reducing VAT on bikes or exempting them altogether, maybe for a "stimulus" period? Or make cycling a compulsory part of the progression to car license qualification.

vorsprung Make it an offense to pass a bicycle with less than a three-foot gap between you and it for all motorised transport except emergency vehicles. Rigorously enforce this policy and advertise it like drink driving was.

sk8dancer Positive images/promotional adverts of people in normal clothes sharing roads with drivers (without hi-viz and helmets).

MkVII How about trains with a guard's van which can actually carry bicycles again?

spiritualscientist2

1. Fit more bike parking. Everywhere. At/near homes or flats. At bus stops. By rail stations.

2. Get everybody involved with road transport on their bikes for a week, to see what it's really like, and to see why so many bicycle-schemes are poorly designed, and poorly installed.

Cyclists v drivers? They're often the same people

HELEN PIDD

Much has been written about a war between cyclists and drivers, as if the two groups were such polar opposites that they could never cross in a Venn diagram. But according to research, people who cycle the most are likely to own at least two cars.

Regular cyclists – those who cycle at least once a week – are also disproportionately likely to read broadsheet newspapers, be well educated, have a household income of at least £50,000 per year and shop at Waitrose, claims the Mintel report, Bicycles in the UK 2010. In addition, they are twice as likely to be men as women.

"Thirty or 40 years ago, people would ride a bike for economic reasons, but our research suggests that nowadays a bicycle is more a lifestyle addition, a way of demonstrating how affluent you are," said Michael Oliver, who wrote the report for market researchers Mintel.

His research reveals that bike sales are being driven by 35- to 45-year-old family men. Where this age group might once have treated themselves to a sports car – in an attempt to hang on to their youth – they now invest in a luxury bike instead.

The report dubs the upsurge in cycle sales among this demographic as "the noughties version of the mid-life crisis".

Men of a certain age now pride themselves on their bicycle collection. In a documentary, Alan Sugar showed off the full-carbon Pinarello machines he has bought for his many residences at a cost of many thousands of pounds each.

Halfords, the UK's biggest bike retailer, confirmed the trend, reporting a rise in interest in all cycles, particularly among top-of-the range products. Premium sales as a whole are up by around 54% in the past two years.

Pashley, a British firm which makes traditional-style bikes, said it had seen sales of some everyday models rise by 50% year-on-year.

However, just 12% of adults questioned by Mintel said they cycled regularly, while 65% said they never rode a bike. One in seven (15%) said they were "lapsed cyclists" who had a bicycle which they no longer rode.

The main reason given for not cycling was safety, with 39% of respondents saying it is too dangerous to ride a bicycle on the road. Women aged 45 or older are the most likely to be put off by the perceived danger of road traffic.

Many people (24%) said they would cycle more often if there were more bicycle lanes, and 14% said while they would like to bike to work, cycling wasn't practical because of a lack of showers or changing facilities.

Ten per cent of the sample of 1,557 viewed cyclists as "a nuisance". That increased to 14% among those who regarded cycling as too dangerous. The most antagonism towards cyclists was reported among consumers in the south, south-west and London regions, but there was no real difference among car owners and car-less respondents, said Mintel.

After the success of British cyclists in the Olympic velodrome in Beijing in 2008, there was hope that a new generation of riders would be inspired by the likes of gold medallists Chris Hoy and Victoria Pendleton. But Mintel's research suggested the effect had been negligible among non-cyclists.

"Successful British cyclists, although arguably more high profile than ever thanks to the success of Sir Chris Hoy, for example, have not managed to inspire the general population, with only 2% of respondents admitting this was an incentive to take up cycling," the report claims.

But at the same time, Mintel's survey reveals that British Cycling – the body which administers the sport in the UK – claims to be the fastest growing cycling organisation in the UK, reporting 25% growth between May 2009 and May 2010.

Another cycling organisation, the CTC (Cyclists' Touring Club), which focuses on leisure cycling, has also experienced recent growth of 8% year-on-year, and now has almost 66,000 members. These members are major enthusiasts; they spend on average £700 plus and own an average of 2.2 bicycles, according to recent CTC figures.

Roger Geffen, campaigns and policy director for the CTC, said the government should do more to make the roads safer for cyclists in a bid to encourage more people to get on their bikes, particularly women.

"We know that the higher the level of cycling, the more the gender imbalance evens out," he said. "In the Netherlands and Denmark, where far more people cycle, 55% of all bike trips are made by women."

Mintel estimates that the bike trade will boom over the next five years. Last year 3.6m bikes were sold in the UK. By 2015 Mintel expects that figure to rise to just over 4m.

But Mark Walmsley of the Association of Cycle Traders said there had not yet been a real cycling boom nationwide. "There have been some pockets of the country which have seen an increase in people buying bikes, for example in London, but nationally, there has been no boom. All of this hype that's going on is rubbish."

COMMENTS

Antecedent Whilst we know that most cyclists are also drivers, we also know that most drivers are not also cyclists. They seem to be the ones oozing the most uninformed invective about the other side.

rpclarkeuk So, 39% of respondents said "it is too dangerous to ride a bicycle on the road". Which in reality translates as 39% believe that "motorists drive too recklessly for cycling to be a practical option".

It is an outrageous scandal that such a massive scale of criminality and violation of the right to travel is condoned by the government and law "enforcement" authorities.

Drspeedy I can't understand why people (non-cyclists in the main) go on about the price of bikes, or 'expensive' bikes. After all, an 'entry level' new car will set you back £5000 at least + VED + insurance etc. A good bike for much less than half of that will outlast it by decades, require much less expensive services and new components over the years – and keep you fit, not to mention provide you with a lot of pleasure along the way.

Mmmmf A decent Pinarello sounds like quite a cheap midlife crisis to me. Cheaper than:

- A Harley

- A Les Paul Standard and a 100w Marshall

- Tupping the secretary in a motel every Wednesday afternoon

Probably better for you, in the long run, than any of them too.

Raddit For the same energy as walking, riding a bike takes you four times the speed and distance. Used like this there is no need for showering, special clothes and expensive bicycles. However, in the UK (and USA) where less than 1% journeys are by bike, cycling is 'owned' by enthusiasts – bike shops run by enthusiasts for enthusiasts, bike magazines proclaiming 'Written by cyclists for cyclists'. This and all the glorification of speed and sport probably puts off most regular folk.

Cyclists are not road tax dodgers

PETER WALKER

I was unexpectedly sent a cycling jersey through the post recently. When we set up the Bike Blog I idly imagined this would be a regular sort of occurrence, but it was the first freebie since we launched.

I mention this not to bemoan my spartan existence, but because the jersey carried the slogan of a new, particularly energetic and PR-savvy single-issue cycling campaign: I Pay Road Tax.

It's the personal response of Carlton Reid, a cycling journalist and author, to that shout from the inside of a car which more or less every rider has heard at one point or another: "You don't pay road tax – why are you on the roads?"

In the words of one particularly unpleasant couple filmed by a cyclist getting hot under the collar after a minor altercation: "You have no say on the roads whatsoever. No pay, no say."

In my experience, such an argument is usually delivered in a triumphant tone that suggests the driver sees this as such an irrefutable, intellectually rigorous put-down that the cyclist can only get down from the saddle, bow their head apologetically and mutter, "It's a fair cop".

Of course, as Reid points out, it's nonsense on a stick. Even setting aside the point that many cyclists also own cars, there is no such thing as road tax, and hasn't been since 1937. Road building and maintenance is financed from other taxation; that fee you pay for the little paper disc which sits on the windscreen is vehicle excise duty (VED), a charge which varies according to the emissions produced.

As IPayRoadTax.com also notes, even if you still choose to view cyclists as tax dodgers, then the same opprobrium should be heaped on the drivers of particularly green cars, war pensioners, disabled drivers, and a number of other groups.

It's nonetheless a difficult message to get across, particularly in the 10 seconds before a set of traffic lights go green.

Hence Reid's campaign, which as well as the website also features a Twitter feed and even an iPhone app. The rather fetching jersey features a series of pictured tax discs printed with a price tag of "£0,00", along with the website address.

Of course, in some ways its a bit contradictory: a educational campaign about the non-existence of road tax called I Pay Road Tax. Reid says on his website: "Shouldn't it be iPayVED.com? Yes. But too few people know what VED is. Everybody knows what road tax is. Or they think they do."

Critics might also argue that this is a minor gripe: OK, a lot of motorists are ignorant; let them be. I'd disagree. I've always felt the road tax argument supports a more general feeling of entitlement among too many drivers. Those who trot it out often seem to genuinely treat cyclists like we're interlopers who should be pushed aside.

But do you have any other ideas for how this point could be made on a jersey? And what other slogans would you like to wear?

COMMENTS

jobysp My slogan would be: "Ha ha – you're stuck in traffic whilst I'm riding around in fresh air on my VED-free mode of transport. Take that tax man."

Bit long, I know, but gets the point across.

sarri I always find it a bit odd that drivers get so annoyed by cyclists, because they also get very annoyed by traffic jams – and if they did ever manage to drive all the cyclists off the roads they'd find themselves in ever longer queues. It'd be great to see a campaign to remind drivers that one more bike on the road is one less car in front of them.

eas956 Hmmm. I pay road tax – VED if you like – on my car. I use my bike on the roads because there's no off-road route I can use to get to work. Can I get a refund on my car tax for those days when my car doesn't turn a wheel, for those days when I use my bike to commute?

stopbanginon Suggested T-shirt to wind up motorists even more: "Bike bought with the aid of the CycleScheme: using your taxes to buy my bike." Not strictly factual but should raise a few eyebrows.

HoistThatRag How about a slogan: "I was once a tw*t in a car like you, but now I'm healthier, fitter, pay less tax and get where I want to go quicker." Hmmm. Doesn't really work, does it? Probably makes you more of a target.

London cycle scheme: On yer bike, looking like Miss Marple

ZOE WILLIAMS

Politicians are amazing, aren't they? I saw Boris Johnson, sitting on one of his new London hire bikes, telling some cameras: "It's clean, it's green, it's the way to get around!" He had the vim and conviction of a man in a 1950s washing powder advert. Did postmodernism never happen? Don't they ever feel a little bit silly?

Goddammit, he's right, though. This is a brilliant scheme: everything about it looks shiny, new and brilliant.

The bikes are roughly the weight of a small shed, emblazoned with Barclays bank logos. You look a bit like a very keen young employee of Barclays bank who's been given an apprentice's bike and is proud to be seen with it, all over town. The seat adjuster is the best designed I've ever seen (by which I mean, you don't need an allen key). Just one monumental burst of energy and you're off!

Naturally, I overstate: it's not like having a racer, but you wouldn't need to be any fitter than, say, your average London mayor to power one. Other cyclists eye you up, before they zip past. You think they might be checking out your cool bike, before you remember which bike you're actually riding. It's a Miss Marple-ish steed, with a comfy saddle and no crossbar – a sit-up-and-beg classic.

The pace is what I believe they call stately – solid as a tram, so ridiculously stable you could indicate with both arms, only of course then nobody would know which way you were going. I decided to overtake a chap at the top of Victoria Embankment and didn't actually manage it until the Houses of Parliament, by which time I'd been following for so long I was technically stalking him. The brakes mean business, and the lights are powered by a dynamo, so they're on all the time. It has absolutely everything you could want from a bike, especially if part of you wants thighs like Sir Chris Hoy.

Would I use it? Not for any great distance, but that's not what the scheme is designed for – the point, reflected in the charges (free for the first half-hour, charged by the half-hour thereafter) is for short journeys. The free half-hour is easily enough to get you from any given bit of central London to any other, and there's room at the front for a bag or two, so it's good commuter or shopping transport.

The main temptation, though, will surely be to get on one when you're drunk. They're much harder to fall off than regular bikes, it would take a superhero to damage one, they're very visible, and they are exactly what you need to get you from the pub that is just closing to the pub that stays open a bit longer.

This must be the most public money that's ever been spent on revellers. It's going to be wonderful, London is going to look like Weimar Germany without the hyperinflation. I can't wait.

COMMENTS

kitten69 At last, someone is getting serious about pollution in the big smoke. Perhaps we should insist all MPs (and lords) cycle from their mainline station to Westminster every morning.

icurahuman2 Make them free and make them many. Also make tricycles for the overweight so they can shift to bicycles once they've burned off a few pounds. Trishaws for the elderly with pedal-powered young unemployed people making a few pennies.

Sophie74 Potentially love the scheme – not happy at being turned into a moving advert for Barclays. Some of us have long memories and are still boycotting Barclays because of their involvement in the apartheid regime.

To listen to the Guardian's bike podcast on the London bike hire scheme go to gu.com/p/2tyqc

Royal Mail's decision to park its bikes defies logic

MATT SEATON

Punctuality is not my strong point and I have to admit that I've arrived rather late to this particular debate. It was only last week that I read an article by the brilliant postie-blogger Roy Mayall about how deliveries by bicycle were being phased out in his district.

In fact, the plan by Royal Mail, to get rid of almost all its bikes and replace them with a combination of more vans and mechanised trolleys, was reported last year. It was followed by a No 10 petition. Sadly, this particular campaign seems to have been underpublicised: when the deadline arrived at the end of last month, the petition had collected only 649 signatures.

Just to recap quickly, bicycles have been used to deliver mail in Britain since 1880. The Royal Mail still has more than 16,000 bikes in service, predominantly sturdy Pashleys (a rare, surviving British manufacturer whose longevity may well owe much to its business with Royal Mail). And as I noted when reviewing Tim Hilton's wonderful, quirky memoir of being a cyclist, there is a special affinity between posties and bikes:

> *Artists rub shoulders with artisans in cycling's classless fellowship of the road – not forgetting, Hilton remarks, the strong representation of posties, whose habits of rising early and clocking off at lunchtime mesh perfectly with the requirement of amateur racing cyclists for 'getting the miles in'.*

If Royal Mail goes ahead with its plan, there will be many losers besides the posties themselves. In recent years, the bicycle aid charity Re-Cycle has shipped more than 10,000 reconditioned Royal Mail bicycles to African countries, where their robust build and sound load-carrying characteristics make them ideal utility bikes.

Doesn't it seem a bit bizarre, you ask, that just when the government is trying to get more of us riding bikes, that a major public-sector employer is ditching a well-tried and tested bicycle delivery system?

Indeed, it does. What is the (departing) chief executive Adam Crozier's rationale for this move, then? As Roy Mayall reports:

> In a letter to the Labour peer Lord Berkeley – which was read out in a House of Lords debate on 29 March – the outgoing chief executive said that bicycles "posed a wider safety risk associated with British street networks where the rider is exposed to greater risks than other vehicle users."

Either that's a touching and hitherto undisclosed concern for his staff's welfare, or it's "elf'n'safety gone mad". Whichever, it's plain wrong – both the government and the British Medical Association (and any cycling organisation you care to mention) could tell Crozier that the health benefits of cycling far outweigh any risk posed by accident. In fact – and this should interest Crozier much more (as he does like his performance-related pay) – there would be a bottom-line benefit to Royal Mail, which would lose far fewer days in sick leave with a healthier, fitter workforce.

But there's yet another contradiction in the Royal Mail management's decision to park its bicycles permanently. As a senior official of the Communication Workers Union, Tony Kearns, wrote in a letter to the Guardian, how will Royal Mail square the circle of signing up to the 10:10 carbon reduction campaign while phasing out zero-carbon bicycle deliveries in favour of adding 24,000 vehicles to its fleet?

The decision seems even more bizarre, given the fact that private-sector firms – even direct competitors with Royal Mail – are increasingly adopting delivery bikes as a way to beat congestion, cut costs, and meet environmental targets.

The last word has to be Mayall's, as I couldn't put it better myself:

> *The bike is a reliable piece of technology, simple and efficient. As a tool for delivery it has proved its worth for more than 100 years. As they say: if it ain't broke, don't fix it.*

We need a national campaign to keep posties on bikes.

COMMENTS

colostomyexplosion I think they don't want to pay the extra pension associated with longer-living retired cycle-posties. If the average cyclist lives 10 years longer and the company runs its own pension scheme (with a big hole in it no doubt) this could be a long-term solution. Cynical? Yes. Completely unbelieveable? No.

thereverent I live a bit south of one of Royal Mail's main London depots and regularly go through there on a bike. The Royal Mail vans are the worst-driven vehicles there.

smogbound I'd never expect any sense from the guys who thought 'Consignia' sounded better than 'Royal Mail'.

willow215 I'm a postman and do a bicycle delivery every day. I joined Royal Mail two years ago so I could ride a bike to make my living, taking a pay cut in the process. I'm fitter now than I've ever been.

I'm dismayed that they're going to get rid of our bikes. I've done the same delivery with a trolley and it takes 30 to 40 minutes longer – 120 years of delivering mail by bike can't be wrong. It is simply the quickest most efficient way to do it. If this plan goes ahead everyone will be getting their mail much later. That is a fact.

Why is it so difficult to take a bike on a train?

CHRIS PECK

Policy coordinator for the CTC, the UK's national cycling organisation

Taking your bike by train in the UK needs a combination of luck, patience and an encyclopaedic knowledge of the rail industry. Why is it so hard to take a bike on a train when the usual alternative would be driving all the way?

I went away for the weekend recently, starting with a train from Guildford to Reading. The trains on this line sometimes have space for one bike, sometimes nothing. I had to guess where the bike space would be and then pray that it wasn't already stuffed with luggage.

Then I had to contend with the volumes of other people, many of whom had bikes, bags, pushchairs and the like as they flooded on and off three tiny coaches in a hurry. Most of the bikes were stashed in the vestibule, ready to fall out of the train if the doors opened.

Irritatingly, the privatised rail system and a lack of interest from the government means that each company has approached the issue of carrying bikes in a different way. Almost without exception, full-size bikes aren't allowed onto trains entering London at peak hours. Similar rules exist for other cities, but those hours – and the level of enforcement – vary wildly.

There is no standard sign to advertise on trains and platforms where bikes can be carried. You can't reserve the single cycle space on the Guildford to Reading train – but if you change on to a long-distance train you must possess a reservation.

Other train companies have different demands on where and when reservations are required and how to obtain them. Sadly the only company that allows you to book cycle reservations online with your ticket is National Express, which doesn't look like it will exist for much longer.

Good cycle parking – which the government is putting £14m into over the next two years – can reduce the soaring bike theft at stations (double the level of five years ago, while car crime at stations has halved) and will no doubt encourage more people to ride to stations.

But better parking only helps if you don't want to use your bike at the other end of the journey, or it's your regular commute. If you're using the train on a day trip or to go on holiday, you'll most probably want to take your bike with you.

Leisure cyclists can bring vital custom to otherwise quiet off-peak trains – I've heard of early-morning weekend trains where cyclists made up over half of the passengers.

Even worse, the government is proposing that the longer-distance high-speed trains to replace much of the existing fleet will have even fewer spaces for bikes – with space for just four bikes on trains for 650 people.

At the moment there is space for just six bikes on the equivalent trains and even that is woefully inadequate. CTC is campaigning against this move – as we have with most other attempts by train companies to deny cyclists' custom.

Sixty per cent of people live within 15 minutes of a railway station, but less than 2% of train trips start with a bike ride to the station. If it was a bit easier to take your bike on the station, surely a few more people might give the trains another go?

COMMENTS

hhazzahh Post war, when have the railways in the UK ever been managed adequately? Cycling is way down the list of sticking plasters to be applied. I went on a bicycle tour to Switzerland. I used a small mountain railway. Middle of nowhere. They had a dedicated 'mixed use' car for bikes – either use the pull-down seat, or hang the bike, a very simple flexible solution.

cowspassage Long distance trains can be as bad. Bike reservations seem to run on a different booking system from passenger tickets and don't seem to open up until some random time very close to when you want to travel. I have travelled on Virgin trains, with a bike booking, only to find when boarding the train that the bike compartment is already taken with other people's bikes. I was then treated as a troublemaker by the guard for being the one with no space to put my bike.

Calli The key word is PRIVATISED. These companies make millions from public subsidy, millions in profits and do not give a crap. The solution is obvious – nationalise the railways, establish national standards that actively encourage bike use. As privatised companies they never co-ordinate and never will, except in minimal provision with the law.

wheelism Just last week five of us travelled across Scotland with our bikes. We couldn't get all five on the first train (capacity six bikes) and so three of us had to wait six hours to get on the next. The guard explained that it was beyond his remit to allow us on, even if we disassembled the bikes (removing wheels etc) as health & safety was monitored by a completely separate private company.

Seeing red: your bike rage experiences

FELICITY CARUS

One night in late autumn, at about 9pm, I was heading home, taking my normal route. I had thrashed out my ideal route between work and home, based not only on distance but also quietness and quickness of roads. At one particularly nasty and unavoidable four-lane junction in south London my safety strategy is always to try to stay ahead of the traffic.

I took off on green from the lights, and managed to reach about 17mph just after a bend. For the driver behind me, this was still not fast enough, even though the lights ahead were turning red. He beeped his horn at me, expecting me to move into a lane that was already full of traffic whizzing by to another destination. I held my position and he beeped again. I turned to look at him. He was on his mobile phone.

At the lights I tried to explain, without a single expletive, that he might have endangered me by forcing me out of his way and into the path of another vehicle, all while driving on his mobile phone. The Highway Code after all defines cyclists as "other road users requiring extra care".

I thought nothing of it – until he stepped out of his car and started yelling at me. I had no idea what he was saying as I moved away from the lights. He overtook me and cut me up, trying to get me to stop. He waited for me in laybys and tailed me for several miles.

I didn't feel like I was in immediate danger, but I didn't think he wanted to invite me for a cup of tea and a nice chat. So I memorised his number plate, just in case.

After seeing his car drive past me for the sixth time, before a particularly dark stretch of road near my home, I called the police.

I was surprised and impressed by how seriously the police took my call. A car was sent to look for the driver within minutes as I waited for the police outside a bar with a rather large, if bemused, bouncer on the door.

My main concern was that the driver might find out where I lived if I continued home on my bike. I admit, it's not really the best use of police time in the capital but they slung my bike in the police van and delivered me and my bike to the door, just as my then-partner pulled up in a cab, looking slightly concerned.

Seldom now do I remonstrate with dangerous or thoughtless motorists, least of all at night. I ride aggressively, but keep my mouth shut, or smile.

Have you ever had a bike rage experience that got out of control?

COMMENTS

cityexile My most memorable experience was being pelted with Brussels sprouts by four lads in a Ford Fiesta, in which case the rage was all mine, and I pedalled after them as fast as I could. I've no idea what I thought I was going to do if I caught them.

goeast I've had plenty, from a driver trying to reverse into me, to me kicking a car once, to me chasing a car through an industrial estate, following the driver into his work and bollocking him in front of his boss. None of these, I add, I'm proud of – it's not smart to get angry with drivers, even if they are absolutely behaving atrociously, and many of them, let's be honest, are.

What I'd say is that the angrier you are, the worse a confrontation becomes. So I definitely go for a Zen/calm approach these days.

vorsprung When I'm cut up, honked at, have a fist waved at me I usually smile and wave at the perpetrator. What I am hoping will happen is that they will think, "Why is he waving? Hang on… is that Bob? Have I cut up Bob???"

mervynreeves A couple of cabbies have given me excellent biological advice after I'd had the temerity to not quite judge the exact location of where the white lane dividing line should be, delaying them a full eight seconds of clear acceleration prior to the next bumper they can pull up behind.

Best response – i.e. the one that really gets them the maddest – is, "Don't take it out on me just because your wife won't have sex with you any more", said with a suitable level of insouciance such as a primary school teacher might admonister a naughty child.

I have taken the subsequent eye-boggling rage as proof that I'm usually fairly close to the mark.

johnnygunn I've got 100,000 touring and commuting miles on my trusty steed, Lucy. Once, in the Black Hills of South Dakota, I was heading down a gravel road as a pickup truck was zooming towards me. I made the palms down motion asking him to slow down. But he continued past me at high speed, kicking up gravel and dinging my leg. So I gave him the universal extended-finger salute.

He screeched to a stop. I have always been known for my diplomatic speech, so I yelled at him, "Well, a minute a go you were in such a hurry, but now you seem to have time to stop." I reached my hand into my handlebar pack. His buddy hollered, "Get back in the truck, he has a gun!" I had a banana.

Mmmmf I had a richly satisfying experience a few years ago. A white van travelling towards me as I crossed a junction jumped a red light and narrowly missed wiping me out as it turned across me.

The van belonged to a glazing subcontractor who, at the time, was on a tender shortlist on a project I was managing, for about £150,000's worth of work. When I got back to the office I politely rang up the sales director I'd been dealing with and told him that, as I had good reason to doubt the quality and wisdom of his employees, I'd have to take his firm off the tender list.

I could tell that there was no doubt that the van driver would be given cause to reconsider his attitude in future.

Midipete I once had a bike rage incident. Not one of my greatest moments, I admit.

After a particularly bad day at work I was cycling back and on a particularly tight corner a big BMW clipped me and knocked me onto the pavement. Needless to say I was pretty pissed off, and as the car was stuck in traffic I got up to remonstrate with the driver. He was still on his mobile phone – presumably trying to turn with one hand had been the cause of hitting me. I knocked on his window and he gave me the finger and turned his head away while still talking on his phone.

This really pushed me over the edge so in order to get his attention I threw my bike at his windscreen. That seemed to work. He lowered his window and started hurling abuse. He still had his mobile phone in his hand and was waving it about. To focus his attention I took the phone, put in on the pavement and jumped up and down on it.

What neither of us noticed was a policeman standing and watching this all unfold. He stepped in and pointed out to the driver that he had been the cause of an accident while illegally using his mobile phone while driving, and he could either take us both in or the driver could apologise, pay for the bust wheel and call it a day. I thought the driver was going to bust a blood vessel, but he did calm down enough to give me £100 for the wheel – more than the bike had cost – before driving off with his now badly-scratched bonnet and cracked windscreen.

The policeman gave me a good dressing down about over-reacting. The fact he was smiling at the time didn't make me feel any less sheepish or foolish.

I have since seen the driver in the FT. He was a rather high-profile banker until about 18 months ago. Hopefully he bought a hands free phone system for his car with one of his bonuses.

When a slap on the wrist is better than a slap on the bonnet

PETER WALKER

It's a shameful thing to admit but there can occasionally be something quite cathartic, even soothing, about shouting at a driver who's just cut you up dangerously. In extreme circumstances a loud but non-damaging slap to a car bonnet or door can do the same trick.

But an email I received this morning reminded me that however tempting such a response might be, retribution is, as the cliche goes, so much more satisfying when served up, weeks later, with a cool temper.

This particular story began on a very early December morning in south-east London. As I waited at the head of a small queue to enter a roundabout a black cab squeezed past – I was, deliberately, in the middle of my lane – and placed itself in front of me.

It wasn't really dangerous given the low speed but it was, at best, pretty discourteous. Mildly irritated, I made a sort of palms up, shrugging gesture intended to say, "What's that all about then?"

The response was unexpected. The cabbie, a grumpy-looking middle-aged man, leaned as far as he could out of his open window and began yelling abuse. As we both negotiated the roundabout this torrent of swearwords – some in highly imaginative combinations – continued. It was bizarre and utterly excessive.

I didn't react in kind but instead made a mental note of the cab's registration number. Later that day I emailed a formal complaint to the Public Carriage Office (PCO), which licenses both black cabs and minicabs in the capital. The PCO, I'd learned a couple of years before, has no power over allegations of dangerous driving among cabbies – that's a police matter – but can look into discourtesy or abuse.

After a slightly awkward exchange of emails a couple of days later where the PCO asked for me details of the precise abuse ("Dear PCO, as far as I recall, it began, 'You stupid f****** t*** ...etc") I forgot all about the incident.

Until this morning. After looking into the matter, a very efficient PCO administrator told me, they had decided to issue a formal written warning to the driver which will remain on his file. Repeated offences could conceivably see his licence suspended.

Now I've got two reactions to this. The first, I'm afraid to say, is pure glee at the thought of this hugely angry man opening the letter informing him about the warning. I imagine cups of tea swept off a table, doors kicked, curses audible from the next street. I only hope he hasn't got a dog.

But I also like to think that perhaps I have, in a tiny way, made London's roads a better place to be. Shouting abuse back would have achieved nothing in the long term. It's possible – and I stress just possible – that a written warning might make the cabbie think twice before doing the same thing to another cyclist, pedestrian or driver, if only to preserve his job.

It reminds me of another incident a few years back when I was very nearly taken out at high speed by a young delivery driver attempting an absurd overtaking manoeuvre at traffic lights. I telephoned the company he worked for, calmly explaining what had happened, what the driver looked like and my strong belief that if he carried on driving that way he'd eventually kill someone. I might have been kidding myself, but the manager who answered the call sounded sincere when they said they'd have some stern words with the driver.

Satisfying, yes. But when faced with a private car, or unmarked van, sometimes only a slap on the bonnet will do.

COMMENTS

TheFoolAngel I am glad that Peter was able to deal with the unacceptable behaviour of that cabbie in a constructive way. I also agree with him that mostly cabbies are generally pretty decent and courteous road users.

UrbanManc Headcams are the way forward … and you must report instances, no matter how futile it may seem.

CycleLal Peter's story reminded me of the only time I have taken the time to report a black cab driver to the police. He seemed to think the green advanced stop lane box equalled his space so when I coasted into it, alongside MrCycleLal, the cabbie proceeded to ram us both (even though the light was still red).

No joking – I actually got trapped and turned from pretty hacked off to genuinely scared. Husband's wheel was bent out of true. As it was on Westminster Bridge a crowd gathered and we got witnesses. Police very nice. Expected nothing to happen but lo and behold he, too got a written warning.

CBR1100XX No matter how much you consider someone to be in the wrong, slapping their bonnet is just inviting trouble.

Chapter 6

Advice and tips

Picture the scene: you're cycling to Heathrow with a child on the back of your bike, and it's a journey you've done so often it's becoming boring. But then a pedal falls off, and simultaneously you hear a thup-thup-thup sound coming from the front tyre as it starts to deflate. And it starts snowing. Would you know what to do?

In this situation as in almost any other, the people who write for the Guardian Bike Blog may have an idea or two – and the people who post comments have hundreds.

If there's one thing the Bike Blog has proved, it's that cyclists are often very grumpy people. But that's not relevant here. If there's another, it is that they have hearts of gold, and will share their knowledge freely.

Cycling is easy and worthwhile and, even in cities, pretty safe. I bore this in mind when I recently went on a beginner's kitesurfing course. The amount of knowledge to be absorbed and jargon learned was intimidating. I would have to come to terms with wind windows, luffing, donkey dicks and chicken loops. But, I reasoned, weren't the intricacies of cycling similarly off-putting for non-cyclists (if perhaps not quite as colourful-sounding)? And I had managed to get quite good at cycling while having fun and not hurting myself very often, even at the start.

Of course, I was wrong. Kitesurfing is ruddy, ruddy difficult and I did little apart from hurt myself for the entire course.

So a wall of jargon can obscure a very challenging activity – or one that is simple even for a relative beginner, like cycling.

And this is where new media come in. The traditional media aren't much help to a would-be cyclist. The press and broadcast news will talk about it in terms of road deaths, riding on the pavement, and eccentric parents who let their young kids go to school on bikes; cycle magazines tend to be aimed at enthusiasts rather than beginners; and repair manuals are page upon page of exotic tools, greasy ball-bearings and odd-looking lugs.

With new media – a user group or, yes, a bike blog – you will find a community of people with differing degrees of knowledge in different areas, glad to offer help and advice. Fire up your smartphone at the roadside, and you have the knowledge you need to fix a puncture even if that was a closed book to you half an hour ago.

Plus, of course, the help and advice on offer on sites like the Bike Blog is often useful even for those who have been cycling for decades. You may consider yourself an expert, but would you know what to do in the situation given at the start?

The answer involves a cardboard box, a full English breakfast, an iPad, mascara, some grass, and a big bushy beard. Now read on.

Ben Thomas

Help make my longer commute more fun

PETER WALKER

I'm still not entirely sure how it happened, but over the past few years my commute has gradually become longer and longer.

A swift dash of almost three-and-a-half miles has somehow stretched to a middle-distance push of almost 10. There have been five different stages; three house moves for me and two changes of office. Every time my home has crept that bit further south while my workplace headed north.

I'm not complaining. For one thing, I know from comments on this blog that many people ride far greater distances to and from work every day. Secondly – and this is the obvious one – I like cycling. There's plenty of public transport options for lazy days. No one's forcing me onto the bike at gunpoint.

But I'm still hoping to beg the benefits of your collective wisdom. The latest house move, a couple of weeks ago, pushed me about three miles further south than ever before. There's various ways I can plot the route across town, but I'm looking at a good 45 minutes each way, more if I use more quiet roads.

So far, with the balmy, dry early autumn weather, it's been a breeze. But I'm getting a nagging worry about how I'll feel, say, in January, when the dark has closed in and every trip involves donning Michelin Man layers of thermals, or the rain teems down. This is when a near-hour ride each way will, inevitably, feel that much more onerous than one taking 25 minutes.

How do I stop the commute feeling like a grind? Much as I may try to escape the city on weekends, urban riding forms the bulk of my cycling miles and I'd hate to fall out of love with it.

My ideas so far are fairly obvious: vary my route, use different bikes. I've even contemplated listening to the radio on my mobile as I go. Lest this sparks a debate on safety, I should stress that I'd do this in one ear only, at low volume.

But what tips can you marathon commuters give me? How can I keep the fun in my ride?

COMMENTS

HelwynBallard Podcasts: as you rightly point out, if you keep the volume low and take out your right earpiece in busier traffic, it's perfectly safe. I listen to hours of them every week on my bike.

unicornhouse When I had a 45 minutes commute a few years ago, I learned some German. Each lesson was 30 minutes, there were 30 lessons to a level and three levels. I listened to each lesson twice, to and from work.

morganics Make one day of the week race day – there and back – and compare your times throughout the winter and in different weather conditions. Make another detour day. Allow a little extra time and make a small detour until you really know how all the roads, valleys, train lines join up between work and home. Become a micro-geographer.

colostomyexplosion Whenever I get to do a lot of riding for a few consecutive days or more, I enjoy the fact that I can get away with that fry-up or takeaway either before or afterwards. Its a good motivator for me to choose the bike over the bus.

Fruit n' Fibre + bus or Full English + bike?

I know what I'd choose.

interestedofnorfolk Take the loser option as I did. Fail your driving test five times and choose a job 15 miles away through the middle of nowhere with no public transport available.

Consolations include a chain ferry ride each way, barn owls, deer, all manner of other birds, assorted farm machinery, beautiful Norfolk countryside and the absence of psychos in vans trying to murder you.

eas956 Sing as loudly as you can. Belt out any song you like and make up the words you don't know.

You feel happier already, don't you?

yogijiva How about really paying attention to your journey? Watching the trees as the leaves turn and drop, noticing the gardens as they change, and the people as they get more and more swaddled up, noticing any changes in the buildings you pass.

There can be a lot of joy in being really present with what you're doing particularly a healthy and wholesome thing like riding a bike.

Rattandy Choose someone from history and cycle in the manner you think they would ride.

What's the right age for a baby seat?

BARRY NEILD

It's with a mixture of heavy heart and genuine concern that I must throw out the following question: what age is it safe to stick a baby on the back of my bicycle?

Feeling slightly frustrated at being foot-bound on a sunny afternoon last weekend, I trundled my eight-month-old daughter's pram into my local bike shop where I purchased some expensive new brake blocks and asked them the same thing.

Their advice: if she's old enough to support her own head (which she is), then she's old enough to ride on the back of bike, providing she's strapped in to a good seat and wearing a helmet.

Instantly I was imagining myself careering around the countryside, behind me a giggling baby in thrall to the same sensations that have made me a lifelong cyclist. The adventures! The bonding! The escape from having to push the bloody pram around the park yet again!

Two things held me back from buying one on the spot. Firstly, there's the heavy heart. For a keen mountain and road rider who has selfishly slunk away to bike the country trails and lanes while baby duties await at home, the idea of a clunking great plastic kiddy carrier sitting over the back wheel is surely the final admission that it's all over.

Then, there's the genuine concern. Is eight months really the right age to be transporting a baby? An American group called the Bicycle Helmet Safety Institute reckons that it's a bad idea before the child is a year old, and is actually illegal in some US states.

Aside from the fact that my daughter will, as soon as she is strapped in and pedalled out into the street, no doubt bawl so loudly I'll be only too glad to retreat to the peace of the park pram circuit, I'm reluctant to risk it. But am I being over cautious?

Update: While there was plenty of "go for it" support for strapping eight-month-old baby Ivy into a bike site, I decided to defer to calls for caution, but only until she reached her first birthday.

Following the advice of one bike blog correspondent, I bought a Dutch-made Bobike chair – a relatively small plastic seat that clips into a Meccano-esque mount on the crossbar.

I'm sure not everyone would be happy having a baby up front behind the handlebars, and the occasional looks of horror I get are not a surprise. But with Ivy's head (protected by a helmet) snug against my chest and my arms either side, to me it feels safe.

I don't take her out often on the bike – only when the sun is shining and the wind is light – and I'm deeply cautious, riding slowly and sticking to backroads and cycle paths.

From the off, Ivy has been unfazed by the new mode of transport, and seems to love it. Downhills are greeted with an excited "wheeeeee!" and she's got the hang of ringing the bell when instructed.

She even enjoyed the time we got swooped on by police demanding to know if my bike was stolen (curiously, they didn't ask about Ivy).

COMMENTS

CowanBricks I've taken my eight-month-old out twice now, but just on a one mile cycle track to the pub for a quick one. She can hold her head fine and enjoys the view from the front-mounted seat. The problem arises on the return when she passes cold out and lolls. Then you ride one handed while providing head support. A struggle on the final hill

Kronky Go for it – I put my daughter on the bike as soon as she could hold her head up properly. But don't have her sat behind you on those big old clunky seats you refer to. You want to get a front mounting seat. They sit between the seat post and the handle bars, kind of on the top frame but the seat mount actually comes with a steel length that goes on top of the frame.

My daughter absolutely loves it – somehow she knows when it's a Saturday and comes to me with her bike helmet: "Let's go bike!"

JenHarvey My daughter also sits on a front-mounted seat and loves it. She even likes to wear her helmet. which is surprising as I can't get a hat on her head for love nor money.

justsomeone I'm a cyclist and a father of two, but there's a serious concern here.

Personally, and I'm not trying to bait a flamewar here, I think it's tantamount to criminal neglect to strap a small child to the back of a bike. When I drive my kids in the car they're strapped in – booster seats, seatbelt, the works. This is a legal requirement, too.

On a bike, they're going to be the first to die if some idiot smashes into me.

utility To those suggesting it is neglect I suggest you need to look at how safe cycling really is, rather than the perceived dangers. I suspect it is the perception of safety that is out of kilter. You probably perform other actions that are just as risky, but don't seem it, without concern.

LordLucan Have always cycled with my kids, from babies in seats right through trailers, tag-alongs and now teaching them to ride on the road independently.

It's worth pointing out that most rear-mounted child seats do offer a fair amount of protection. I've managed to drop a bike with a heavy two-year-old in the rear seat who was fine because the seat kept legs and arms inside the plastic surround.

AdamVaughan Barry – I put my daughter on the back of my bike when she was 12 months. I would've put her on earlier, but my wife wasn't keen. My daughter loves it, especially whizzing down hills.

I think in terms of when the baby's ready – you have to judge that yourself. If they can sit upright and you can strap them in securely, go for it. I think around eight months and up is probably about right.

In terms of general safety ... I cycle on London's roads daily and don't think they're very safe, so I generally only cycle on quiet roads locally in south London when she's on the back.

Anecdotally, one thing I have noticed is that (most) drivers give me a wider berth when my daughter's strapped on the back of the bike.

When can children cycle on their own?

PATRICK KINGSLEY

At what age should children be allowed to cycle unsupervised? For paranoid parents, maybe never; for others, perhaps nine or 10. But for one south London couple it's even younger: Oliver and Gillian Schonrock allow their two children to cycle to school together – aged only five and eight.

Not for much longer, perhaps: the Schonrocks have been censured by their school headteacher for allowing them to ride unsupervised the mile-long distance between Alleyn's junior school and their Dulwich home. The Schonrocks say they merely want "to recreate the simple freedom" of their own childhoods; Alleyn's headmaster Mark O'Donnell thinks it might be a matter for the social services.

Who's right? For the department of education, it's a grey area: there are no official guidelines. But for Oliver James, child psychologist and author of parenting manual How Not To F*** Them Up, the issue is more clear-cut. "I'm pretty gung-ho when it comes to my five-year-old," he says, "but I wouldn't let him ride alone. I think it's a pretty odd thing to do. It should be banned really, though I couldn't say at what age." James is also concerned that the Schonrocks' children are at risk from attack. "Not from adults – there's a huge exaggeration in people's minds about paedophilia – but from other children. It depends on where you live, but other children pose a genuine threat in terms of knives and muggings."

Justine Roberts, who runs parenting website Mumsnet, is more worried about the cars: "For me the biggest risks aren't the strangers, but the traffic. Personally, I wouldn't let my four-year-old cycle to school even with me in tow. But all children are different, and in the end we ought to trust the parents."

According to Professor Frank Furedi, a sociologist known for his opposition to paranoid parenting, the Schonrocks should be praised. "Riding along the pavement is obviously well within the capability of many eight-year-olds," he says. "And some five-year-olds will definitely be mature enough to start to go to school on their own. Of course there are some children you wouldn't even let near a bicycle, but it sounds like these particular children will have benefited tremendously from the responsibility."

COMMENTS

Ortho A real non-story. If the parents and the kids are happy about it, which they seem to be, I can see no problem with this and no room for criticism. The school should mind it's own business – if it has no more pressing worries than this, it is a very unusual school.

PwabjXP This just shows the total absurdity of modern Britain. We have the fattest, least happy children in Europe because we don't trust them to do the things we did when we were children. It is utter stupidity. The health benefits of cycling substantially outweigh the risks.

artmim If you could see the speed and lack of care that some drivers show in the vicinity of our school, despite the signs and flashing lights then you would say the headteacher has a point.

LordLucan There's no way of knowing whether you would make a similar judgement yourself without knowing the route. Unfortunately, my kids have to cross a 40mph road on their way to school with no controlled crossing so I guess I'll be cycling with them for the foreseeable future.

LewRolls It is only permissible if they wear helmets, high visibility jackets, protective knee pads and follow a route with surveillance cameras every 10 metres. Even then the parents should sign a disclaimer, take out third party insurance and have a background check performed by social services.

BsAsBlue Getting children to cycle alone to school should be a goal, not a concern, for the UK. It is a common sight in Germany and Holland.

Punctures: facts and mysteries

BEN THOMAS

Thup thup thup thup thup thup thup thup. It's not a sound any cyclist wants to hear. You still wake up sometimes, don't you? You wake up in the dark and hear the punctures thup-thup-thupping? I heard the thup-thup sound coming from my tyre just now. Bad news, but on the bright side, it means I've got another item to add to my list of Puncture Facts and Mysteries.

What I know, as of today, is that I'll be more cautious when I stop to check on the thup-thup sound. It might be an RBPT (ruddy big pointy thing) scraping on the mudguard as it goes around. The pointy thing might be the only thing keeping the air in the tyre, so I'll have a closer look before slapping it off and getting back in the saddle.

Like all the other items of knowledge on my list, this latest one is (a) based only on limited personal experience and (b) a touchstone of absolute truth, to be imparted down the pub whenever punctures are discussed.

Facts:

- Punctures come in threes; if you get one, you've a 46.8% chance of getting another each time you go out until you reach your three.

- People who work in bike workshops don't use tyre levers, because their combination of knowledge and forearm strength is enough. Always.

- It's a good idea to carry a spare inner tube.

- You should let the glue go slightly tacky on the repair patch before you put it on.

- If you haven't got a repair kit, you can pack your tyre with grass and go a few miles that way. I think.

Mysteries:

- What's the 3cm rubber enema tube in puncture repair kits for?

- How long do you really need to wait between putting the patch on and inflating the tyre? Or is it OK to inflate the tube straight away, because it compresses the patch between tyre and tube?

- I don't do that thing that my dad showed me with the crushed chalk any more. The repair works without it. I also don't wait for the glue to go slightly tacky. Should I feel as guilty as I do?

COMMENTS

mojoangel Us folks who do work in bike shops do use tyre levers. But only to get the tyre off the rim. Never ever, ever use a tyre lever to put the tyre back on – especially that last little bit, because it will pinch the new or repaired tube, and you will be back to square one. You need to use your thumbs – and bicycle mechanic magic!

The other thing that many cyclists do not do is KEEP THEIR TYRES PUMPED UP HARD! This simple act prevents many punctures, keeps the life of the tyres (and rims) greatly extended – and the ride is much better, with less, energy sapping, rolling resistance.

The little "3cm rubber enema tube" is for the old-fashioned Woods valves, which no-one uses any more. Except the Dutch.

ske1fr Bicycle mechanic magic?

In that case I'm going to break the bike mechanic/Magic Circle rules. No magic involved. The rim is generally a smaller diameter along the centre of its cross section than along the shoulders, yes?

So if you pull the the bead of the tyre into the centre of the rim with your fingers as you push it on with your thumbs, you'll find it slips on quite easily.

Yes I know, I'm a marked man now.

Pidd Oooh, getting that last bit over the rim is a bugger. I have been known to go and sit quietly for five minutes when I get stuck at that point and gather strength to Go Over The Top.

My top puncture repair tip is to never repair a puncture. I always replace the inner tube. A new tube costs no more than a fiver and it's far less of a faff.

The other golden rules: punctures always happen when it is least convenient, and almost always in the rain.

mikemanorhouse Use a bit of washing up liquid and water on the inside of the tyre bead to help it slide back onto the wheel rim

puntoebasta When that last little bit getting the tyre back on is really, really tough, it helps to use a scrap of cloth. Wrap it round the tyre and, using the flat of your hands, "roll" the bead over the rim. Always works. Eventually.

LaMochi A totally girly thing to do, I know, but I smear a small bit of terribly ugly electric blue eyeshadow over the location of the

puncture to mark it. It shows up well and doesn't transfer
or rub off as easily (especially if you use cheap, nasty dime-store
eyeshadow) as chalk does. And most females usually have at
least one colour of eyeshadow they regret buying, so there's
almost always some at hand.

How to stay warm in the saddle

PETER WALKER

In case you hadn't noticed – perhaps you're reading this tucked
up in bed – it's cold. Very cold, in fact, even in London, although
of course our hovering-close-to-zero conditions are balmy
compared with other parts of the UK, let alone further afield.

As I pedalled to the office early this morning, swaddled in
thermal tops, I pondered the various ways, over the years, I've
learned how to keep warm on even the most brisk of mornings.
I should stress that these are mainly of relevance if you're
planning a slightly longer, or high-speed ride. For a spin down
to the local shop, then of course everyday winter street gear
does just fine.

So, in no particular order, here are my top five tricks. I'd love to
learn yours.

1. Invest in some proper thermal socks, particularly if you're
   planning any long rides. There are few things more miserable
   than standing by the side of the road trying to stamp some
   feeling back into your toes. My venerable pair of cosy
   woollen bike socks finally disintegrated just before Christmas
   and my girlfriend bought me a pair of ultra high-tech Swiss-
   made ones. The shiny exterior finish looks a little S&M, but
   my God, they're warm. And they'll last for years.

2. The nuclear option for cold feet is, of course, neoprene
   booties. These look even more Torture Garden than the socks,
   but on a really chilly day there's nothing better. If even that

doesn't work than another bike blogger recommends heat pads in the shoes.

3. Don't forget the ears – if you ride lid-less then a hat does the job fine, but with a helmet there's nothing better than a thin-but-thermal headband underneath. Don't forget to take it off with the helmet, though, as otherwise you will look like a 1970s ski bum.

4. Get a proper base layer. Merino wool will be your new best friend on a 7.30am January commute. Other than being extremely warm, its sweat-dissipating properties stop that clammy, boil-in-the bag feeling.

5. Don't overdo it. This might seem counter-intuitive, but particularly on the top layer, less can sometimes be more. You warm up surprisingly fast as you ride and going for the full Michelin Man look means the one advantage of sub-zero temperatures – the ability, if needed, to skip a shower when you get to work – is suddenly gone.

COMMENTS

simonwinter I used to cringe at the thought of long johns, but they're really awesome. My dad got me some for Christmas. They keep me warm when riding but they also breathe incredibly well meaning I can keep them on all day under my jeans.

acrascall A Buff is an essential winter piece of kit that can be used as a ear warmer, neck warmer and many other variations!

Takkk Best way to keep warm? Pedal faster…

hrababble A big bushy beard works a treat.

Beating the snow on your bike

MATT SEATON

Snow, for many, is already here. And after I'm done writing this, I'm going to put the knobbliest tyres I have on my bike for this morning's commute.

I've got used to riding with a big crowd of cyclists on my way to and from work, but I suspect that as it has snowed overnight in London, the rank and file of two-wheeled commuters will be thinned out substantially.

But really, there's no need to leave the bike at home, just because of a bit of the white stuff. In fact, with bus, train and London underground services reduced by the inclement weather, cycling might be about the best bet for getting to work vaguely on time.

I just came back from a couple of weeks in north-east US. It snows there any time from November to April, and easily a foot at a time. In New York, where they snowplough the avenues and the main cross streets with incredible efficiency (courtesy of the sanitation department, which uses garbage trucks kitted out with blades and chains on the wheels), I saw no shortage of cyclists pedalling through the snow and slush. Up in Vermont, I rode on dirt roads carpeted in packed snow and sand: with a windchill of -20C, the biggest issue was avoiding frostbitten fingers; staying upright was no problem.

Only ice is the real no-no, but riding a bike in snow is not only easy, it's even fun. And you get the added kudos because people think you're incredibly intrepid getting to work, as though you'd just pedalled to the South Pole or something. With all the hype about the winter weather, I did start websearching for some serious winter tyres – the type with metal studs that will bite and give grip even through hard-packed icy snow. There's so little demand for studded tyres in the UK that these products are hard to source, and by the time your order arrives, the snow will almost certainly have disappeared. So I'd suggest that unless your commute takes you over the Cairngorms, a pair of studded tyres for £70 is a slightly over-the-top technical fix for a problem that occurs a day or two a year at most.

Assuming, then, that we're doing cycling in the snow the cheap and cheerful way, I've got a few tips, but I'd be interested in yours, so please share below.

- The more tread on your tyres, the better. You can ride in snow on slicks, but I wouldn't choose to. If you have a mountain bike, with chunky off-road treads, this is the day for it.

- Let some air out of your tyres, whatever sort they are. Ride them soft: you'll get more grip.

- It's natural, when you're a bit anxious about conditions, to ride leaning forward and tense, with your hands on the brakes. But try to relax the hands and arms, and keep your weight back.

- As in any slippery conditions (such as very wet roads), do your braking early and as much as possible in a straight line. Definitely only use the front brake in this way; otherwise, use the back brake more. And you can also use the back brake to test the amount of adhesion you have.

- Try to steer "with your hips" rather than your hands: in other words, make directional changes progressively and with your whole mass on the bike, rather than by sudden sharp steering inputs at the handlebars.

- As snow gets grooved by car tyres and refreezes, you can encounter rutted tracks and momentary "tramlining" effects. Deal with this by allowing the front wheel of the bike to go where it wants; again, keep your weight back, stay relaxed and don't be too ambitious about your speed.

- Mostly, on British roads, the snow is cleared or turns to slush quickly, but beware of transitions from snowy side streets to clear roads: this is where you're most likely to encounter ice or tricky ruts.

- I generally ride around town with some sort of hat, rather than a helmet. But in the snow, I'll wear a helmet – there's just a little more likelihood of a slip. Most likely, it would be slow-speed and harmless, but I'd factor in the extra risk by wearing a helmet.

- Unless you have mudguards (with good clearance!), wear old clothes: that slimy black slush is perplexingly indelible and a dirty stripe up your arse is not a good look in the office.

- The most dangerous time, as with any analogous activity (skiing, skating, downhill mountainbiking etc), is when you get over-confident. The day I got a little cocky on the back roads in the Green Mountain State, I found myself sliding down the road on my butt. So hey, what do I know?

COMMENTS

supersoni Some more tips:

Remember you're allowed to put your feet down if you slide.

Stay behind cars at junctions. Cars that accelerate too fast on snow/ice will slide sideways – you don't want to be there.

Give drivers a wider berth than normal. Their windows are probably fogged/snowed up, and they are more than likely going to be concentrating very hard on the road right in front of them, more likely to weave around to avoid ice/ snow drifts, and might not check mirrors as much as usual.

cycleloopy It helps if you try and use the highest gear possible so it creates less wheel spin and less pedalling. You are using the same principle as a car in snow: move off from stationary in second or third gear if you can.

LordLucan Apparently some people use cable ties around the tyre thru the spokes, would only work with disk brakes for obvious reasons. Have never tried this myself.

Trois Good advice here, but slightly surprised that there is no mention of avoiding the front brake. Cycle slower and use the rear brake to slow and stop. A front wheel skid is almost impossible to recover from, whereas a rear wheel skid is manageable.

Why it's easier than ever to maintain your own bike

PETER WALKER

It was only changing a bottom bracket and re-greasing some bearings in a rear wheel hub, but I could hardly have felt more proud if I'd welded together a new frame from scratch.

Despite being a long-term cyclist I've rarely ventured into the more fiddly bits of bike maintenance. Change a gear cable, maybe replace a cassette and chain? Fine, but nothing much more complex than that.

So what prompted me to get my hands greasy? Firstly it was cheaper, even after I'd bought the special tool required. Also it was faster. One of the unexpected drawbacks of cycling's recent popularity is the sheer difficulty of getting repairs done.

While sales in some bike shops remain mixed, there is a nationwide shortage of trained bike mechanics, Mark Warmsley from the Association of Cycle Traders told me recently. My local store is so busy it won't even service bikes it hasn't sold.

Finally, for the would-be bike mechanic there's an ever-growing resource of tips and tutorials, particularly on the web. To take just one example, the fantastic Bicycle Tutor website has step-by-step videos on everything from fixing a puncture to assembling a mail order bike. Park Tools, manufacturers of high end bike tools, have a still more exhaustive (if video-free) online maintenance archive.

What if you haven't got a laptop or iPad to take into the garage with you? Bike repair books are getting increasingly user-friendly as well, a point emphasised to me when a new tome arrived in the post.

The immodestly titled Ultimate Guide to Bicycle Maintenance starts with the basics – what tools might you need? – and stretches all the way to the complexities of mountain bike suspension systems. It's logical, clearly illustrated and even has warnings for the over-confident. One says: "If you ruin or cross-thread your bottom bracket, your frame will be severely compromised. Ask yourself, is this a job for a qualified mechanic?"

Good advice, which I only read after I'd taken the plunge myself, luckily without any severe mishaps.

Now I realise that many people have no interest whatsoever in maintaining their bike – for them it's a means of transport, not a weekend hobby. But for dabblers like myself, it's becoming ever more easy.

Are you now a confident hand with a spanner and greasy rag, or frightened by even the thought of ballbearings? If the former, how did you learn: the old-fashioned way (from a friend/relative) or from a book or online?

COMMENTS

mikenetic Given the high cost of even relatively basic servicing it's worth investing in decent tools yourself – even specialist tools you might use only a couple of times (such as crank pullers) work out to be pretty cost effective. The major bike retailers have some good value complete toolkits. If you can stretch to it, a foldable workstand is a great investment too.

RedBarchetta From experience: always buy decent tools. Park Tools stuff may seem expensive but you will live to regret getting a cheapo item from Asda's cycle shelves.

Jacksavage Au contraire – it is now harder than ever to repair your own bike. I have ridden (and repaired my own) bikes for 45 years and I can assure you they are getting more and more complicated and difficult to service and repair.

Exquisite, fast and efficient when new, today's road bikes wear out at a terrific pace if you put in a lot of miles on them, and the spares are eye-wateringly expensive by comparison with say, 30 years ago. More and more special tools are required. Parts that fit only one manufacturer's model are more and more prevalent.

trickygjobs I hate to say this, but basic maintenance is fun. Yes it is.

The most basic 'once over' to check your bike is fit to ride takes about 30 seconds.

A – Air in tyres

B – Brakes – are they working

C – Chain – is it oily

D – Does it feel safe

The last point is a little ambiguous, but you will have picked up on squeeks and niggles as you ride. The simplest service can just begin with solving any problems that arise from this check. I would also include lubricating those pesky cables.

Keeping your bike safe on a plane

MATTHEW SPARKES

I recently returned from a tour of the Balkans. The plan was to land at Sarajevo, cycle to Split in Croatia, ride up the coast and across to Ljubljana to fly home. But that isn't exactly what happened, because the airline mislaid my bike.

After a suspiciously long wait at Sarajevo airport for the cardboard box I'd carefully packed it in days earlier, I was told it was still in London.

Two frustrating days later, and Germanwings finally delivered a now very tatty box containing a travel-weary bike. The frame was dented and scratched, the rack bent, the gear lever minus its plastic end and my bell was broken. And because of the delay I had to take two trains to catch up, so missed a lot of my planned riding.

Fear not, the trip was salvaged and I enjoyed lots of sun, sea and sightseeing, but it was slightly tarnished.

Annoyingly, this also happened the last time I flew with a bike – although that time the damage was limited to two chainrings and a set of handlebars.

So, keen to avoid another bill from the bike shop next summer, for myself and the readers of the Bike Blog, I have asked every keen tourer I know for tips on getting a bike from one airport to another, minus dents, delays or drama.

Firstly, if you are flying in and out of the same airport then you can use a hard case which offers a lot of protection. These can be expensive to buy but some bike shops will rent one for around £30 per week.

However, most bike tours involve riding from A to B and the cardboard boxes that new bikes come shipped in are the best choice. They can be popped in a recycling bin when you arrive and bought cheaply or had for free when you get to the other end.

So, without further ado, here's the collected wisdom of a big handful of cyclists. Please add any tips you have in the comments.

- Add extra layers of cardboard to the corners of your box and use plenty of tape to hold it tight.

- Take extra tape in your hand luggage – customs may need to look inside the box, and aren't required to help you seal it up again.

- Take off pedals, wheel skewers and anything else pointy that may puncture the box.

- Use lots of padding – foam pipe cladding from a DIY shop is perfect for protecting your frame and very cheap.

- Change to the biggest rings at the front and back – this will take up as much slack as possible in the chain and tuck the derailleur in.

- Once you've removed the wheels, protect the frame by using the plastic clips that come attached to forks on new bikes – if you don't still have yours ask for some at the local bike shop

- Weigh your bike – if you're over the allowance weight you may be stung with a large surcharge. Bathroom scales are perfect for this – but make your life easier by boxing it up first, as it's not easy to balance a bike on one when it's built up.

- Mark your seatpost with a bit of tape – this will help avoid any fitting issues at the other end.

- Pop any small, loose items like pedals or skewers in a small sandwich bag and tape it to the inside of the box. If there's a small hole then you could lose them.

- When booking your flight look carefully at bike surcharges, which vary hugely. For example, Iberia charges a €75 flat rate for every flight, so a return trip will cost €150. With KLM you get a 20kg allowance, and if a bike is under this it is carried free.

- Over-sized luggage can take a long time to check in, so arrive early or you may find your box has not made it on to your flight, even if you have…

COMMENTS

bristoltraffic I've found naked bikes (flip the pedals round, turn the handlebars 90 degrees) works as people roll the bikes in and around. There's less incentive on the handlers to throw the bike when you can push it. Just clean everything first so that nobody else suffers chain marks on their fancy luggage.

Fluffymike

- Let the tyres down
- Take the pedals off
- Turn the handlebars around

Done it loads of times. There's usually some bonehead at the airport who'll try and stop you loading the bike because it's not in a carbon-fibre carry-case or wrapped in a hundred cubic feet of expanding foam, but if you argue long and hard enough, you'll both get on the plane eventually.

PeterWalker My top tips:

- I line the sides of the soft case with bits of plastic corrugated sheeting bought from B&Q. Very light but very tough.
- Tape a load of clothes (which you need for the trip) inside a plastic bag to the bottom of the bike, protecting the big chainring, in case it's dropped.
- Plaster the entire bag in 'Fragile!' stickers.

It's worked for me so far, touch wood.

Olympic gold medal-winner Victoria Pendleton on why being the "wrong shape" for cycling didn't stop her

INTERVIEW BY JOHN CRACE

John Crace: You're not the conventional shape for a cyclist are you?

Victoria Pendleton: For sprinting I'm definitely not the right shape. I mean when I started everyone was pretty certain that I would be moving to the road swiftly and the fact is losing weight to be an ideal road cyclists was easier than trying to develop enough muscle mass to be comparable to the ladies on the sprint. Despite not fitting in the traditional norm, my power to weight ratio is very good and naturally on a bike I have a very low drag co-efficient. I don't know why but I've been in a wind tunnel and it's good because I have narrow shoulders and my hips are quite narrow. That's nothing I've trained to do specifically, it's just the way it is.

I'm quite heavy for the size of me – people are always surprised by how much I weigh because they think I'd be a lot lighter. I've got quite dense powerful muscles but they don't take up much room. They're quite efficient. I'm a little engine on a bike! The advantage is that I'm only pushing 62 kilos on a bike when there could be girls I'm racing against who weigh up to 80. I've also done a lot of endurance sports so I can recover quicker than some of the girls in the competition.

Despite the fact that people thought I was wrong for the sport, I'm a tenacious little being and I really wanted to do it. I want to the best and I want to win and whatever you say just inspires me to work harder and prove you wrong. I never felt limited and I don't want people to tell me what I can and can't be. I want to be exactly what I want to be.

JC: So you're stroppy?

VP: No, I've got very strong views and don't want people visually looking at me and telling me what I can and can't do. I've got a lot of criticism from coaches in the past thinking I don't take it seriously because I still look like a girl. I haven't cut my hair short, I still wear make-up and high heels on the weekend so perhaps it's perceived that I'm not taking it seriously because I'm not trying to become more of a masculine individual.

JC: How do you start, is it extremely scary?

VP: It's exciting! It's not scary. I mean if you look down the top of the banking on the apex of a bend you'll think "wow, that's really steep how does that work". But when you're riding around it's not that bad so as long as you just look ahead you'll be fine.

JC: What's the secret to riding the track?

VP: Just to stay relaxed, if you tense up or start panicking about the bends, the steep gradients that's when you start slipping and making mistakes. You've got to be very relaxed and keep your eyes on where you want to go.

JC: So in a sprint race do you just keep your eye on the road or do you watch others?

VP: You watch what the others do but when you commit to a move it's a hundred per cent and there's no keeping anything in the tank. You lay your cards right down and just go for it.

JC: Now that you have won the World Championships and the Olympics, how do you motivate yourself up to do it all again?

VP: I think it's been made very easy for me this time obviously because of the London Olympics. If it was in any other city it may have been a harder decision to make but there is no decision because it's such as fantastic opportunity. Why wouldn't you? You'd be crazy not to. I mean if you were in the physical condition that I'm in now why wouldn't you continue from the last Olympics to the next one. Four years is not a lot of time. And the opportunity to compete on home turf is amazing, it's going to be amazing to be part of it let alone have the opportunity to have success there.

JC: When you retire say after London, will you ever look at a bike again?

VP: Yes, I'm looking forward to the day when I can ride by bike without having a specific objective. Just to go out and ride for any length of time and not worry about if I have done enough, if I need to do more or if I went fast enough. It will be good just to pootle along at my own pace, take in the countryside and kick back with friends who maybe cycle a bit but are not up to training standard and have a chat and be a bit social. I do look forward to the day when I don't have an objective because right now I know what I need to get out of each session. That's what I do, that's my job isn't it?

This is an abridged version of an interview that appeared on the Guardian's bike podcast. You can hear the unedited interview at gu.com/p/29jdd

Chapter 7

Cycling the world

One of my most vivid cycling memories dates some years back when I spent a fascinating – if hair-raising – afternoon riding around Bangkok. The Thai capital isn't known as a bike-friendly city and for good reason. Aside from the sapping heat and humidity its labyrinthine road network is an anarchic melange of cars, lorries, three-wheeled "tuk tuk" taxis and motorbikes, all careering at breakneck speed with no apparent order or reason. Some tourists enlist local assistance just to cross the road.

But I loved it. Aside from seeing bits of the city I'd never have otherwise ventured through I felt truly part of Bangkok life, however briefly. Tuk tuk drivers laughed at my folly but gallantly gave way amid the gridlock. Moped riders good-naturedly raced me away from traffic lights. I spoke not a word of Thai but we were – in our very different ways – all in it together.

That's a slightly tortuous way of explaining that when it comes to global cycling I take a slightly different view to many British riders. Yes, I'd love the endless network of dedicated cycle lanes of Denmark or the Netherlands. But part of me stubbornly resists: wouldn't it be just a little, well, dull?

Hence my unorthodox choice later in this chapter of car-is-king Sydney as one of my personal favourite cities in which to ride, an opinion roundly mocked by readers at the time.

But I'll stick to my guns: for me, the wide world of bike riding is about much more than civilised trundles down sanitised northern European boulevards. Take, for example, a traditionally traffic-choked metropolis like Bogotá in Colombia. This has a long-running vehicle-free day every week, something I was ignorant of before reading Mike Power's eloquent description.

Another interesting trend is how some of the more aggressive cities are being gradually civilised through the advent of municipal bike rental schemes. The hugely popular Vélib' network has gradually turned cyclists in Paris from a curiosity to a near-ubiquity. Even some cities in North America have caught the bug.

If you've never taken your trusty machine beyond domestic shores I'd urge you to do so. It's more than an eye-opener – it can be an inspiration.

To illustrate I'll finish with another slightly self-indulgent reminiscence. One early bike trip abroad saw me riding, laden with panniers and inching endlessly upwards, along a Swiss Alpine pass. Although August it had been raining all day. I and all my possessions were soaked through and I was shivering with cold and dejection. Through the sodden mist I saw a Belgian-registered motorhome overtake me before stopping on a bend about half a mile up the hill. The door opened and out descended a family, a couple and their three young childen. They waited patiently and as I inched past broke into a volley of claps and cheers. Two minutes later their motorhome passed again, the family having resumed their trip. I'm not ashamed to admit that my view of the road became slightly misty, and this time it wasn't just because of the rain.

Peter Walker

New York trails

MATT SEATON

Move anywhere new and there's a lot to deal with. Like, where's the nearest supermarket? Is there a decent pizza place nearby? Help, I need a hardware shop. You'd think there'd be a farmer's market round here somewhere!

But for the cyclist, there's an additional layer of novelty and discovery, pregnant with opportunity, fraught with risk. Move anywhere really new and you have to acclimatise to a whole new culture of bike use, road craft and traffic lore.

Anyone who's lived abroad must have come across this phenomenon. In the far east or in African countries, the unfamiliar conditions would be just a subset of the gulf of cultural difference you'd have to assimilate. But I suppose I didn't expect the US, so intimately known in many ways from movies and TV and sharing a common language, to be so different for cycling.

I recently relocated to New York, and I'm still finding my way. Literally. To begin with, I only had the racing bike I flew in with – too precious to leave locked up on the street of a strange city. So, I was walking everywhere. And at first, walking was great. Pedestrians see more, and notice stuff that cyclists – with their necessary, life-preserving scoping of the road ahead – can't afford the luxury of looking at.

Sometimes, walking through Chelsea (Chelsea, New York, as in the Chelsea Hotel of Patti Smith and Leonard Cohen fame) on the way to work, I'd look up and just have to stop and stare at some exquisitely echt-Gotham example of ziggurated art deco apartment building, which, to New Yorkers, are so ten-to-a-cent as to be a practically invisible part of the city's backdrop.

But as the weeks went by, and the novelty wore off, I became frustrated. Between my apartment on West 35th Street and the Guardian office on West 27th, there are only so many combinations of zig-zagging navigation across this small portion of Manhattan's grid before you get bored with the same nondescript commercial midtown side-streets. I really craved a bike, not just to streamline my commute, but to experience New York fully as a cyclist.

Cycling is popular, but perhaps more as a sport than a mode of travel. There's a steady stream of bike traffic at rush-hour over the bridges from Brooklyn, but in Manhattan itself there's little of the massed ranks you get in London at intersections, morning and night.

There are bike lanes on some of the avenues, and recently Broadway got a segregated bike lane for a large portion of its considerable length. But it's not much used. And the only times I've tried it, the main hazard is meeting one of my fellow immigrant workers who's using the bike lane in the wrong direction to deliver takeout food on an electric bicycle.

There are amenities besides bike lanes: there are bike parking stands on most street corners. But until now, there's been no Paris- or London-style rental scheme – although the city transportation commissioner has announced a bikeshare plan with 10,000 bicycles, which it hopes to have up-and-running in 2012. And while there are fantastic cycle routes around virtually the entire perimeter of Manhattan along the shoreline, especially up the west side along the Hudson river, the car still rules the roads – even in this city where, uniquely for the US, fewer than half the inhabitants own a vehicle.

The avenues – five- or six-lane highways, mostly one-way (either northerly or southerly) – are exhilarating to ride down, but slightly scary. For one thing, your instinct as a cyclist is to choose one side of the road or the other, but the problem is that cars and cabs that want to turn into a side street have to give way to pedestrians crossing those intersections. So you're constantly finding yourself blocked or cut up by cars trying to turn off the avenue but stopped.

So that forces you to move into a middle lane. But that means you're mixing it with hundreds of yellow cabs, which will travel as fast as the traffic conditions permit, and then some. (And who knows what the posted speed limit even is: it might be 35mph, but 45–50mph is normal and there are no speed cameras and zero enforcement.)

Those yellow cabs are trigger-happy with their horns when they see a cyclist, but that's OK, because at least if they honk you, you know they've seen you. In London, you feel that drivers – especially bus and cab drivers – have grudgingly conceded the reality that cyclists are part of the traffic: they expect to find their passage somewhat impeded by cyclists and have evolved the skills to get along with them, and get by them when they can.

In New York, there isn't, so far as I can see, a critical mass of cyclists to have "calmed" the traffic. So you sense that the taxi driver zooming up behind you discovers you suddenly as a viscerally annoying anomaly, not as an expected, normative, minor nuisance. As confident a cyclist as I am, it's got me a little spooked – being buzzed by these impatient sociopaths.

But if there's little apparent enforcement of speed limits for motorists, the cops seem to care even less what cyclists do. This may, again, be an aspect of the lack of critical mass: if there were waves of cyclists ignoring red lights and riding the wrong way down streets, then perhaps NYPD's finest would be bothered. As it is, you can pretty much do as you wish with impunity.

Even in solidly Democratic, liberal New York, it seems, there is some of that American frontier, let-me-alone-to-live-as-I-please spirit. So I'm slowly unlearning the habits of an adult lifetime of obedient adherence to the rules of the road – because if you stop for a red light on a bike here, people just think you're weird, or French, or something.

If traffic regulation is somewhat anarchic, there are great things, too, about NYC's grassroots bike culture. Chief among these is the absence of chain stores. There is no Halfords, Evans Cycles or Cycle Surgery here. Instead, bike shops are all small to middling independents, each with their own quirky character, implied clientele and niche locality. I keep discovering new ones – which suggests that the trade is flourishing. I chanced on the easy-to-remember A Bicycle Shop a week or so ago in Chelsea. Besides the mandatory photograph of local hero (and long-time Lance Armstrong teammate) George Hincapie, I saw they had a few used bikes at the back of the store and I had to browse. Fifteen minutes later, my wallet was $250 lighter, but I rode off on a really quite excellent urban junker.

It's the only bike I've ever owned that has a "coaster brake" of the rear hub variety where you have to backpedal to slow down.

So that adds an additional learning experience to the general novelty of cycling in Manhattan. But the feeling of liberation was immediate: I had wheels again! Now all I have to do is learn how to ride here.

COMMENTS

hhazzahh Besides the yellow cabs (they are driven with efficient recklessness, and that is not a contradiction in terms), it is the scale that can be daunting. The roads are arrow-straight with immense buildings lining the road, and huge cars/SUVs surrounding your space. You can feel quite small as a visitor on a bike...

greendakini The trick when riding on Manhattan avenues is to stay pretty much in the centre of the left lane. It's important not to let taxis and cars intimidate you so that you hug the parked cars. The cabs may honk but they will not cold-bloodedly run right over you. But they will elbow you to the side if you let them, where you are vulnerable to being doored, a real danger. In New York, bicyclists have the right to a full lane, just like cars.

luckycountry I've lived in Manhattan for nine years and you couldn't pay me to ride a bike here. The standard of driving is appalling. I wondered why until I had to pass a driving test which consisted of driving around a block in the Bronx and performing a three-point-turn. I was in the car for seven minutes. No barriers to being a car driver in the USA. Uncle Sam wants you to be a gas guzzler, not a cyclist.

Sehr gut: Why cycling in Berlin is a dream

HELEN PIDD

Having found myself enjoying an unexpectedly long sojourn in Berlin, courtesy of flight cancellations, I decided to make the most of it by hiring a bike to pootle around one of my favourite places in the whole world.

Berlin is not, on the surface of it, a classic cycling city. The public transport system actually works, so you don't need to saddle up to be sure of reaching your destination on time. A portmanteau of two capitals, it is also huge, and so getting from one side of it to the other by bike can really test your legs. Plus there are cobbles all over the shop. Despite all this, it is a really marvellous place to cycle. Here are 10 completely subjective reasons why.

1. The streets are crazily wide

   Thanks to a combination of Allied bombing and the Communists' insatiable appetite for tearing down lovely old buildings and replacing them with brutal new ones, many of Berlin's streets are incredibly wide. Yesterday I pedalled from Alexanderplatz (site of the 1989 protests) down Karl Marx Allee, the archetypal example of East German roadbuilding. Constructed to show off Communist town planning after WWII, this imposing boulevard is almost 90m wide. Even the pavements are broad enough for tanks to drive down two abreast.

2. You can cycle on the pavement

   Well, you usually, can, anyway. All but the narrowest pavements have bike paths built into them.

3. No one tells you off for not wearing a helmet

   Helmet use is on the up in Berlin. When I was a student here seven years ago, I don't remember anyone wearing a helmet, but I've noticed the odd one this past few days. At least once a week in London a friend or colleague will ask: "Where's your helmet?" Not here.

4. You are allowed to cycle through parks

   The other day I cycled through Tiergarten, one of Berlin's biggest parks, and no one tried to stop me. I've never managed to bimble through the middle of Regent's Park without getting at least told off.

5. You only get fined for cycling crimes if you cause an accident

   Again: usually. According to a cycle-themed edition of Prinz magazine which I have before me, if you cause an accident going through a red light which has been red for longer than a second (love that German precision), you can be fined €100 and get a point on your driving licence. Hurt a pedestrian while hurtling through a pedestrian zone and you can be charged €20. Pay €30 if you cause havoc cycling in the wrong direction. Interestingly, you can also be fined €25 for talking on your mobile while cycling, and if you are caught cycling drunk you can be taken to court.

6. It's almost completely flat

   On Monday I cycled all the way from Neukölln in the east right through to Wannsee, the placid lake where the Nazis planned the Final Solution. It was probably 30km or so each way, and only when I hit the woods near the lake was there more than the vaguest of inclines. Incidentally, if you ever come to Berlin in spring or summer, you must visit the ginormous strandbad (lake beach) at Wannsee. Germans are a bit wussy about temperatures so when I went for a dip, there was just me and one old lady. Nudity is optional.

7. All flats have bike parking

   We can take some credit for this again with our bombing. Traditional Berlin tenements (Mietskaserne) are built with courtyards perfect for storing bikes.

8. You can take your bike on tubes and trains

   As long as you buy your bike a ticket.

9. Drivers expect you to be there

   In Britain drivers still seem to be surprised and puzzled to see a cyclist. Here, whenever cars are turning right – usually straight into the path of the cycle lane, as in Britain – the drivers look first to see if cyclists are coming through.

10. It is really easy to hire a bike

I plumped for Fat Tire Bikes, which has shops at the zoo station and Alexanderplatz. It cost €12 for the first day, €10 for the second and €8 thereafter. This sturdy orange bike has taken me from east to west, north to south, on pavements and rough tracks. Sehr, sehr gut.

COMMENTS

Eremit I came to northern Germany eight years ago intending to stay a short time and I'm still here – the cycling provision and tolerance shown by drivers offers me a quality of life that I can't find in the UK.

quacky It's not all tolerance, sweetness and light for the cyclist in Germany, I'm afraid. By law (even during daylight) a bike must have a dynamo lighting system (batteries won't do), and various reflectors front/rear/spokes. The police do spot checks and will issue tickets for infringements. I have been pulled up myself.

acme Everything that Helen says about Berlin is also true of Munich. You can hire bicycles cheaply at the station and cycling for the amateur is pleasant, easy and safe. With well signposted cycling lanes everywhere and cycling used as a means of transport by a range of ages and fitness levels

Millerntor I am a cyclist in Hamburg and can vouch for everything in the article. I did get a €5 on the spot fine for wearing an iPod while cycling to work which was nearly increased to €50 when the police lady found out I had Coldplay's first three albums on shuffle. My defence was that I was listening to "Fix You" from the X&Y album therefore I was fully in control of my senses.

My favourite cycling cities – if not everyone else's

PETER WALKER

All urban areas have a different character, and this extends to the often wildly different experiences you get from cycling around them. This can often be very personal. Here, in no particular order, are my five favourite cities I've cycled around, and a few reasons why. I'm sure many will disagree, so how about you?

Copenhagen

Not a very original choice, admittedly, as Copenhagen is hailed widely – even by its own somewhat immodest tourism website – as the world's most cycling-friendly city. As the tourist officials point out, more than 1m km are ridden there every day, usually by helmet-less types pootling around in everyday clothes, not Lycra-clad warriors. I lived there for a period as a child, and was instantly entranced at being able to ride to school, aged 10, near the centre of a capital city, in the safety of bike lanes, something more or less unknown at the time in the UK.

Beijing

China may be falling out of love with cycling, whatever Katie Melua believes, but the bike remains probably the best way for a newcomer to discover Beijing. Yes, many bikes have been replaced by aggressively-driven cars, but this transformation has not been as complete as in some other Chinese cities. A lot of big roads still have wide bike lanes and you can spend hours trundling round the smaller streets, particularly in the few remaining hutong districts. Plus, it's pancake flat.

London

A choice with some reservations, as I'm guessing is often the case for one's home town. But I still love riding around London, whatever the occasional behaviour of drivers and, of course, some of my fellow cyclists. Travelling around the Big Smoke, cycling is the only mode of transport where I can time my arrival more or less to the minute. And even now, the view from Waterloo Bridge at dusk is enough to make me pull over for a few minutes of silent gazing.

Sydney

A much more personal choice, mainly as, in my experience, it's really not a very bike-friendly city at all, particularly the decidedly skittish taxi drivers. It mainly merits a place for one thing: the cycle lane over the Harbour Bridge. Once you've ridden across on a sunny day you're hooked. If you're brave – and no one else is around – you can even ride down the 45-degree slope in the middle of the stairs when you reach the end.

Paris

Another place not usually seen as a cyclists' paradise, although the Vélib' rental bike system has helped change this somewhat. Aside from the fact that Paris's compact geographical spread makes cycling very practical, I mainly like the relative lack of Lycra and aggression among fellow riders. Yes, people occasionally jump a red light or trundle along a pavement, but it's done with some sensitivity to pedestrians.

COMMENTS

SkippyKangaroo As a Sydney rider I think the ramp at the north end of the Harbour Bridge is emblematic of what's wrong with cycling there. The only dedicated cycle lane in the whole of the city – and they put a set of stairs at one end of it

hobbes2009 I'd suggest Vancouver. Mostly courteous drivers who stick to the speed limit. Beautiful Stanley Park for pootling around and counting raccoons; the UBC Endowment Lands for some very easy but really pretty off road trails; Granville Island Market for fantastic food.

Roryer1 If we can include any city, even smaller ones, then I would say Groningen in the north of the Netherlands – 60% of all trips there are made by bicycle. The whole centre is shared space for pedestrians, cyclists and cars, while there is clear segregation of traffic on the ring roads and arterial roads, with bus lane, car lane, bicycle lane and sidewalk.

wddr And so my favourite cycling cities:

Copenhagen and Amsterdam for the everyday nonchalence of cyclists there.

My adopted city of Helsinki for the exhilaration of riding on packed snow at minus 10 degrees in winter (and then realising it's just normal for the natives).

San Francisco for the short steep hills and the fantastic rides just over the Golden Gate bridge.

New York, simply because the sight of an old Chinese guy riding the wrong way up the middle of five lanes of traffic seems to be an everyday fact of life.

SteveJC Basel, Switzerland. I love it. Comprehensive network of cycle lanes and a huge number of streets that are two way for bikes and just one for cars. Large pedestrian area, lots of velo parking, bikes can be taken on buses and trams, beautiful riverside and close to the Vosges and Jura, and of course the Alps are just two hours away.

Basel is never mentioned, but its so much better than Zurich and Geneva.

AlmightyThor No one has mentioned Chicago yet – regularly voted best cycling city in the USA. There's a cycle lane along Lake Michigan that can take you all the way into Wisconsin. Absolutely breathtaking.

PeterLoud Look no further than Milton Keynes.

Bogotá's Ciclovia shows how to run a car-free capital

MIKE POWER

It's a bright Bogotá morning and I'm sprinting, standing up out of the saddle pushing hard on the pedals to cross La Septima (7th Ave) and 19th Street, normally one of the most nightmarish junctions in this traffic-swamped, car-crazy town. But I'm doing it for a laugh, not to escape quickly, as today's a Ciclovía.

Ciclovía is a weekly, city-wide, car-free day in Bogotá that puts 76 miles of roads, including La Septima – the city's main commercial centre – off-limits to cars. It's been running since 1974, and offers a brilliantly bonkers insight into this wild Andean capital.

More than 2 million people come out every week to cycle, hang out, flirt, pose and eat on the street. It's transport policy in a Critical Mass dreamworld, and the weekly event makes Boris Johnson's once-a-year cycling ambitions for London look like the lily-livered, business-loving, small-thinking, can't-do claptrap they truly are.

Three out of four lanes in La Septima are closed and today are filled with elderly strollers in superfly shades carrying massive radios listening to tango, children scrambling round on toy bikes, punks on skates, stern-faced Lycra warriors on $5,000 Treks, moody goth skateboarders and, fabulously, one man and his pitbull in matching leather harnesses, panting in unison.

And all along the sidewalk, you can buy mangoes, coconut juice, salpicon (a delicious fruit slurry) as the guys selling mystery-meats-on-a-stick fan their embers with their baseball caps. In public parks there are free yoga and aerobics classes, known as the Recrovia. Today in the National Park, there was what looked suspicously like a vast and riotously good-humoured three-legged race.

Ciclovía's impact has spread far and wide, with similar events all over Latin America, but here it's had an unintended but very welcome consequence: social integration.

"Ciclovía is one of the few places where Colombians of different classes mix," says Mike Ceaser, who owns a bike rental business, Bogotá Bike Tours. "You've got a lot of poor people and very few rich, here. Rich and poor only meet as workers and employees in Colombia – janitor and bank manager, maid and home-owner. But the Ciclovía is democratic. Here, everyone's on a bicycle, mixing, meeting on an equal level," says Ceaser, a former journalist who set up his bike shop when the US newspaper industry started cutbacks.

In Latin American cities, class and wealth define everything, with galaxy-sized gaps between the dirt poor and the astronomically wealthy, and here it's no different. Bogotá's income division is north-south. The rich live in the north, and the poor in the south, but people switch territories during Ciclovía. Cycling in Bogotá does not carry the eco/health/lifestyle cachet it does in the UK – if anything, it's seen as a poor man's way to save money on bus fares. Wealthy Colombians won't commute to work as they think it makes them look poor. But everyone loves the Ciclovía.

Any cyclist wanting a good look round Bogotá should stop by Ceaser's shop in the old colonial heart of Bogotá, La Candelaria, where he has around 40 bikes and helmets for hire and expert tour guides on call. It's a fantastic way to see the city – safe, easy and affordable. Today, I covered 10 times the ground on two wheels as I would have done by foot, or taxi, or bus. As I pedal, smiling Colombians laugh at the tall gringo in the biggest, yellowest helmet they've ever seen, panting and purple-faced as the altitude takes its toll: Bogotá is the world's third-highest capital city, at 2,640m above sea level.

Don't worry if you hit a spot of bother on your bike, though. The route is attended by hundreds of paid guardians carrying medical kits and bike tools. (When the call first went out for the guardians, just 20 CVs were received. When the city authorities rebranded the job as Bikewatch guards, after Baywatch, asking for athletic and active people to apply, they got 1,500 CVs, says former city official Enrique Peñalosa).

Be aware though – bike theft is rife, and bike parking spots are few and far between – and even when they look official, you may not be able to lock and leave.

The city also has a vast network of bike lanes – though they are in a pretty poor state and are often used by sidewalk vendors to sell anything from scavenged mobile phone parts to barbecued corn on the cob. And the Ciclovía's main route is under threat: the mass transit bus service, Transmilenio, may expand into some of the roads where the cyclists currently reign.

But it seems to have luck, albeit of a grim variety, on its side. A few years back a Bogotá senator, Fernando Castro, tried to move the hours of Ciclovía to run it from 5am to 12 noon, cutting back the most popular hours with the public. During the senate hearing arguing for the move, in a scene straight out of a magic realist novel, the car-loving, chain-smoking senator keeled over at the dispatch box and died later that day.

If a city as busy and poor as Bogotá can close its roads every Sunday of the year, and every one of the dozens of holidays enjoyed here, why can't London, or Manchester, or Liverpool, or Glasgow or Cardiff or Newcastle? Is it so radical a concept to promote healthy, non-polluting, silent forms of transport that bring people together, rather than locking them behind airbags and safety glass, for just half a day a week? Must we measure everything so drearily in pounds lost to business?

I guess revolutions are best left to the Latin Americans.

COMMENTS

busybeingborn Excellent. Good on the people of Bogotá. If there is anything that is destructive of community identity in our society it is the car. If only our city councils were enlightened enough to allow just one day a week (or even one day a month) when our roads were free of cars. Imagine a day free of car fumes; it isn't hard to do.

wildfrontear This article combines magic realism and cycling and is my favourite thing that I've read in the Guardian this year.

RedBarchetta This will never happen in the UK. Imagine the uproar if it was decided that London's roads were to close for a day to accommodate cyclists? The mewling and moaning by drivers whining on about how all those smug red light jumping bastards on bikes are all of a sudden being treated like they are something special?

colostomyexplosion I think the barrier to doing this here is that the pro-car dependency lobbies would be worried that removing all the motor traffic for a day will allow people to see just how compromised their everyday lives are by the subjugation of the needs of pedestrians and cyclists to the benefit of motorised transport.

Just imagine being able to cross a road without being forced to wait because someone else chose a "more important" form of transport. It would make it even more plain to see how much motorised transport has compromised our town layouts and how much time space and resources are devoted to serving it.

muppetcrusher Ciclovía is a great project but even now some of the activists out there fear that it hasn't had the impact they wanted. Just like Freewheel/Skyride was a diversion from proper reallocation of road space away from the cars, Ciclovía hasn't resulted in massive shift in ordinary trips. Indeed there is a fear that people now only use their bikes for Ciclovía and don't see the bike as a transport option.

Car-free cities: an idea with legs

STEVE MELIA

*Coordinator of Carfree UK and a researcher at the
University of the West of England*

A quarter of households in Britain – more in the larger cities,
and a majority in some inner cities – live without a car. Imagine
how quality of life would improve for cyclists and everyone
else if traffic were removed from areas where people could
practically choose to live without cars. Does this sound
unrealistic, utopian? Did you know many European cities
are already doing it?

Vauban in Germany is one of the largest car-free
neighbourhoods in Europe, home to more than 5,000 people.
If you live in the district, you are required to confirm once
a year that you do not own a car – or, if you do own one,
you must buy a space in a multi-storey car park on the edge
of the district. One space was initially provided for every two
households, but car ownership has fallen over time, and
many of these spaces are now empty.

Vehicles are allowed down the residential streets at walking
pace to pick up and deliver, but not to park. In practice, vehicles
are rarely seen moving here. It has been taken over by kids as
young as four or five, playing, skating and unicycling without
direct supervision. The adults, too, tend to socialise outdoors far
more than they would on conventional streets open to traffic
(behaviour that's echoed in the UK, too).

Most of the European car-free areas are smaller and "purer"
than Vauban: vehicles are physically prevented from entering
the streets where people live. Exceptions are made for
emergency vehicles and removals vans but not for normal
deliveries, which are made on foot, trolley or cycle trailer. A few
peripheral parking spaces are available to buy (usually around
one space for every five homes) and a few are reserved for car
club vehicles. In all the examples I have studied, cycling is a vital
means of transport.

Car-free areas of this kind, with anything from a couple of hundred to more than a thousand residents, exist in Amsterdam, Vienna, Cologne, Hamburg and Nuremberg, among others. There is even a small one in Edinburgh.

There is another form of car-free development, so familiar we have until recently overlooked its potential. Most pedestrianised city or neighbourhood centres in Britain are almost entirely commercial. But a few farsighted councils, such as Exeter, have brought back housing and residents, without cars or allocated parking, into city centres that would otherwise be deserted after 6pm.

Groningen, the Netherlands' capital of cycling, has the largest car-free centre in Europe: half-pedestrianised, entirely closed to through traffic, with 16,500 residents, three-quarters of whom have no car in the household. Forty per cent of all journeys within the city are made by bicycle.

Carfree UK, which I coordinate, was set up to promote European-style car-free development in this country. We are not anti-car, we are pro-choice. We have recently run public meetings in London to set up a new car-free association for London, which is beginning to look at areas of the city from which traffic could be removed. We know considerable potential demand exists for traffic-free housing in London, and probably in a number of other major cities. Where else do you think might be suitable?

COMMENTS

Mezzum Practically speaking I'm sure you could have car free areas in most major UK cities.

For most people I would imagine the idea of getting around their city without a car is not the problem, it's when they have to travel further afield they start to experience real difficulties.

Car free cities are a fantastic idea, less pollution, less costs, less obesity... However, in the UK we need deep and protracted investment in our public transport networks. Without this investment the idea is dead in the water.

davetrom In central London boroughs only a quarter of households have cars, so why do residents put up with everyone else's smelly/noisy cars on their street?

Step one: let's reclaim some parts of the streets. Take one car parking space and install six secure bike lockers.

Step two: block the road to through traffic and smell the air quality getting back to normal.

Step three: get a couple of car share vehicles in the street and encourage people to ditch their car.

Step four: lobby the new generation of EasyCouncils to put the cost of permit parking up x10 to be more in line with the cost of the land used by the vehicle.

Step five: capitalise on the new empty road space to plant trees, meet demand for cycle lockers etc.

tattywelshie Anyone who has visited CenterParcs would have experience of car free living, where cars are not allowed to drive around the complex, and it is absolute bliss! I don't know why new-build housing estates do not at least try and promote car-free living into their schemes. There is a massive stigma attached to cycling, which in my opinion needs to be got rid of otherwise cycling will never become a fully integrated part of our lifestyle in the UK.

Vive la vélorution

LIZZY DAVIES

It's 2am on a Friday night and I need to get home. There are no taxis, the last metro left 10 minutes ago and, tottering on my three-inch heels, I'm not keen on walking it, either. Unlike when

I was a Londoner, and no night out was complete without an excruciating night bus at the end of it, this is no cause for despair. I simply do what every savvy Parisian does now: I take a Vélib'.

With its cumbersome frame, clunky gears and ungainly handlebars, the Vélib' – a sturdy, three-gear roadster weighing almost 50lb – is an unlikely saviour of chic urban transport, but saviour it is, none the less.

Since the scheme (whose name is a contraction of vélo and libre) was introduced to Paris, following the success of a similar initiative in Lyon, it has gone from maverick novelty to sturdy staple for everyone from skint students in need of a free ride to bankers in need of a workout. With more than 20,000 bikes on the streets, a rank every 300 metres and more than 2 million journeys made every month, the Vélib' scheme has managed to turn a city of tumultuous traffic and angry drivers into a haven for adrenaline-junkie cyclists.

Parking spaces are being taken over by Vélib' rental ranks, commuters can pay for their bike journeys with their integrated transport swipe card and hundreds of kilometres of cycle lanes are being built. It is nothing short, the French have decided, of a vélorution

But the rise of Vélib' has not been without its hiccups and verdicts have been mixed. One commentator, in Le Figaro, declared that the scheme had "fallen victim to its own success".

The cracks appeared in the months following socialist mayor Bertrand Delanoë's launch of the scheme in July 2007. Although the Vélib' had increased general bike use by more than 90%, reports indicated that uphill activity was almost zero. The ranks in Montmartre, where the highest point is about 130m, were often empty. JCDecaux, the company that runs the scheme, decided to allow those brave enough to leave their bikes at the top of the hill with free extra minutes in the saddle.

The company also realised that bikes were being stolen and rarely recovered. Reports emerged of the specially made models being found in eastern Europe, even Africa. So far, 8,000 have "disappeared" and a further 16,000 have been damaged beyond repair. JCDecaux has admitted it is struggling to fund a system with such a rapid turnover.

Sociologists, when asked why the harmless bicycle has become the target of such anger, have blamed the phenomenon on class resentment. The people who have taken most enthusiastically to the Vélib', they point out, are Paris's privileged bourgeois bohemians, or "bobos", who inspire as much loathing as they do envy.

"It's a bit like the 4x4s that people have a go at to get at the rich," said Sebastian Roché from the National Centre for Scientific Research. So has the vélorution reached the end of the road? Not quite. In Paris, fans are staying loyal despite the odd bad experience and in cities around the world, authorities are using the Vélib' system as a model for their own bike-hire efforts.

JCDecaux is operating in Luxembourg, Brisbane and Dublin. Brussels, Milan and Montreal have also cottoned on, while towns and cities across Britain have been experimenting with pared-down versions of Vélib', with varying degrees of success.

Cheltenham has removed its 30 bikes after a year of low usage while Bristol's Hourbike, the closest the UK has to a city-wide scheme, is having trouble getting its residents to tackle its undulating terrain despite the presence of four hubs around the city centre and a Vélib'-style pricing system in which the first half-hour is free.

It is in London that cycle campaigners hope the real breakthrough will come. With keen cyclist and mayor Boris Johnson in the saddle, Transport for London (TfL) is vowing to create an efficient and well-funded rental system to rival the French capital's, with 6,000 bikes for hire by May next year.

Part of a £111m package invested by TfL and the mayor's office to make the city more cycling-friendly, the idea is to have 400 bike-docking stations spread over nine London boroughs and several royal parks. As in Paris, cycle ranks are to be located no more than 300m apart and, as in Paris, the scheme is expected to trigger a noticeable spike in bicycle journeys around the capital – around 40,000 extra trips per day, according to TfL.

Despite Johnson's best efforts, the scheme's future remains unclear. Some city councils are reportedly reluctant to support the plan because of fears their budgets will squeezed, although TfL has insisted the launch will go ahead. If it does, and Johnson has the chance to prove his belief that "a cyclised city is a civilised city", get ready to say au revoir to that night bus.

Update: The London scheme eventually launched in July, not May, but proved popular – in just 10 weeks the millionth ride was clocked up.

COMMENTS

kirstend Barcelona's bikesharing scheme has experienced similar success without as much theft/vandalism – perhaps it's because Bicing seems to cover all classes and age groups

kanawish The Vélib' system now has a incentive program in place for people to bring bikes back to stations with higher elevation. Some higher elevation stations are marked as "V+" stations. If you bring a bike back into one of those stations, you get a time credit of 15 minutes on your account.

The non-cyclist whose hire bikes changed urban riding

SUZANNE GOLDENBERG
The Guardian's US environment correspondent

For a man who may be on the verge of revolutionising the urban cycling experience, Michel Dallaire has spent relatively little time on two wheels.

Dallaire, who designed the Bixi public hire bike, as used in London, regards himself as a skiier rather than a cyclist. His longest ride was a "really painful" 36 miles, and negotiating London's traffic seems a terrifying prospect.

"The traffic in London with these huge buses, two storeys high and they drive so fast," he said. "The bicycles sometimes are just in front of these big buses and they ride 40km, 50km in the city and of course on the wrong side of the street."

But Dallaire's Bixis, the frames marked with their disinctive silver swoosh, seem unstoppable, moving on to Boston, London, Melbourne Australia and Minneapolis after a hugely successful debut in Montreal.

The sharing scheme registered more than 1m rides in its first four months in Montreal. The Montreal parking authority, which runs Bixi, put 2,000 more bikes on the streets and added more docking stations. The bike system could end up being the most widespread design of Dallaire's 43-year career.

"I saw people I knew who I never imagined would be on a bike in town, and some people cycling for the first time," said Suzanne Lareau, the president of Velo Quebec, the cycling advocacy organisation. Many users have their own bicycles but are afraid of getting them stolen if they ride into town, she said.

Others say the Bixi gives them a sense of freedom. They can duck out of their offices for a quick lunch, ride into work without fear of being caught in the rain on the way home. In the summer months, it's another transport option along with buses, and metro. "It's part of a cocktail of transport," said Catherine Mayor, spokesman for the Angus Technopole, a green redevelopment project on the site of an old locomotive shop.

Membership costs $78 for a year, or $5 a day. The first half-hour rental is free, with prices rising thereafter. Dallaire attributes at least part of the success to the uniform design of the Bixi, which turned the bicycles and docking stations into part of the urban landscape. He said the sturdy look of the bike inspired confidence – and prevented vandalism.

Dallaire, who worked with a local manufacturer, DeVinci, as well as Velo Quebec, also hid the cables inside the bike's main frame to prevent them being tampered with.

London's bicycle sharing scheme is not identical to the original Bixi, which uses solar power and modular design for the bicycle docking stations, which are shut down during the winter months.

The docking stations, which hold six bicycles, are mounted on aluminium plates which can be picked up by cranes and plunked down on pavements, allowing the authorities to easily shift bicyles to areas of high demand. London's docking stations are permanent, using power from the electrical grid.

There were setbacks too in Montreal, with one in five bikes reportedly vandalised. Roger Plamondon, the head of the parking authority, refuses to release figures for theft or vandalism, saying he does not want to encourage copycats. But he admits the early days were a challenge.

"We had people trying to sell them in a garage, we had people trying to sell them for the aluminium," he said. "But we had people calling us and telling us come and pick up the bike, the bike is not supposed to be there."

A spokesperson said thefts in the early days were at 3% to 5%. About 50 of the 5,000 bicycles are under repair at any given time.

Dallaire was called in to modify the locking system, and the authorities say the changes cut down on thefts.

"It has really changed the dynamic of the social community," he said. "It has changed Montreal. It's more friendly, people are more together – and it is so practical."

COMMENTS

olafp The Milan bike-sharing scheme – www.bikemi.com – is going well, and keep in mind that Milan is one of less bike-friendly and environmental-conscious cities on the continent.

lagatta I'm just back in Montreal from Amsterdam, and ironically global warming is making our fair city far more cycleable. I'm a non-athletic, 50ish woman and cycled well into December this year, and could have resumed in February if I weren't too intent on my European work trip and walking everywhere. I've been on my bicycle every day since the beginning of March.

Cycle hire schemes?
A UN plot, says US politician

PETER WALKER

To their users, bike hire networks like that in London and the popular Vélib' scheme in Paris might seem no more than a convenient, fun way to get around a city. But they're wrong.

Dan Maes, the Republican frontrunner to challenge for Colorado's governorship has discovered the truth about such cycle schemes: they are a grand United Nations plot to enslave the US.

"This is all very well disguised, but it will be exposed," Maes told supporters at a campaign rally.

"This is bigger than it looks like on the surface, and it could threaten our personal freedoms. These aren't just warm fuzzy ideas from the mayor. These are very specific strategies that are dictated to us by this United Nations programme that mayors have signed on to."

His target is a programme called the B-Cycle in Colorado's capital, Denver, a planned network of 400 red bikes to be placed at docking stations around the city and accessible using swipe cards. B-Cycle already operates in Chicago and hopes to expand to other US urban areas.

Maes argues that Denver's bike scheme, and other policies promoted by the city's Democratic mayor, John Hickenlooper, such as encouraging employers to install showers for cyclists, are the brainchild of the International Council for Local

Environmental Initiatives (ICLEI), a UN-linked organisation connecting 1,200 communities worldwide.

If the Tea Party-endorsed Maes wins the Republican nomination he will face Hickenlooper in the election to be governor.

Maes conceded that some might find his theory "kooky". He explained: "At first I thought: 'Gosh, public transportation, what's wrong with that, and what's wrong with people parking their cars and riding their bikes? And what's wrong with incentives for green cars?' But if you do your homework and research, you realize ICLEI is part of a greater strategy to rein in American cities under a United Nations treaty."

A spokesman for Hickenlooper said Denver joined the ICLEI in 1992, more than a decade before he became mayor, and had "limited" contact with the organisation.

Update: Maes won the Republican nomination but got just 11% of the vote in the election for governor, behind not only Hickenlooper but also the fringe Constitution party.

COMMENTS

BalbKubrox Not in the least surprising: when I was working in Norway back in the late 1990s I shared an office with a Texan god-botherer who categorically refused to use the town of Stavanger's excellent public transport system on the grounds that buses are intrinsically "cammunist". Our team had a pool-car allocated to it: which she promptly appropriated to herself on the grounds that an American shouldn't have to rub shoulders every morning with the ungodly and possibly socialist-voting Norwegian riff-raff.

AnneDon I suspect his objections are the common ownership and the lack of a petrol engine. If there's no profit and no exhaust fumes, Republicans can't cope.

RedPanda Does Nurse know he has access to the internet?

Proof that God is a cyclist

BEN THOMAS

You might think that Los Angeles, the city that has spent a century being defined and shaped by the car, would be an unfriendly place for cycling.

You would be right. But proof that God is a cyclist came last month when Los Angeles' mayor, Antonio Villaraigosa, decided for some unknown reason to go for a bike ride. The prolific LA cycle blogger Ted Rogers was one of those registering their surprise: "For his first four years in office, Villaraigosa never let the word bicycle pass his lips in public."

The story gets better, although not for the mayor, who experienced an immediate road-to-Damascus conversion. The shattering revelation came on Venice Boulevard, where a taxi pulled out across his path and he fell from his bike. Today, with eight metal pins keeping his broken elbow together, the mayor is Los Angeles' latest convert to cycle advocacy.

He declares that he wants to change the city's culture in favour of cyclists; yesterday he held a "cycling summit" at the city's transport HQ and went some way to winning over what Rogers calls "a highly sceptical house of roughly 300 bicyclists". His suggestion at the meeting that helmets should be made mandatory – he was wearing one when he had his accident – was reportedly met with "audible dismay", according to the LA Streets Blog.

But he has pledged $3.2m (£2m) for cycling in the city this year, and committed to building 40 miles of bikeways each year for the next five years. The event, says Rogers, was a first step, but it was a "huge, and hugely successful" one.

As providence appears to be smiling on cycling at the moment – with bike hire schemes popping up all over the place – which other cities around the world are most in need of change? And for that matter, who's next for cycling conversion? Jeremy

Clarkson? Or celebrity chef James Martin, he who infamously claimed he had startled a group of cyclists into a hedge while testing a high-powered but silent electric car?

COMMENTS

GGBandrew Proof indeed! However, some of my most enjoyable cycling down the coast of California was along the beach in LA. A dedicated cycle path in the middle of the beach – awesome. The only problem was getting in to LA. Cycling through Malibu was lethal due to the inconsiderate SUVs and the neighbourhoods to the south offered alternative threats. Let's hope the funds are well spent and the locals adopt cycling in the same way as Santa Barbara and San Francisco.

vancouverite LA is changing. The sketchy area around the Jewellery Quarter and the Fashion District is changing rapidly. The beautiful beaux arts and deco buildings that have been empty for years are being transformed into stylish apartment blocks. The young apartment dwellers are causing infrastructure like cafes and restaurants to appear where there were once empty lots, and these carless youngsters are getting around by bike. The mayor is just reacting to a change that is already happening (and probably seeing votes in it).

OakenGrove Ouch. Poor chap. I really hope he nailed that taxi driver to the wall. There are some abuses of power I would fully support and making bad drivers disappear to Guantánamo Bay would be one of them.

"Cycling can be lonely, but in a good way"

DAVID BYRNE

I cycled when I was at high school, then reconnected with bikes in New York in the late 70s. It was a good way of getting around the clubs and galleries of the Lower East Side and Soho. At that time almost no one else was riding, but I didn't care what people thought.

There's a certain amount of freedom involved in cycling: you're self-propelled and decide exactly where to go. If you see something that catches your eye to the left, you can veer off there, which isn't so easy in a car, and you can't cover as much ground walking.

The physical sensation of gliding with the wind in your face is exhilarating. That automatic activity of pedalling when you have to be awake but not think too much, allows you to let subconscious thoughts bubble up and things seem to just sort themselves out. And the adrenaline wakes you up if you weren't properly alert. If I'm commuting to work by bike, I'm fully awake by the time I get there, having dealt with a little bit of New York traffic en route.

I had an accident once when I had been out at an art opening and had too much to drink. I lost sight of my girlfriend and was turning around trying to see where she had got to, then slipped and broke two ribs, which I realised the next day and woke up in incredible pain. But that's nothing compared to some collisions bikers have, although it's definitely getting better. There are more secure bike lanes and drivers are beginning to have a better awareness of cyclists.

What usually takes me to other places is business, and when I get time off I'll always set a destination to visit. In Berlin recently, I decided to go to the Stasi headquarters, which was out of the centre and a bit of a ride. It was a great thing to see, but it's as much about the landscape along the way.

I've got lost plenty of times. We were touring on the border of Switzerland and France and I was going down various paths on my bike when I ended up in the other country. I had cut through some vacant lots, under an express way, through a fence, then suddenly spotted the border crossing. Luckily I had my passport on me.

It's difficult to have conversations biking, although quite a few of us on the tour have bikes and we try to ride together. Cycling can be lonely, but in a good way. It gives you a moment to breathe and think, and get away from what you're working on.

David Byrne's chronicle of his adventures on two wheels, **The Bicycle Diaries,** *is published by Faber & Faber. The Talking Heads songwriter was talking to Rosie Swash. You can listen to the full interview at gu.com/p/2a2ed*

Chapter 8

Staying safe

Talking to a Danish friend recently about whether or not cycling was inherently dangerous, she said it never even occurred to her that riding a bicycle could be considered a perilous activity until she moved to London. "Back home in Denmark, cycling was simply the easiest way to get from A to B and everyone does it," she said. Then Therese crossed the channel and suddenly people were telling her how brave – if not bonkers – she was to pedal around the place.

While it is supremely tedious to bang on about the joys of cycling in Copenhagen/Amsterdam/AN Other City More Civilised Than Our Own every time the subject of road safety comes up, the point she made was a good one: how and when did cycling start to be thought of as so risky? Especially when, as Chris Peck points out so neatly in this chapter, it is actually safer than gardening.

Those who hate cyclists claim that we bring peril on ourselves by behaving badly in the saddle. But the truth is that only a tiny proportion of accidents involving cyclists are caused by riders jumping red lights, failing to wear a luminous vest or not having bike lights, as Peter Walker explains. The fraught topic of whether it is ever acceptable to breeze through a red light is covered in the legal chapter, but for what it's worth, my view is this: don't do it because it gives the rest of us a bad name. And if we want taxpayers to stump up for better cycling infrastructure, we need to persuade the (predominantly car driving) general population that we are not irresponsible idiots. If you get hit with an on-the-spot fine for misbehaviour: good. If you didn't spot the policeman, you're clearly not nearly observant enough to be ignoring the rules of the road in the first place.

But I digress. The one topic – apart from, perhaps, red light jumping – which exercises bike blog readers more than any other is the great helmet debate. Both subjects end up being shoe-horned into the comments section of almost every blog, however tangentially. We've included just one helmet-themed post in this chapter, however: a discussion of whether David Cameron was right to thumb his nose at the safety police by daring to ride his bike with a bare head one day.

Good on him, I say, though like Cameron, I sometimes wear a helmet myself (if it's raining/the roads are slippy after rain or frost/I'm doing a sportive or triathlon and have to). I am often accused of recklessness on the days I go without – predominantly by non-cyclists rather than fellow brethren. I always respond in the same way: it's a personal choice, it's not illegal and, incidentally, were they aware that the most common injuries to cyclists are to their shoulders, not heads, as UK hospital admission statistics show?

And while we're here, shouldn't pedestrians be given helmets since walking is actually more dangerous than cycling? According to the UK government's road casualty data, in 2007 there was one fatality for every 32 million kilometres cycled. That's slightly fewer per kilometre than for pedestrians, who suffered one fatality every 28million kilometres. So there.

Helen Pidd

Helen Pidd is the author of Bicycle: Love Your Bike: The Complete Guide to Everyday Cycling.

Why gardening is more dangerous than cycling

CHRIS PECK

Policy Coordinator of the CTC, the UK's National Cyclists' Organisation

When I started cycling in London eight years ago I felt I was virtually the only one, battling for space with taxis and buses. It was a fight with few allies. Today, things are very different – I'm one of the pack surging away at the traffic lights. Official figures show more miles were travelled by bike in 2008 than for each year since 1992. Cycling has almost doubled on London's main roads in nine years and increased by 30–50% in cities such as Bristol, Leicester and Leeds.

But it's really remarkable that despite the increase in cycling, casualties suffered by cyclists are still down by around a third. To anyone who doesn't cycle this might seem a bit odd. Shouldn't more cyclists mean more crashes and injuries? As those who cycle will know, however, the more cyclists there are the safer it will be for everyone.

CTC (the UK's national cycling organisation) found that the same phenomenon occurs if you examine different areas within the UK. Cambridge, where a quarter of people cycle to work, or York where it is about one in eight, have a much lower risk of injury for cyclists than places where you hardly ever see a cyclist on the streets.

Why does this "safety in numbers" effect occur? The vast majority of cyclist injuries result from crashes with motor vehicles, and most of these appear to be primarily because the driver "looked but did not see". Cyclists (and motorcyclists) have even given this type of crash a name – Smidsy, an acronym for the drivers' refrain, "Sorry, mate, I didn't see you!" These type of crashes start to decrease as cycling levels rise.

Take the hypothetical case of Bob the Driver, who last rode a bike when he was still in school uniform. Bob drives up to a junction with a major road, glances right and, not seeing anything car-shaped, pulls out into the path of the "unseen" cyclist. Crash and injury result. If, as Bob approached the junction, there was a stream of cyclists crossing in front of him, he probably won't make the same mistake.

As more people cycle, one of the new cyclists may be one of Bob's relatives or friends, or even Bob himself. When riding a bike he is less likely to pose a risk to others than when he is driving – and more likely to understand cyclists' needs.

Even though cycling gets less risky at the same time as more people taking up cycling, there may come a point where the overall number of injuries to cyclists actually increases. There are far more people killed cycling in the Netherlands than in the UK, for example, even though the population is smaller. But the Dutch cycle ten times further than here, and the risk per mile is substantially lower. After years of badgering, the government has finally agreed to present casualty data as risk per mile rather than numbers of injuries and deaths.

At a population level, of course, not cycling is far more dangerous than cycling. The life expectancy of non-cyclists tends to be two years shorter, with 39% higher all-cause mortality than cyclists. But most people still associate cycling with danger. This is partly because this seems to be the main message of government and local authority advertising.

I'm often told I'm brave to ride a bike but few people consider it brave to get out into the garden and do a bit of weeding. Yet in reality this is a more dangerous activity than getting on two wheels. An hour spent gardening is more likely to result in injury than the same time spent cycling. So remember, next time you step outside to clip the hedge, beware of the risks you are running!

COMMENTS

Yifan I too get the "you are so brave" comment from non-cyclists all the time in London. Interestingly, in China, this "cycling is dangerous" concept is also developing among the middle class, who, one generation back, were all keen cyclists. But with the proliferation of taxis and private cars, many have left cycling and look back to their pedaling days as some youthful bravado.

Amsterdamize What's often missing from making comparisons is the fact that the Dutch couldn't have accomplished this (over the last 40 years, mind you) without comprehensive and long-term national policies, proper funding and (often unpopular traffic-calming and taxing) measures. You have to enable safe cycling with proper infrastructure and facilities, legislation, education, (positive and factual, not fear-mongering) promotion, etc. 'Safety by numbers' doesn't magically appear and establish a sustained growth without addressing all these aspects, you'll quickly hit a ceiling.

It requires dedication and commitment, regardless of party lines. Not something easy to come by, but nobody ever said it was.

Luke1972 Seeing as I cycle to my allotment it isn't looking good for me is it?

Celebrity chef stirs up cycling hate campaign

HELEN PIDD

The celebrity chef James Martin – the Yorkshire one off Saturday Kitchen who puts butter in everything – has incurred the wrath of cyclists including Bradley Wiggins after writing a cyclist-baiting article in the Mail on Sunday.

Martin, who moonlights as a motoring correspondent for the paper, wrote of his hatred for "herbal tea-drinking, Harriet

Harman-voting" cyclists (surely we Guardian types have copyright on such insults?). He was fed up, he said, of the "city-boy ponces in fluorescent Spider-Man outfits, shades, bum bags and stupid cleated shoes" who pedal around the lanes near his country residence "with their private parts alarmingly apparent."

So far, so predictable. But in a review of the Tesla electric car, he went further, gleefully describing how he had utilised the speedy and silent approach of his test vehicle to sneak up on a pack of weekend cyclists, honk his horn and drive them off the road. "The look of sheer terror as they tottered into the hedge was the best thing I've ever seen in my rear-view mirror," he wrote.

The cycling community is now in full counter attack. Tour de France sprinting ace Robbie McEwen urged everyone to "either key [Martin's] car or punch him in the face"; Taylor Phinney, the US world champion, called him a "douche bag". Most bruisingly of all, Bradley Wiggins, the Olympic gold medallist, tweeted that he had always preferred rival cooking show Something For The Weekend anyway. Ouch!

Tesla, which loaned Martin the car, wasn't happy either. "In this case, we're not even using it [linking to the review from our site]. It is really odd. I have to sadly admit this is not the first time a journalist in the UK has brought up this issue of wheatgrass-eating hippies riding bikes. [But] this is definitely the most extreme version of it," said Rachel Konrad, Tesla's communications manager.

Before long, Martin's Wikipedia entry had been hacked and the Daily Mail website had removed the facility to comment on the story so that no one else could call him a moron. The cyclists' organisation the CTC also waded in, urging the cyclists terrorised by Martin to contact the organisation's accident line. An inevitable Facebook group was formed, with over 1,000 people signing up to declare I Hate James Martin, and dozens of angry cyclists began to bombard his agent and publisher with emails.

Wiggins' wife, Cath, announced she had written to the Press Complaints Commission and urged everyone else to do the same until Martin apologised. Almost 400 others also complained and although the PCC agreed the piece had caused "considerable offence" it ruled that it had not breached the PCC code of conduct.

When the Guardian contacted Martin, he declined to comment, but a source close to him said he was only joking – it was "a humorous piece like Clarkson and caravans" apparently. He did later issue an apology on his website though.

> *May I take this opportunity to apologize [sic] for any offence I have caused through the article in last weekend's Mail on Sunday. It was never my intention to offend the many cyclists who share our roads across the country. What was intended to be a humorous piece was clearly misjudged. Further more I do not condone any form of reckless driving.*
>
> *Once again, I am sincerely sorry for any upset caused in relation to this article.*

I must admit I quite like Martin. I got his book on puddings for my birthday the other year – the pear tart is a winner – but picking on cyclists is pretty lazy way to get a laugh.

Did you find it funny? Should cyclists stop taking themselves so seriously and not take the bait for once?

COMMENTS

rogerleeds What a prize tit.

LordLucan Personally I don't think that Clarkson crosses the line in the same way that this fool does. Fair enough rant about cyclists and caravans, but don't write your twisted violent fantasies in a national newspaper and expect to have people write it off as being humerous.

gfewster Seriously, lighten up. I drive a car, I cycle, I ride a motorbike. Car drivers aren't actually out to kill those of us on two wheels, they're just ignorant and generally lazy. Everyone could do with raising their driving/riding standards.

fatboyflying I thought this sort of lame prejudice had died out with the Black and White Mistrel Show. I suppose prejudices don't disappear – they just change. Cyclists are the new target, clearly. Or the fat. Or the Welsh. I'm all three – bring it on, Martin!

mojoangel Hopefully, his career will now go down the frying pan.

Lorry drivers: expect cyclists in unexpected places

KEVIN GRAHAM

A lorry driver for Lambeth council in south London

I'm not just a lorry driver, I'm also a cyclist who rides to work. But I still found a recent course on bike awareness for lorry drivers really useful: it taught me, for example, how to identify the blind spots where a cyclist could be, particularly at junctions and roundabouts. Everyone on the course sat in the cab and looked for driver blind spots, and then we all got the chance to be a cyclist as well. I think the drivers who don't usually ride a bike learned even more than me – it was a bit of a shock to them when they got on the bike.

I know my colleagues are careful anyway, but the experience made them more aware – everyone should take the course. But it's not only drivers who need to learn, cyclists should be trained, too. Some cyclists – you could call them the ignorant riders – come up on the inside at junctions, where the driver is signalling to turn left, and try to squeeze past just before they turn. Some, unfortunately, don't make it.

I'm definitely more careful as a driver because I'm a cyclist myself. As a cyclist, if I'm not sure what the driver is going to do, I stay back. I never come up on the nearside of a lorry. I try my best not to filter between lanes. I use proper hand signals, bright clothing, and always have lights on my bike – just simple safety measures.

If I had to give one piece of advice for another lorry driver it would be always to use the mirrors and expect cyclists to be in what seem like unexpected places.

For cyclists, I'd just say this: stay behind a lorry, and if you have to overtake one in slow-moving traffic always pass it on the right-hand side. Pull out when you're a good five metres behind the lorry so the driver can see you coming.

Remember, if you cycle, you do it because you want to get places quickly, but you want to get there safely, too.

Lambeth council organises training for its drivers on how to be more aware of cyclists.

COMMENTS

goinganextramile Not overtaking a lorry on the inside unless you're absolutely sure it's stationary in traffic is very good advice, but could someone please explain to me why Bus drivers seem to target cyclists by deliberately pulling alongside us, promptly signaling left and beginning to move over. Where do they expect me to go? I've had no end of disputes with this tactic.

Chris0 A good perspective to hear from and I wish all lorry and bus drivers had the sensibilities of Kevin.

Unfortunately the tendency of the road planners is to filter cyclists to the left. That's where the cycle lanes are, and also how they are supposed to get to the advanced stop lines. It's not surprising that less experienced cyclists take risks by going on the left of lorries when the message they get is that it is where they are supposed to be.

Beware the 'iPod zombie cyclist'

PETER WALKER

There is, apparently, yet another two-wheeled menace stalking our urban streets – the "zombie cyclist". This is the not-in-the-least hyperbolic name for the phenomenon of riders listening to iPods and the like, coined in the Sunday Times and now enthusiastically picked up by the Daily Mail.

Both articles take as their starting point a warning against listening to music as you cycle from Edmund King, president of the AA, who is supposedly a keen rider himself. They then weld this clumsily to government statistics released earlier this month which showed a year-on-year rise of 19% in cycling deaths and serious injuries for the three months to June.

While they note there is nothing concrete to connect the two things, the inference is there. The Daily Mail story starts off, "The fashion for wearing iPods while cycling has been blamed for a rise in the number of riders being killed or seriously injured," but then presents no evidence to back up this hypothesis.

Now, cycle safety hysteria in the press is nothing remarkable. As one Times reader comments: "Beware of zombie journalists inventing scare stories to sell newspapers." But beneath the papers' bluster, do they have a point when it comes to headphones?

Personally, I don't like using them when riding on the roads. I experimented once or twice listening to speech-only podcasts at low volumes.But even that made me feel disconnected, shut off from that ever-changing hum and roar of traffic, the frequencies of which, as a cyclist, you're always half-consciously scanning for something unusual or amiss

However, that's just me. As a number of readers of both articles point out, it's not as if every car driver listens intently at all times. One writes:

> Drivers often have the windows shut and music on in their cars. Surely this is the same as a cyclist using an iPod. Certainly if I can clearly hear their music as they drive past me then they can't hear outside.

That would seem to make sense. I often rely on a well-timed yell of "Oi!" to alert a driver that their half-tonne slab of metal is drifting inexorably into my path. There are times when the volume of music coming from inside means they clearly won't hear me. A gentle kick to a door panel usually wakes them up, but it's not a trick you want to use every day.

What are your thoughts? If a cyclist sets off through the urban streets with his or her ears assailed by Slipknot cranked up to full volume, are they just asking for trouble?

COMMENTS

Oseph I used to do this on the way to school and it made me much more aggressive and much less aware of my surroundings. Stopped doing it when I nearly got hit by a bus.

Coolio I don't think hearing is too important, you should be able to spot any hazards ahead of you and an approaching car behind you should always be passing wide, if they are overtaking then it's up to them to do it safely. Even if you came to a big pothole and had to swerve to avoid it, you should look over the shoulder anyway instead of relying on hearing to detect trouble. Remember the deaf are perfectly able to drive and cycle safely.

bazhay Fair enough that some car drivers drive with loud music in their cars, they are surrounded by a bubble of metal, a cyclist isn't. You can't say "if they can do it why can't we!"

If you wear headphones while riding you take away one of your most valuable senses, its tough enough riding on the roads as it is without that disadvantage.

Dornier Cyclists get killed by motor vehicles, not by iPods. Why is it the cyclists behaviour that is criticised? When people get killed by guns, we control guns.

piemagic Cycling with headphones strikes me as one of the most efficient forms of suicide out there.

Risky cycling rarely to blame for accidents

PETER WALKER

A tiny proportion of accidents involving cyclists are caused by riders jumping red lights or stop signs, or failing to wear high-visibility clothing and use lights, a government-commissioned study has discovered.

The findings appear to contradict a spate of recent reports speculating that risky behaviour by riders, such as listening to music players while cycling, could be behind a near 20% rise in cyclist deaths and serious injuries in the second quarter of this year.

The study, carried out for the Department for Transport, found that in 2% of cases where cyclists were seriously injured in collisions with other road users police said that the rider disobeying a stop sign or traffic light was a likely contributing factor. Wearing dark clothing at night was seen as a potential cause in about 2.5% of cases, and failure to use lights was mentioned 2% of the time.

The figures were slightly higher when the cyclist was killed, but in such cases only the driver's account is available.

The data, which was analysed by the Transport Research Laboratory (TRL), showed that more than a quarter of all cycling deaths in 2005–7 happened when a vehicle ran into the rear of a bike. This rose to more than one-third in rural areas and to 40% in collisions that took place away from junctions.

The 64-page analysis found that police attributed responsibility for collisions more or less evenly between drivers and cyclists overall, but this was skewed by the fact that when child riders were involved their behaviour was named as a primary factor more than three-quarters of the time.

With adult cyclists, police found the driver solely responsible in about 60%-75% of all cases, and riders solely at fault 17%-25% of the time.

The cyclists' lobby group CTC said the report showed that the government needed to focus more on driver behaviour rather than on issues such as cyclists wearing helmets. The TRL published a separate DfT-commissioned report today in which it was estimated that the universal use of helmets could save between 10 and 15 lives a year, a conclusion disputed by the CTC.

"The main cause of crashes seems to be 'failed to look properly', whereas very few cyclists are injured or killed acting illegally, such as failing to use lights at night or disobeying traffic signals," said Chris Peck, from the lobby group.

"We believe this report strongly supports our view that the biggest problem for cyclists is bad driving. With that in mind we are greatly concerned that the government still seems fascinated with analysing and promoting cycle helmets, the value of which appears to be inconclusive. We believe that the government should now focus on tackling the causes of injury which appears to be mainly inconsiderate and dangerous driving. Reduced speed limits, stronger traffic law enforcement and cycle-friendly road design are the solutions."

TRL recommended that more research be carried out into the relatively high numbers of young casualties, finding that those aged 10 to 15 were most at risk of injury for each mile cycled. Riders aged 16 to 29 were more likely to suffer harm than any other adult group.

The data – which covered incidents on the highways – showed that 3% of all collisions leading to deaths or serious injuries took place on bike lanes, and almost 80% of casualties happened during daylight hours. Just over 15% of all such accidents involved the cyclist alone.

COMMENTS

GerryP In 50 years of careful cycling all the accidents I have had have been motorists either pulling out of junctions into me or turning across the road in front of me. Indeed as a driver I also plead guilty, having pulled onto a roundabout and clipped a cyclist who I just did not see, allbeit it was a dry sunny day and I was not speeding.

The Government would do well to study why motorists fail to see cyclists who in theory should be clearly visible. I suspect there is a neurological reason for us to filter out the cyclist image, maybe on the basis we do not expect them there.

DelphicSybil Most of my near misses – as a careful cyclist – have actually involved pedestrians stepping out into a cycle lane without looking, often with their back to the oncoming traffic.

dianab My son cycles. He has done most miles in our Midlands city with the usual rubbish cycle lanes, fairly low number of cyclists on the road and high number of bike-blind drivers. He is now cycling in Cambridge – and is traumatised! Not only by the erratic and dangerous behaviour of other cyclists but also by the drivers who seem to see the bikes solely in order to aim at them.

AnnaLangley I'm not surprised by this finding, and fully agree that we have a motoring culture that is both reckless and selfish. I cycle every day, and get very hacked off with the cyclists who flout the law, for the reason that it stokes hostility toward all cyclists, indirectly making cycling more dangerous for the rest of us.

Cars and cycle lanes: too close for comfort

PETER WALKER

Along with running red lights and wearing helmets, the use of cycle lanes is one of those controversial perennials more or less guaranteed to start a debate – if not an actual argument – among cyclists.

The latest salvo comes from a study which purports to show that where there is a bike lane, motorists tend to give less room to cyclists when they overtake.

Ciaran Meyers, a postgraduate student at Leeds University's Institute for Transport Studies, hopped on his Marin Mill Valley hybrid with a camera mounted on it to measure passing distances.

On a 50mph section of the A6, north of Preston in Lancashire, the readings found that motorists, on average, gave Ciaran an extra 18.1cm of space where there was no marked cycle lane compared to when there was. On a 40mph section of the same road the difference was 6.8cm, whereas on the 30mph section it was down to 3.7cm, seen as not statistically significant.

John Parkin from the University of Bolton, who was also involved in the study, had the following explanation:

> In the presence of a cycle lane, a driver is likely to drive between the cycle lane line and the centre line in a position which is appropriate for the visible highway horizontal geometry ahead of the driver. A cyclist within a cycle lane does not seem to cause a driver to adopt a different position in his or her lane. This has important implications for the width of cycle lanes and implies that their width should never be compromised.

I suppose that one thing to note is that these were painted cycle lanes rather than kerbed ones – I can only presume drivers would have been more cautious otherwise.

It's an interesting study nonetheless, and one that makes me think of a much-reported project from several years ago when another university researcher concluded that cars skimmed closer to cyclists wearing helmets. If you remember, Dr Ian Walker also donned a blonde wig to conclude that cars gave even more room to non helmet-wearing female cyclists, or at the very least to stubbly men wearing unsuitable blonde wigs.

So what is it with bike lanes? I encounter a few on my ride to work, and I have to say I don't really like them. I've never really been able say why, but perhaps it is because I sense unconsciously that when I'm in one drivers somehow see me as safe, or zoned off, and so in less need of attention. Of course, some drivers also clearly believe they're just another place to park.

Could the real problem simply be that too many UK bike lanes have clearly been designed by people who last rode a bike several decades ago?

You can view an online gallery of readers' pictures of badly designed cycle lanes here gu.com/p/2cxn5

COMMENTS

jonevents With some of the "cycle lanes" it seems like the councils have needed to hit some quota, so paint a few metres of "cycle lane" which is no good to man nor beast.

loupblanc I lived 2 years in Finland and I still dream of cycle paths like they have over there. It's the best network of cycle paths I've ever seen but I fear we'll never see the likes of it in this country.

Painted cycle lanes are a joke.

frootle I don't bother with cycle lanes. They appear and disappear like spring showers, and often slow you down by forcing you to give way to the traffic.

RoJoCo I dislike cycle lanes because they reinforce the 'apartheid' that exists between bikes and other road vehicles. Drivers will never get used to sharing the road with cyclists so long as these artificial divisions are present. Most cycle lanes are afterthoughts, anyway, and are generally littered with all kinds of road debris (usually glass from shunts involving, er, other road vehicles).

EnglishInHolland Over here in the Netherlands they are wonderful. I commute here faster than I ever could in the UK as the cycle paths have priority over almost everything so I only have to stop once on my 30 km each way commute. At the same time, the environment is so safe that parents have no fears about letting their children cycle. As a result, school cycling rates are virtually 100%.

The 75th anniversary of the UK's first cycle lane

PETER WALKER

So you think bike lanes are modern phenomenon? Wrong. Exactly 75 years ago today (December 14, 2009), the UK's first dedicated bike path – or "safety track for cyclists", as a Guardian report called it – was opened alongside the A40 in west London.

Even then, the UK was lagging behind other nations in Europe, notably The Netherlands, where such paths had been around for some time.

The fantastic archive Pathé news footage of the opening ceremony includes a cyclist, one Oliver Dietrich, who trundles nonchalantly along on a vintage penny farthing, puffing at a cigar.

But what most strikes me most is how roomy the bike lane, now long since gone, appears. Built from concrete, the path, one of a pair on each side of the road, was just over 2.5m wide and stretched for an uninterrupted two-and-a-half miles. The film shows riders using it three abreast. Try that on one the narrow, glass-strewn slivers of bumpy tarmac carved reluctantly into the edges of modern urban roads.

Perhaps equally depressing is the way that many of the same arguments have been raging between cycling and motoring lobbies every since.

The A40 lane received a "frigid welcome" from cyclists' groups, the Guardian noted in December 1934. They were worried that such innovations marked an attempt by a then-tiny minority, drivers, to push everyone else off the roads.

Chris Peck, from cyclists' organisation the CTC, has been looking over the organisation's archives:

> I'm afraid that in 1934 the CTC was dead against cycle tracks of all kinds, even this one. We were still very much of the mind that we should try and recapture the roads from the motorists, so the construction of cycle tracks was seen as defeat. Indeed, the CTC suggested an alternative, "motorways" – built only for cars – leaving the rest of the road network for cyclists to continue to use. The CTC eventually got its wish: the motorways were built and led to a flood of more cars onto the old roads, making them even more hostile for cyclists.

Peck notes, too, that the letters pages of the CTC Gazette were soon filled with debate, with many critics pointing out one flaw of such lanes – how do they remain safe when they meet a side road?

Something else has also stayed the same: envy towards cycle lanes in Europe. Soon after the A40 path was opened, one A. Lancaster Smith wrote to the Guardian, "I believe that in Holland these tracks are laid down beside a great number of roads. What one nation has done another can do." Sadly, as we all know, Mr Lancaster Smith was proved wrong.

There is one more thing to note. The Guardian's story from 1934 records that an astonishing 1,324 cyclists had been killed on the nation's roads the previous year, almost a fifth of all road deaths. In London alone, 11 more had just died in a single week just before the bike lane was opened. It's a very long way from the 115 who died nationally in 2008, even if the massive reduction in bike use over the decades means that it's hard to say whether cycling has got that much safer on average.

In an editorial praising the new bike lane the Guardian argued:

> To provide tracks for cyclists is no more of an infringement of their liberty than to provide pavements for pedestrians ... It is true that cyclists will no longer be able to ride three and four abreast, but that is acknowledged to be a dangerous practice

for all alike, and the right to be killed can hardly be maintained with conviction.

A final bit of historic context from Peck:

It could be said that CTC's campaign in the 1930s to retain cyclists' rights to the road network was too successful. Cyclists were never restricted from the non-motorway road network and in part because of this local authorities never built adequate facilities for them when those roads became bigger and bigger and the volume of motor traffic soared.

At the time CTC was also still fighting to prevent regulations that would, eventually, force cyclists to use rear red lights. CTC believed that cars should at night be obliged to travel at a speed which would enable them to stop should they encounter another user in the road – it should be their responsibility to notice the unlit road user, not the responsibility of the cyclist or pedestrian to carry a light.

COMMENTS

Smogbound I agree with the idea that our roads should be made safe for non-car users of all kinds. The idea that cyclists have been forced off the roads onto special tracks designed to reduce the opportunity for car drivers to kill and maim them is appalling.

felixcat I have read that motorists in the Thirties feared that they would be confined to the proposed motorways, just as cyclists today fear being forced onto cycle tracks. If the tracks were motorway standard we might feel differently.

thechief15 There are many examples of the traffic calming "cycle lanes" across Nottingham, and instead of making roads safer all they actually achieve is convincing most drivers the 0.75m of red tarmac is all the space a cyclist needs. Better still are the 3 examples where they run alongside parking bays in just the right spot for those wishing to assist the motorist with door removal.

Safety track for cyclists – a frigid 'welcome'

THE MANCHESTER GUARDIAN,
SATURDAY, DECEMBER 15, 1934

Mr Hore-Belisha MP, the Minister of Transport, yesterday opened ribbon tracks for cyclists along the grass swards of Western Avenue, Ealing. There are two tracks, one "up" and one "down." They are 8ft. 6in. wide, and have been constructed in concrete at an approximate cost of £7,000. They extend for two and half miles, from Hanger Lane to Greenford Road.

After declaring the cycle tracks open by cutting a tape, Mr Hore-Belisha presented the bicycle recently given to him at the Motor Cycle and Cycle Show to Mr V. P. Chant, a member of the North Ruislip branch of the British Legion. With representatives of the National Cyclists' Union, he inspected the cycle tracks, and later cut another tape and declared a new section of the Western Avenue open.

Mr. Hore-Belisha said Western Avenue was the most perfect example of artificial road construction in this country. It was 120ft wide, and its borders had been acquired to a further depth so that it might not be spoiled by building development. There were twin carriage-ways divided by a central reserve, so that the risk of head-on collisions was virtually eliminated. Shaded footprints had been laid down for pedestrians, and a special staff had been recruited for the care of the wayside trees.

The Vulnerable Cyclist

The provision of the two cycling tracks would give effect for the first time on a great traffic artery to the principle that classes of traffic should be segregated in accordance with the speed at which they could move. He was confident these cycle tracks would be given an unbiased and friendly trail. "Are not casualty lists, and the number of accidents involving cyclists, themselves arguments for the provision of experimental tracks of this kind? Of the 7,202 persons who died as the result of road accidents last year 1,324 were pedal cyclists. Out of the 184,781 non-fatal accidents pedal cyclists were involved in 43,789. A distressing feature of these figure is that they disclose that about half of those who were killed were under the age of 21. The evidence before me shows that accidents to cyclists are increasing."

In a later speech at a luncheon at the Empire Stadium, Mr Hore-Belisha said there should be no complaint of ribbon development on the section that they had opened that day. He was glad that an agreement was in prospect whereby the adjoining county of Buckinghamshire would complete the most difficult section of the Western Avenue, so that it would join with the widened London–Oxford road and Denham.

Hostility of Cyclists' Union

Mr. Hore-Belisha referred to a statement issued by the National Cyclists' Union after the opening ceremony. In this it was explained that the union accepted the invitation to send representatives to the opening of the cycle paths believing it their duty to be present and hold a watching brief on behalf of cyclists. In the acceptance of the invitation, the statement declared, it was clearly stated that they did not thereby lend themselves in any way to the support of the scheme. The statement then set out a number of the objections of the union to the provision of cycle paths.

Mr Hore-Belisha said he had hoped that the tracks would have been given and (sic) unbiased and friendly trial. "I observe that our cycling guests to-day – at least those who are represented by the National Cyclists' Union – have used their other guests as suitable receptacles for a circular in which they say that they come here to hold a watching brief. They who hold a watching brief should watch for results, but they have made up their minds in advance that these cycling tracks are an assault on their privileges and deprive them of their rightful use of the highway. Nothing has been taken away from them, but something has been given."

"I do not see why it should be considered less reasonable to provide a cyclists with a cycling track than a pedestrian with a pavement. I have never heard that a pavement is a deprivation for pedestrian of the use of the King's highway."

Of the thirty-five persons killed in the Metropolitan police area during the week ended December 8, eleven were pedal cyclists. This is the largest number of pedal cyclists killed in one week since an analysis was first published during the last period of October.

Editorial – The Perfect Road

THE MANCHESTER GUARDIAN,
SATURDAY, DECEMBER 15, 1934

No one likes giving up anything that has once been enjoyed, and it is fairly certain that the age which has discovered speed will only surrender it as a last resort. But if we accept speed on the roads as a factor that has come to stay, the acceptance places all the more importance on its proper control if accidents are to be avoided. A step towards the improvement of this control was taken yesterday when Mr Hore-Belisha, the Minister of Transport, opened a new section of the Western Avenue in Middlesex, which he described as "the most perfect example of arterial road construction in the country." Sufficiently wide to be divided into two separate ways by a "reserve" strip, with all the improvements that have been perfected on other roads, it also has two bicycle tracks for the sole use of cyclists. This last feature, which has long been urged in this country and successfully employed abroad, is being tried for the first time on an important arterial road in England. As Mr. Hore-Belisha pointed out in his speech, the number of road accidents in which cyclists are involved is steadily increasing, and when it is known that 1,324 out of the 7,202 deaths on the road last year were of cyclists there should be few to quarrel with the experiment. To provide tracks for cyclists is no more an infringement of their liberty than to provide pavements for pedestrians and if in the future it is decided to divide the road still further into lanes for slow and fast moving traffic there will surely be no complaint from the lorry-drivers that they are being driven off the road. It is true that cyclists will no longer be able to ride three and four abreast but that is acknowledged to be a dangerous practice for all alike, and the right to be killed can hardly be maintained with conviction.

Welcome to Sevenoaks and put your watches back 25 years

JOHN M. MORRISON

If I told you that the busy main road near my house was safe for polar bears because there is no record of polar bear casualties on it, you would probably think my reasoning was flawed. Yet this is the kind of logic we use every day to discuss road safety. The relentless focus on casualty reduction has led to a kind of tunnel vision which increasingly has no relevance as to whether roads are really safe for non-motorists.

I live in a leafy commuter area of west Kent which is mostly rural and has some of the lowest cycling levels in the UK. The roads are full of motorists racing to catch trains to London. Speed limits are mostly ignored, bus use is very low, car ownership is high and many children are ferried to school by car. The majority of local councillors are hostile – or at best indifferent – to the idea of promoting the bike as an alternative to the car, for environmental or any other reasons. Welcome to Sevenoaks, and put your watches back 25 years.

Campaigners who want our district to be a safe place to cycle are battling not just against local resistance; we're finding that the national ideology of road safety, based exclusively on casualty reduction, isn't much help. If the only trigger for introducing speed cameras or traffic calming is a record of accidents, preferably serious or fatal, then it's impossible to change the status quo. Cutting the number of accidents involving children on bikes isn't a meaningful target when the children riding bikes aren't there in the first place.

Many roads may be accident-free but they are "safe" only for car drivers, not for more vulnerable users such as children, pedestrians and cyclists. Safety for motorists has been achieved at the cost of marginalising other users, who are regarded as exotic interlopers – rather like the polar bears. Bikeability schemes at school won't reverse this, because parents rightly take the view that the roads are just too dangerous for their children; far easier to pop them in the 4x4 for the half-mile journey to school or the shops. Nobody seems to see the obvious contradiction between casualty reduction and the government's other goal, promoting active travel.

How do we get rid of this catch-22? Road safety experts are right to say that one child's life lost on the roads is one too many. But if the government is serious about bringing about a "modal shift" towards active travel, especially in well-heeled areas like mine, it will have to accept that accident statistics don't tell the full story. This means a U-turn from the current blinkered expert approach, which dismisses public perceptions in favour of "evidence-led working". For a quarter of a century, the Home Office, taking a different approach to the Department for Transport (DfT), has acknowledged that police statistics on recorded crime don't give the whole picture, and has supplemented them with the British Crime survey. This annual research asks 50,000 people not just about their experience of crime but about how they perceive danger and risk in their areas.

If public perceptions of crime are important enough to inform Whitehall policy-making, why aren't public perceptions of road safety? Why can't the DfT conduct a British Road Safety survey which would ask similar questions, widening the focus towards danger reduction and risk perception rather than the narrow measure of casualty reduction?

Let's start asking parents if they think their roads are safe for their children to cycle on. Let's ask nervous potential cyclists about the perceived dangers of swapping four wheels for two. Let's ask pedestrians if the roads are getting safer to cross. I've been reading a lot of road safety research recently, and it seems to be a cosy little world where all the experts share the same car-centred views. I'm not part of the road safety establishment, just a cyclist who wants to feel safe on the road.

COMMENTS

simonaspinall The cheapest, best, most effective and efficient way is increasing the law in favour of cyclists, more monitoring of cars using CCTV traffic solutions (I work in CCTV and believe me there are incredible advances in technology to record misdemeanours) and actually prosecuting drivers when they commit a dangerous driving offence, which does not happen at the moment.

Combine this with raised motoring taxes, shutting a lot of city centre main areas to traffic and not building any more roads and people will soon get the message.

Fuchsiaperfect I have a theory that modern cars are just too insulating from the outside world and that some drivers don't connect with people on the outside.

David Cameron's 'topless' ride to work

PETER WALKER

Some might argue that there are plenty of reasons to dislike – or disapprove of – David Cameron. I couldn't possibly comment. But cycling without a helmet? For me, that's just not one of them.

Within – seemingly – half an hour of Cameron being photographed pedalling from his London home to the House of Commons, wearing a reflective belt but insouciantly bare-headed, the criticism began.

The Conservative leader should have been "setting a good example" by wearing a lid, the head injuries charity Headway said. "We are deeply disappointed," a spokesman said. The Royal Society for the Prevention of Accidents also weighed in, saying it always encouraged cyclists to wear helmets.

Now, the press shots of his morning ride raise one puzzling question: why does he have a helmet hanging from the handlebars? Is he planning a few pints later and wants to play it safe on the commute home? But when it comes to the bare head, plus everyday-looking clothes, I have no quibbles.

I've heard the for-and-against arguments over helmets more times than I care to remember. I wear a lid more or less every time I get on a bike, a habit that makes me feel exposed whenever I am cycling topless. But I'm resolutely against any moves towards compulsion, even of the guilt-based, you-should-set-an-example-to-others sort.

The isle of Jersey recently passed a law making it compulsory for all under-18s to wear helmets when cycling, in my view an absurd piece of legislation.

Here's Roger Geffen from the national cyclists' organisation CTC, who puts the arguments better than I ever could:

*The idea that it is somehow "dangerous" and "irresponsible"
to cycle without a helmet is a total myth. It merely puts*

people off cycling and contributes to the increase in the level of obesity and other inactivity-related illnesses, which kill tens of thousands of people every year. If we are to encourage people to take up cycling – with all its benefits for our health, our streets, our environment and our wallets – then we need to promote it as a safe and enjoyable way to get around for day-to-day travel, wearing normal clothes.

This isn't something you're likely to hear very often from the Guardian, and I stress it's a single issue-only accolade, but here goes: three cheers for Cameron.

COMMENTS

urbanwriter Compulsory helmet laws enable small-time by-laws, promulgated by small-time bureaucrats, and enforced by small-time authorities, to define life as something we need to be protected from.

Babz Far from being applauded David Cameron should be reprimanded for riding a cycle without head protection, when parents are trying to instill safety into children what message does this give? He may be protected by the police car behind him but other cyclists, children and adult, are not so fortunate and must take their chance amongst traffic.

cycleloopy Cycling without a helmet should remain a choice. There is clear evidence, from Southampton University, that cars do pass closer to you if you wear a helmet because motorists take you to be a more confident cyclist just because you are seen to be wearing all the gear. On the other hand, wearing no helmet and cars, strangely, give you a wider berth because you are seen to be more vunerable.

averagejoe66 I never wear a bike helmet. A helmet would not protect you if you were crushed by a 50 ton artic. IMO they only give a false sense of security and are a scam by the nanny state lobbied by helmet makers to part people from their cash.

Berlinenglishman Counter-intuitive though it may be, the injury rate amongst cyclists goes up when helmets are made compulsory (Australia is an example). It seems that, (a) motorists cut up cylists in helmets, (b) motorists become less aware of cyclists because the number of cyclists goes down when helmets are made compulsory.

nattymumbpo Is that Gordon Brown with his foot on the accelerator behind him?

Chapter 9

Trivia and obscure interests

Cyclists sometimes ride in pairs, occasionally in groups, but mostly we ride by ourselves. One of the fundamental pleasures of riding a bike, after all, is having the power to go where you want, when you want, at a pace of your choosing. To ride a bicycle is to be the master of one's own destination. Even in periods of history when cycling has been a truly mass phenomenon, cycling has always enabled, if not encouraged, a certain "go your own way" individualism.

On a bike, you are neither the slave of public transport, stuck on fixed routes obeying someone else's timetable, nor the prisoner of traffic and congestion in a private car. Riding your bicycle, you can weave and dodge, take a detour, explore, ride along a canal, up a bridleway – your freedom, barring a minimal acquiescence to the rules of the road, is practically unfettered. Even bicycles themselves are easily and quickly customised, expropriated from its shop-bought status as mass-manufactured object to a personal conveyance that, with its almost infinite variety of possible paint jobs, handlebar tapes, light accessories, replacement saddles, and all kinds of optional fixtures and fittings, can express its owner's personality in a way that one would be hard-pressed to achieve with, say, a Ford Focus.

Add to these basic facts about bicycles the 19th- and 20th-century social history that runs in tandem – of cycling's polite revolutions against the strictures of traditional dress, gender roles, class mobility and industrial urbanism – and you have rich potential for all kinds of cycling-related eccentricity, anarchism and bohemian behaviour. There is a line that connects nonconformist artists and thinkers like George Bernard Shaw, HG Wells and William Morris directly through to Iris Murdoch, Ivan Illich, Critical Mass theorist Chris Carlsson, and David Byrne. The bicycle seems to lend itself to an independent cast of mind every bit as much as it does to an independent mode of travel. There is an optimistic idea of social progress inherent within its constructivist architecture of two circles and two triangles, but always on the condition of personal freedom.

All this is by fancy way of saying that what cyclists used to be derided for – being eccentric in our habits and habitments, our interests and pursuits – is nothing to be ashamed of. Quite the reverse. We bikies should embrace our inner crank (appropriately enough, given the mechanics of our machines). Ride a bike and, by definition, you take the road less travelled. And one filled with byways: cycling may still and always be a minority activity, even though virtually everyone knows how to ride a bike, but there is no "subculture" of cycling. We are made up of minorities of committed minoritarians, with innumerable subcultures: fixies and single-speeders, commuters and racers, bicycle activists and leisure riders, sportivistes and Brompton addicts, Lycra-fetishists and tweed-dandies, roundheaded helmet-wearers and hatless cavaliers...

Whatever sort of cyclist you are is entirely up to you. You go your own way.

Matt Seaton

Matt Seaton has written three books about cycling:
***Two Wheels*, *On Your Bike* and *The Escape Artist*.**
He is also a regular contributor to *Rouleur* magazine.

Stripping off for the World Naked Bike Ride

MATTHEW SPARKES

When it comes to bikes, I'm always game for a new experience. But the World Naked Bike Ride, an annual protest about the vulnerability of cyclists, always seemed like a bridge too far.

As a concept it's brilliant – it reminds everyone that we are nothing but frail flesh and bone, exposed to the dangers of the sturdy metal traffic. But I was a tad shy.

I must have been carried away by the sunshine then, because I found myself in Hyde Park, stripping off and throwing my clothes on the rear rack.

And I was not alone – more than 1,100 people joined me. The curious audience in the park outnumbered riders by about twenty to one, and among the riders men outnumbered women by a similar ratio.

I spoke to Sarah Reader, a 23-year-old from London, who was swapping her clothes for body paint with two friends. "It's a bit of reclaiming the streets," she told me. "I cycle ten miles a day and London's built up such a car culture."

"When I first heard of it I didn't think it was a political thing, but when you think about it, it will make cyclists visible."

"I think it will be incredibly liberating and it's a bit cheeky. We might start off with underwear then ditch it later on," she said.

Neil, who was painted bright green from head to toe, told me that for him it was a mixture of an environmental protest and a celebration of the human body.

"The only thing that's daunting is that you're riding along and you go through narrow streets crowded with people. You'll find yourself riding almost on your own," warned Neil.

And, true to his word, the first 500 yards of the ride was an intimidating gauntlet. Huge crowds lined both sides of the path out of Hyde Park, leaning dangerously close to the riders and snapping thousands of photographs.

Once we got on the open road there was more time to chat. The reasons for taking part were as diverse as the bodies on show. Some were motivated by the BP oil spill to take part as an anti-oil protest, others were there as cycling activists and a large portion were nudists first and foremost. It is, after all, a great opportunity to get your paler bits out and not be arrested for it.

One man had decided to jog the seven-mile route instead, which produced a rather hypnotic pendulum effect. Another, a bike paramedic, did it on his work machine and nothing but a reflective vest. Safety first.

There were one or two minor crashes, but thankfully no serious injuries – although the naked paramedic would, I'm sure, have been swift to treat them.

Perhaps the worst part of the day was when a chap at the end realised he had lost his wallet, trousers and boxer shorts on the way round. A steward came to his rescue with a pair of union jack pants bought at a souvenir stall.

It made me wonder: what would happen to anyone unfortunate enough to get a puncture? Would the ride stop, or would they be abandoned, naked, to fix it on the side of the road?

The public mostly took it all in good humour, although some looked so shocked that one has to wonder if they had ever seen a naked body before. At least one passerby spontaneously got naked and joined in. Apparently this happens every year.

If this all sounds interesting, but a little intimidating, then its worth mentioning that the ride runs a "bare as you dare" policy, so there were some pants and bras around. I saw plenty of people who had arrived on this basis stopping on the route and going the full monty.

"It's interesting that the average age was much lower than previous years, lots of young people. A lot of university students are getting in on it, especcially those that are studying environmental science," said one of the ride organisers, Martin Ireland.

He said that since coming to London in 2004 there are now franchises in Brigthon, Bristol, Edinburgh and Oxford, and many others.

It was a liberating, enjoyable, scary and interesting experience, and I recommend you have a go if you get the chance.

COMMENTS

Rhod Just when you thought cyclists couldn't get any more irritating or objectionable, they do. They look pretty grotesque in Lycra, but naked? Oh dear…

00SilianRail00 My girlfriend and I saw this procession making its merry way down Tooley Street, and I can't understand why anyone would have a negative reaction to it. It was such an unexpected sight, and everyone involved was so evidently having such a great time, that we couldn't help but be caught up in the fun of it all. Not quite caught up enough to join in, admittedly, but then we didn't have our bikes with us…

alocin42 I was at the Bristol ride on Sunday and it was amazing! The first time I'd ever done something like that and I somehow got roped into being painted blue from head to toe. Everyone who took part was very welcoming and it was a fantastic experience – I'll definitely be taking part again next year!

fbilleter Maybe there would be fewer bike accidents if everyone rode nude. Drivers would definitely pay more attention.

Do you ever "catch the bus"?

MATT SEATON

OK, disclaimer time: let me first make a "I make no apologies for this" kind of apology. This blog is very much in the category of confession to a guilty secret. I'm not recommending this behaviour; I'm not saying it's clever or cool. But it is fun, and I'm definitely not the only one who thinks so.

Second disclaimer: it's not my idea. The inspiration comes from my favourite cycling film, Breaking Away. I won't bore you with a plot resumé but let me just recommend you watch the sequence in which our cyclist hero picks up a ride behind a tractor-trailer, takes a tow in the slipstream and covers the 50 miles into Bloomington, Indiana in about half the time it normally takes him. (The truck driver actually gets a ticket for speeding!)

Here goes, then: one of the unspoken pleasures of urban cycling is catching the bus.

And I don't mean leaving the bike at home and using your bus pass. I mean getting tucked in behind a doubledecker on a clearway and slipstreaming it at 30mph. The trick is to "catch the bus" when it's just pulling away from a stop, so that you can get close and match your speed as it accelerates. Obviously, this is only worth doing when the road ahead is reasonably clear and it's only possible if the driver hasn't got a lead foot.

But if you're lucky, and especially if it's out of rush hour and the bus doesn't have to pull in at every stop, then you can get an effortless high-speed tow for half a mile or more. And the buzz you get from a bus ride is … well, it's a buzz.

Risks? Well, yes, it's not risk-free. You have to ride close enough (a few feet) to be out of the wind and get the full suction effect. That means you need to be quick on the brakes and agile enough if the bus suddenly decides to brake or pull in. It also means you get no sight of the road surface ahead, so you need to "ride light" over dodgy drain covers and the like. And you won't want to pick a smoky bus unless you don't mind turning your lungs into kippers.

But if you're confident and sensible, there's nothing to it; and I've never had a "moment". The only annoying thing that happens sometimes is missing the bus – and being overtaken by one with someone else riding behind it at twice your speed and wishing you were there.

Own up now. Have you ever tried it?

COMMENTS

acinetobacter I much prefer getting onto the wheel of another cyclist, preferably one who looks like he/she is faster than me.

effemm Definitely a good laugh, I do it all the time. And if your city has plenty of bus lanes (as mine does) you can get a good long ride, even in heavy traffic. It also helps if you know where the bus stops are. I don't worry *too* much about buses doing anything unexpected – they're big and heavy and surely can't stop *that* suddenly. Can they?

amantius An added benefit is that it does not rain behind the bus!

Lazygirl Not in a million years. I wonder if my utter bewilderment with this concept has something to do with the fact that I don't have testicles.

What sort of bike do you get for just £70?

HELEN PIDD

In a recent eye-catching marketing campaign, Asda boasted that it was to start selling "the cheapest bicycle in the UK". Having bought into the notion that to get a half decent new bike you had to pay at least £300 for it, I was intrigued to find out what you'd get for less than a quarter of that amount – Asda's adult machines cost just £70.

And so it was that I have spent the past month juddering around London on a 26in British Eagle 18-speed women's mountain bike in a patronising purple shade.

My first outing on the Purple Eagle ended on a sour note when the handlebars started turning in an entirely unhelpful and counter-intuitive way every time I rounded a corner. The headset was horribly loose, and I had no tools on me to fix it.

Herein lies the first problem with buying what bike snobs refer to as a BSO (bike-shaped object): you have to build it yourself. The Eagle comes in bits, meaning you have to attach the pedals, front wheel, handlebars and saddle to the frame. Asda's PR folks made mine, but the lesson is the same. Are you sure you know how to put it together properly? If not, you can either take it to your local bike dealer and hope they won't laugh you out of the shop when you ask them to do it for you (and if they oblige, you'll pay at least £20 for it). Or you can risk getting it wrong. The best-case scenario is that, like me, you end up walking home. Let's not contemplate the worst case.

The second problem was the grip-shift gears, which are operated by twisting the end of the handlebars. Very quickly I wished that British Eagle had concentrated on getting three gears right rather than making 18 substandard ones. Every time I went over a speed bump I changed gear; even on the flat there was always an irritating clicking sound which spoiled every ride. On the scale of annoyance, it was rather like being at the cinema and having someone kick the back of your seat all the way though the film.

To test the bike properly I decided to take it on a grand tour of north London's Three Peaks: Crouch Hill, Highgate Hill and Muswell Hill.

Yorkshire folk will no doubt dismiss these bourgeois mounds as mere hillocks, but tackling them on my weighty (18kg), graceless machine felt like I was scaling Pen-y-Ghent on a pedal-powered tractor. The good thing about mountain bikes is that they have super-low gears, but as the Purple Eagle could never stay in any gear for long, I may as well have been on a single speed.

After 40 miles or so of gentle bimbling, I took the bike into my local bike shop, Two Wheels Good, and got the owner, Jonathan Boyce, to give it a once over. He groaned as I wheeled it in – "We see these a couple of times a week and so often the repairs cost more than the bike," he said, adding that he gave me "four to six weeks" before the bike was too jiggered to ride. Jonathan's advice for those on a budget is to scrape together £100 to buy a decent secondhand bike rather than waste money on the Purple Eagle or any of its relatives.

Here are some of the flaws Jonathan noticed:

1. The Purple Eagle is a ladies' bike. So why the men's saddle?

2. The components are rubbish and made out of the biking equivalent of a supermarket own-brand. The derailleur, gear shifts and more are made by a brand that sounds like Shimano but isn't. It's even written in the same font.

3. The brakes are made from plastic, rather than more expensive aluminium, and so will flex and bend, wasting energy.

4. The handlebar stem is the old "quill" style (instead of attaching to a steerer tube it fits directly into the headset and screws onto the forks), rather than an a-head stem.

5. The rear derailleur is hooked onto the axle, rather than bolted straight to the frame, making it almost impossible to adjust the gears properly.

6. The cheap plastic pedals will "simply fall apart before long".

7. The rear wheel was badly out of true.

8. The front wheel wasn't round, and was wobbling about the place as if the bearings have already gone. Apparently this shouldn't happen on a decent bike until you've done at least 1,000 miles.

But the biggest problem I had with the Lumbering Eagle was that it was horrible to ride. Every time I was due to set out on it, I cast a jealous glance at my lovely, nimble racer and prepared myself for the unpleasant ride ahead. This is the real downer with cheap bikes: they put you off cycling.

COMMENTS

ToddMNash I regret the decision to buy a cheap bike when I moved to London. I've had it six months now and it barely gets from A to B anymore without having some sort of physical meltdown. I can't even make a short trip without taking my tools. I've had to replace the crank twice, the back brake no longer works and the gears, well they weren't much good in the first place.

NotAgainAgain There needs to be some form of European standard to ensure people aren't put off cycling by shoddy crap. Somebody who knows nothing about bikes will end up buying one, ride it once or twice, and then find the whole experience horrific and not ride it again. Thinking that they hate cycling. When in reality they hate the shoddy piece of crap they are on, but would actually enjoy cycling if they had a decent bike.

BarryMcC If anyone wants to buy one of these "mountain" bikes and come hit the trails in Wales with me, you are welcome. You'll end up hurt. Very hurt. But, I'm a trained first-aider, so I'll be able to look after you whilst the helicopter comes. Your £70 steed won't fare so well, I'm afraid. But, I'm no miracle worker.

BlackandAmber I've never understood why people will pay £20,000 for a car without blinking and seem to think £200 for a bike is a bit much. I'd say anything less than £250 is a complete false economy and it's likely to put you off cycling rather than encourage you

WoolEyes I beg to differ. I bought a similar bike for £70 from Tesco in Oct 2005. I still have it today and I cycle approximately 2,500 miles each year, so I've covered a little under 10,000 miles on this bike. It has required routine repairs, no more/less than any othere bike, say £40 each year. It has the same nasty plastic brakes etc as the Asda bike, but it all works. Never buy an expensive bike unless you are going to use it a lot and are a good cyclist. A lightweight bike is still slow if you are unfit, and a heavy bike is fast if you are fit and know how to ride well.

Mmmmf Christ. I can't believe the number of people who think it's outrageous to spend a decent amount of money on a decent bike.

"Hey – look at me – I paid 26p for my bike and I've ridden it to the moon and back and it's still fine".

Get a life.

It's hilarious how all these Guardian readers who would balk at buying a four quid high street sweatshop tee-shirt suddenly get all bloody righteous about paying a sensible price for a sophisticated piece of machinery made by people who aren't on the minimum wage.

MarkBrownACT Last night Asda's latest TV advert showed these wonderful machines. Unfortunately the advert showed the bike with its front forks facing backwards!!

Not even Asda know how to set-up their own bikes. This is indicative of the problems which arise from what we in the bike industry call "flat-pack bikes". However, unlike flat-pack furniture this could seriously damage your health.

I believe this TV advert has now been pulled but it really goes to show how dangerous it is for these retail giants to move into non-food sectors where they have no expertise.

Heaven help the poor customer with little or no cycle experience and lacking the wrong tools who try's to build this "bicycle" for themselves.

Mark Brown
Association of Cycle Traders
(representing the UK's specialist local bike shops)

Trying out a £10,000 Tour de France dream machine

PETER WALKER

My first reaction was almost mild intimidation: I'm not worthy to ride this bike. Next came a thought perhaps even more absurd – what if I'm mugged?

All I was doing was preparing to leave the office for my usual seven or so mile ride home. This time, however, it would be aboard a machine which costs comfortably more than any material possession I've ever owned, property excepted.

I was being lent for the weekend a Colnago C59, depending on your reckoning somewhere between £8,000 and £10,000 of absurdly light and precise carbon fibre sleekness.

By happy coincidence, on the day I returned the C59, another model was being ridden – much, much faster – across the Pyrenees by France's Thomas Voeckler en route to a dramatic Tour de France solo stage win.

This was, of course, part of my worry. Would I feel like an imposter, even an idiot, pootling along on such a specialist, space age bike through the back streets of south London?

Not really. This being London, the overwhelming response was blank indifference, although a couple of roadies couldn't help sneaking a crafty glance as we waited at red lights.

My fears of being dragged from the bike by a gang of young cycling-obsessed ruffians in matching Bouygues Telecom jerseys were, of course, equally absurd.

Now for the two questions everyone who heard about the bike asked me: how can it cost so much? And what's it like to ride?

The first is quite simple – it's so expensive because it's been deliberately made that way. The frame, which combines carbon fibre tubes with traditional-style lugged joins, supposedly for extra stiffness, will set you back £3,300 alone. Chuck on some carbon wheels and a few Campagnolo Record bits and pieces and everything soon mounts.

The PR company who loaned me the bike are, in fact, deliberately touting it as "the Ferrari of the bike world", a pricey totem for the Colnago brand. It was they who came up with the £10,000 figure, though someone else conceded that £8,000 would be more realistic when it eventually hits the shops.

All this money gives you a bike which is astonishingly fun to ride. Far from the C59 being intimidating – metaphorically sneering in disdain when a relative snail like me gets aboard – on the open road it instead whispers sweetly into your ear. "Come on, you can go a bit faster," it says. "Why not climb out of the saddle for this hill? It'll be fun."

And of course it is. But is it £10,000-worth of fun? This is where the difficulty comes in.

My own road bike, if I'd bought it new, would have cost a shade over £1,000, and it's no real surprise that the C59 is a faster, lighter, more responsive, ride. But once you get above, say, £2,000 or £3,000 the "extra performance" axis of the graph flattens out considerably. I'm nowhere near quick enough a rider to make such a relatively vast outlay worth it.

That's not to say I'd laugh at anyone else for buying one. It's a lot of money for a bike, but more or less commonplace for a car or motorbike, and they won't be a hand-built collectors' item.

I wouldn't recommend they lock it up on the street, though.

COMMENTS

Teratornis I don't think the speed of the rider matters as much to justifying the outlay as the amount of time one spends on a bike. Professional racers like to ride the best bikes available, because high-quality bikes are less annoying. Pros who ride 400 or 500 miles per week are spending a very large fraction of their waking lives on a bicycle.

NotFromLondon People spend £70k+ on a flash car, when an average £15k one would do the job just fine... others spend hundreds on designer clothes, when Primark stuff works ok...

Why?

I'm not sure it really matters why. I do think these things are rarely "worth" the cost in pure monetary terms, but the bottom line is the pleasure they bring to peoples lives. If there's something you love, you're happy to invest time and money in it, almost without questioning it.

mroli Law of diminishing returns innit. Basically for most riders, you are going to get all the bike your ability requires for about £1k. Personally, I'd rather have eight bikes costing £1k, e.g. road bike/TT bike/cyclocross bike/folder/tandem/fixed gear/winter hack/cargo bike than one bike costing £8k.

faffster You could never, ever be seen pushing that up a hill!

Maradonerkebab It hasn't even got a stand. What a rip-off.

Why do bike shops frequently offer service with a sneer?

PETER WALKER

Pushing my bike into the bike shop, I inquired tentatively about booking a service at some point in the coming days.

The proprietor's response was crushing: "No chance mate. We've got a six-week waiting list and we don't even touch bikes which weren't sold here."

"Hang on. So I could live here for 10 years and you'd never do a single thing to this bike?" I asked.

"Yup," came the reply.

In some ways it's something to be celebrated, the fact that a bike shop is so busy they're turning away custom. But the brusque – in fact almost smug – way I was dismissed took me back to the bad old days when staff in cycle shops seemed to take positive pleasure in patronising, belittling or otherwise abusing customers.

Much like the perennially snooty staff at independent record shops, during the start of my cycling career it seemed obligatory for bored bike shop assistants to delight in displaying their vast knowledge as they simultaneously showed me up as a novice or a fool, perhaps both.

Most terrifying was Condor Cycles, the revered institution on Gray's Inn Road in central London, in business since 1948 (I should stress immediately that these days Condor staff are the epitome of patient friendliness).

Even buying a new inner tube was an ordeal. "Schraeder or Presta?" the assistant would bark before I'd even finished my question, referring to the two different types of valve, the respective names of which even now I can never remember.

I'd pause for half a second. With a world-weary sigh the assistant would reach under the counter and bring out a dusty wooden block into which an example of each valve had been mounted. "BIG valve or LITTLE valve?" came the follow-up, spoken as if to a five-year-old.

Five years ago, my girlfriend, then a novice bike commuter, picked up her cheap, secondhand machine after repairs at an independent shop in east London.

After a 10-minute wait, the mechanic dragged the bike up from the basement workshop. "I've spent half my day servicing this piece of shit," he grumbled along the way, clearly realising the bike's owner was in earshot. "Who'd ride this? It's not even worth mending."

Her experience was not unique. A number of female friends and colleagues recount being patronised in bike shops over the years.

Now, of course, this is much rarer, a culture change brought about in no small part by the rise of chains like Evans and Cycle Surgery, who, while condemned by some as soulless and ubiquitous, understand newcomers make up a big part of their customer base and train staff accordingly.

But why do some old-school bike shops tend to be so rude?

COMMENTS

Wildcherrybomb There's an old guy who works in our local bike shop who treats me like I'm braindead scum. I went to get a part for my bike once and he wouldn't believe that the original part had fallen off and gotten lost. I had to argue with him for a good 10 minutes about it before he'd actually sell me the part! I don't know whether it's because I'm a woman or because he's just an obnoxious git.

redorc Learn how to service your own bike – that's what I did when I had a similar experience – it's really not that hard.

Yamaman Now hold on!

I was discussing bike shops with a mate over the weekend and we both agreed that they are generally full of really friendly staff. I've lost count of the number of times I've popped in to pick up a few nuts and bolts or other little things and never been charged. And I usually always find them full of useful advice on what's needed to sort something out.

Cycling in the pub

PETER WALKER

I have to admit it was a first – finishing a pint just before taking part in a competitive cycling event. But then again, it was the first time I'd ever had a bike race inside a pub, or for that matter, a race where your bike never moves an inch.

All in all, my first taste of Rollapaluza was something of a night of new experiences.

First set up around a decade ago, Rollapaluza has set out to revive the long-lost sport of indoor roller racing, in which pairs of competitors sit on bikes fixed to treadmills propelled by the rear wheel and "race" each other over a hypothetical fixed distance.

Initially a fun pursuit for friends on London's cycle courier scene, it's now expanded to a full-time business which organises try-out races at schools and community festivals, as well as corporate events.

The first surprise was the sheer spectacle: a couple of hundred people packed into a back room, yelling encouragement above thumping music as pairs of competitors raced each other on a stage, legs spinning at furious speed. A huge dial with two moving hands indicated their respective approach towards the 500m distance point, while a digital clock indicated their time.

With my heat yet to come, I asked one of the Rollapaluza organisers, Winston, for tips. "Just pedal really, really quickly," he advised. Glib though it sounds, that's really all there is to it – the roller is set to minimal resistance, so the key is not in strength but the ability to keep to an absurdly high pedalling cadence for a brief but extremely intense spurt.

While cycling enthusiasts often did well at Rollapaluza events, Winston said, it's not just a pursuit for the Lycra-clad – recent winners included sporty bike novices such as a 400m runner and a martial arts fan.

I hoped a quick drink would help loosen my fast-twitch muscles, but in the end my relatively respectable time of just over 25 seconds was a good two seconds slower than my opponent, and I was eliminated at the first hurdle. But it was undeniably exciting, especially with a beer-fuelled crowd cheering me on from a few feet away.

What also struck me was the sheer scale of the turnout – on a damp Wednesday night – and the passion of the mainly young competitors and fans. The pub's small front garden was festooned with bikes, locked to every available fixed post or fence.

Winston explained that one of roller racing's qualities is that it provides an easy, fun way for people to try out a cycle sport. It seems he was right.

Hear Peter Walker try out Rollapaluza on the Guardian's bike podcast gu.com/p/2f9vv

COMMENTS

chaz1 What the Rollapaluza guys have shown is that the sport can be reinvigorated though bringing racing to the people. With a dying audience, what else was there but bring the track to the pub, to where people are? It was worth a try, and it is working.

simonaspinall Ride your bikes outside you soft southern fairies.

thechief15 Cycling in pubs?

What's wrong with a game of darts or a few hands of dominoes?

Cycling the recumbent way

PETER WALKER

"That downhill section was great!" my friend Barry exclaimed, beaming. "It felt like I was doing the Cresta Run." And this was just a spin around a park. There was, however, a key difference – it was a ride on a recumbent.

Such machines, where the rider leans back on a full-size seat and pedals with their feet in front of them rather than beneath, have something of an image of being the preserve of a hobbyist niche – at least in the UK. Certainly, when I'd previously seen them in London, more often than not the rider turned out to be a green-living (perhaps even dreadlocked) man of a certain age, often carting a bag of organic groceries.

Luckily Inspired Cycle Engineering (Ice) were on hand to dispel my tired stereotypes. The Cornwall-based company makes a series of sleek and reassuringly high-tech recumbent bikes and trikes, most of which they sell overseas, particularly to US customers.

They lent me the particularly space-age Vortex, £2,500-plus of shininess, where even the seat is carbon fibre. It's a trike, with a pair of 20-inch wheels at the front and a full-size 700c road one on the back, meaning a novice like me could forget about balance and concentrate on mastering trying to steer with a narrow handlebar positioned somewhere down below my mid-thighs.

A first tentative test ride on a quiet local road brought the first recumbent revelation – people don't half stare. Children, in particular, could hardly look more aghast if you'd just paraded past them on a rhinoceros. On their website, Ice venture the theory that this novelty makes their machines safer to ride in traffic than their minimal height would indicate, as surprised drivers pay you more attention.

It's fair to say, though, that the Vortex, with its bum-scraping rider position, isn't built for the city commute. It's an open-road machine, one many buyers apparently use for long-distance touring.

A combination of time and logistics, sadly, meant the closest I got to this during the brief loan was some laps round the six-mile or so circumference of Richmond Park in west London, a popular club cyclist training route with a couple of steep, if brief, climbs. To bring a vestige of scientific rigour to the test run, Barry brought his normal road bike and we swapped machines every lap.

In general, recumbents are viewed as faster than traditional bikes as the low riding position is more aerodynamic. On the Vortex, however, this is partly negated by the trike's blunt front profile, and it was notably slower than the bike, particularly on hills, where the only option was to select a low gear and patiently spin those legs.

In compensation, it felt faster. Much faster. Skipping at speed down a hill and leaning against a corner with your buttocks about an inch from the tarmac is about as close as you can get to rediscovering the thrill your 10-year-old self experienced sledging on a tin tea tray. You can see why people get addicted.

A bit counter-intuitively, it's also extremely comfortable. "This feels like a bath chair," Barry said as he lowered himself down into the contoured seat for a first lap. "My biggest worry might be nodding off."

There was one more surprise to come: at the end of the ride we felt a whole series of unfamiliar aches. Recumbents use muscles in a different way to traditional bikes, it seems, perhaps partly explaining our relative slowness on the Vortex.

The verdict? I wouldn't swap my bike for it on a city commute. But if I had, say, a four week tour planned somewhere rural (and a sudden, if unlikely, deluge of cash for the trike and associated racks and panniers, also made by Ice) I could think of little better.

Hear Peter Walker testing the Vortex on the Guardian's bike podcast gu.com/p/2gy8f

COMMENTS

RedBarchetta Sorry, but no matter how much fun it may be it's suicidal going anywhere on one of these things on a road. You are just so low down so as to be practically invisible.

iMalone I've cycled all my life and 6 years ago I bought a recumbent trike and I've rarely ridden an upright since.

My experience is that all the claims about perceived risk are bogus, I've never felt safer on anything I've pedalled whether on the open road or in rush hour traffic.

bassireland Are you not just at exhaust fume height?

Can cycling shorts ever look sexy?

HELEN PIDD

The other day my friend Audrey sent me one of those rare forwarded emails which genuinely made me laugh out loud. "Why bicycle shorts are always black!!" was the exclamatory subject header. Inside the email were two photographs. The first showed what looked to be the US national cycling team. The second depicted what I assumed to be the Polish squad. The Americans were wearing black shorts, the Poles, pillar box red. The joke was that on the latter picture, the red shorts shrinkwrapped the riders' genitalia like over-packaged supermarket fruit, while the black ones preserved a little more of the Americans' dignity.

This gently pornographic spectacle got me thinking about cycling shorts. Can they ever really, actually look good and not merely perverted? Before you start thinking what a superficial filly I am, let me say this: I know that tight Lycra cycling shorts are designed to enhance performance, rather than the wearer's privates. And yes, I realise that you don't care what you look like when you're out on your bike. But has any man in the history of the world actually made them look safe-for-work?

I know that people got all dribbly over Chris Hoy's thighs at the Beijing Olympics. But I just felt I had seen too much. When I catch certain colleagues in the Guardian's subterranean bike shed wearing cycling shorts I feel as if nothing will be the same again. It's like when I went swimming once as a child and walked into the communal showers to see my RE teacher as naked as Eve before she ate the apple. And though I love my boyfriend very much, when he turned up to a fancy dress party recently dressed as Lance Armstrong (the theme was the letter "L") I felt slightly nauseous when he took to the dance floor in his pervy bib shorts. People didn't know where to look. It's a good job they didn't touch – they would have discovered the panty-liner-like Chamois within.

But am I missing something here? Does anyone want to defend cycling shorts from a purely aesthetic point of view?

COMMENTS

ignominious Standard road cycling shorts look just fine, when you're on a bike. Like any other piece of Lycra cycling equipment, once you get out of the saddle you look like a fool. Even pro cyclists tottering around the interviews after the most impressive and grueling stage of the Tour de France can't help but lose a fraction of your respect for looking a bit silly.

ChasnDave Cycling shorts? 2 words... No! & Wrong?

StopSharkFinning The worst are those guys who wear Lycra underneath some baggier shorts. Come on, guys!! Grow some nuts!! Lycra is king!

ts808 As a fashion conscious individual I have to say that Lycra should only be worn when on a bike, accompanied by a helmet and sunglasses, rendering one totally anonymous.

theblondone I like a Lycra clad man, because he shows confidence! And I don't know, I just tend to look people in the eyes or at least face region, not at the crotch, so can't really understand what the issue is off the bike.

Cyclists! The public think you are cool and normal

HELEN PIDD

News just in from the world of academia: cycling is no longer considered the preserve of the sort of hippies historically associated with the Guardian. It is even widely thought of as "cool".

Prof Alan Tapp and a team of researchers from the University of the West of England have the stats to prove it. With the help of YouGov they asked 3,855 people for their opinions on bicycles and the people who ride them.

What makes this survey worth listening to is that the vast majority of those who took part don't actually cycle much, if at all. Of course we think we're hip, but to hear non-cyclists (and therefore likely motorists) say so is just not just a novelty but also very encouraging for the future of cycling.

The results make fascinating reading. Most respondents consider bike riding as normal (65%) and only 7% reckon cyclists are strange. Amusingly, those who cycle the most are disproportionately likely to think others consider them weird – 24% of those who use their bike at least once a week said they believed most normal people think cyclists were "a bit odd". Which does explain the proliferation of "I'm mad, me" types one occasionally encounters in the bike lane.

Just 10% of UWE respondents agreed that "urban cyclists are just left-wing hippies", which surprised Tapp, who told me, "I expected there to be quite a high proportion of the total who still had the negative view of cyclists as weirdy-beardy Guardian readers."

While more people in the survey said cycling was "cool" than "uncool", cyclists themselves are not quite as trendy as they think – 59% of regular cyclists agree that cycling has become cool nowadays, compared to 37% of lapsed cyclists.

A heartening 69% of those questioned overall said cyclists should be taken seriously, and many admitted that when they are stuck in traffic jams they sometimes wish they were cycling (43% compared to 29% who disagreed). Fifty per cent of those surveyed disagreed with the statement that "Roads are for cars not bikes" (compared to 28% who agreed).

At the same time, though, more people than not said they would be unwilling to drive more slowly if it encouraged more people to get on their bikes. And 54% do not want to see pro-bike measures that penalise car drivers.

But as someone who genuinely believes that cycling makes me more cheerful, I was pleased to see that when the researchers asked people whether they were happy, current cyclists said were far more likely than lapsed ones did (39% compared to 18%).

Regular pedallers were also more likely to describe themselves as independent, confident, free-spirited and rebellious than those who no longer saddle up. But then we would say that, wouldn't we?

Despite the general approval of cycling, Britain's top riders are far less well known than celebrities who cycle. When shown a list of people who ride bikes, far more people recognised David Cameron as a cyclist than the Olympic gold medal winner Victoria Pendleton (59% compared to 27%).

Those surveyed by YouGov were a random selection of society who seem fairly representative in terms of their cycling habits: just 6% said they cycled "very often" (i.e. at least once a week), 5% "often", 28% "sometimes or occasionally nowadays" and 46% were lapsed cyclists. Half were men; half were women. Fifty-five per cent were in the social class ABC1 and 45% were C2DE. Just over half said they owned a bicycle.

COMMENTS

alantapp Overall I think the research was genuinely heartening for cyclists – lets face it 10 or 20 years ago we would never have had nearly half the population thinking "cycling is cool nowadays". Our research team is trying to help develop pro-cycling marketing ideas designed to be used by advertisers to promote the positive feelings around cycling – things like freedom, stress busting, the joy of being outdoors etc are coming up a lot. Any ideas welcome.

MrBronze There should be a survey on whether people who drive cars are considered cool too.

Personally when I see a solo person in every car in a huge line of badly designed indistinguishable boxes, paying for petrol and listening to Magic FM as I cruise by in the bus lane to the head of the queue I think " … those are the least cool people in the world".

dianab Bet they didn't survey the people who leave comments on my local paper website! Cyclists rate up there with the Iranians & North Koreans …

What's in your bag

BEN THOMAS

As a nosy child, I was notorious for asking ladies what was in their handbags. Sometimes I tried to get them to empty them out. I didn't think it gave me an insight into what kind of person they were, I really just wanted to have a look (and if possible ask follow-up questions).

Now I want to ask you. Think of it as an exercise in crowd-sourcing. It might show there are as many different types of cyclists as there are cyclists themselves. It might help other, less-experienced riders know what to keep with them. It might just show that I'm still nosy.

If you want to analyse what your bagfull says about you, even better.

I'll throw mine open first:

- Repair box (three tyre levers, Cooltool, Leatherman Micra, spoke key, paracetamol, anti-nausea tablets)
- Puncture repair kit (glue evaporated)
- Plastic mini pump
- Computer, lead, dongle
- Sarnies
- Railcard

- More paracetamol (there's none in the jungle after all)
- Cable lock
- Mobile phone
- Spare T-shirt
- String bag

Anaylsis: I'm a forgetful borderline-neurotic impulse-shopping geek who commutes to work and sweats a lot.

Over to you.

COMMENTS

OxfordBiker Lots of those red rubber bands discarded by posties, great for holding in your jeans at the ankle, emergency light fittings, stopping locks bouncing around etc.

Plastic bags for shopping, seat covering on wet days, putting things in when it rains cos my panniers are no longer waterproof.

Bungee straps

spare batteries

bike spanner

waterproof jacket

tissues

old biros

shopping lists

old till receipts

lolly sticks from consumed ice lollies

pennies picked up from the ground by bike stands

if only I had enough foresight to include plasters and a first aid kit...

banzaibee In my Lycra top I carry:

1 bag of nuts

Analysis: (I am a squirrel).

Davos119 My trusty Ortlieb Back Roller Classics:

One currently contains a paddling pool.

The other contains one running shoe, my dead mother-in-law's pink fleece, a table cloth, a bread knife, a broken knecklace, some casette tapes and a toy mouse (for the cat).

I really must (a) have a clear out and (b) start commuting by bike again.

imhotepa "As a nosy child, I was notorious for asking ladies what was in their handbags."

And then you became a journalist?

I see.

Cyclists are sexy – apparently

PETER WALKER

As well as giving you thighs of steel and an unhealthy interest in gear ratios and carbon fibre widgets, did you realise that an interest in cycling will make you more attractive to the opposite sex? Well, a PR-generated "survey" claims so, meaning it must be true, right?

The findings come in a poll carried out to publicise the 2009 Cycle Show at the Earls Court centre in west London.

The survey asked women which "typical male sporting pursuit" they find the most alluring. Astonishingly, for a study commissioned to promote a bike show, cycling came out on top. In all, 36% of the women asked found men who cycle attractive, against 17% for football and 14% for rugby. If we believe the findings, the words women tended to associate with cyclists were the likes of "kind" and "intelligent", as against "aggressive" and "selfish" for football lovers.

Even if we take the findings at face value – and that's a big leap to start with – I find this notion of the cyclist-as-sex-symbol a bit hard to take. Yes, as a pursuit it keeps you fit, and does wonders for the legs. But while the likes of Chris Hoy are suitably chunky, are we really expected to believe that women prefer the rake-thin physique of most pro road riders – make that skeletal for the road cycling climbers – over the more even musculature of, say, footballers?

And let's face it, those funny tan lines are never a good look. Shaved legs on men, meanwhile, remain a niche area of appeal.

The survey is, however, definitely right on one front. You might think you look great in the full, body-hugging Lycra gimp suit, but chances are your girlfriend disagrees – according to the poll only 7% of the women asked rated it a good look.

COMMENTS

archibold Let's be honest if you can look good in a full Lycra suit you can look good in anything (making no personal claim on this front, just an observation).

zukini So … ladies… I'm available… If you can catch me!

No doesn't work.

Kreike I believe a mountain biker coined the phrase, "Friends don't let friends wear Lycra."

johnball It's true women do like guys on bikes. While living in Holland Dutch women would occasionally flirt with me while we were both waiting at the traffic lights on our bikes. I never knew what to do about it though as the light would turn green and the moment would be lost. My friend had a Mazda MX5 at the time and he hated it when I mentioned it.

Wrennie Shaved legs are just wrong – on males and females. I've yet to see a shaven leg that doesn't make the owner look strangely amphibious.

Teratornis The empirical approach would be to shave just one leg, and see which side gets the most action.

serac Hairy legs?? Love 'em!!! In fact, I reckon they're really sexy! Roll on the summer!!!

Is cycling the new rock and roll?

PETER WALKER

He used to wear kilts, now it's Lycra. It was news to me, but it seems that when not reviving foppishly dressed 80s chart toppers Spandau Ballet, Gary Kemp is now a road cycling addict.

In one of the more unexpected interviews carried by Cycling Weekly magazine in recent years, the band's guitarist and songwriter reveals that he is a recent convert to the sport, taking part in the Circuit of the Cotswolds sportive over the summer. A check of the online results shows he did the hilly 102-mile course in a respectable 7 hours 5 minutes.

Of course, being a millionaire pop star, Kemp didn't begin his new hobby on a second-hand £300 machine purchased on eBay. He tells the magazine that he rides a titanium Litespeed – a brand which won't see much change from £3,000 – and then also bought an equally flash Colnago C50, "to find out what it would be like to ride a carbon". It might sound profligate, but it's much cheaper than the usual pop-star pursuits of fast cars and lavish parties.

Anyhow, the interview got me thinking about cycling rock and pop stars. The most famous examples are, of course, Kraftwerk, where founder Ralf Hütter developed the habit of leaving the tour bus 100 miles or so from its destination and cycling the rest of the way. His obsession with the sport reportedly became so all-encompassing it threatened the group.

But apart from that, things get a bit sparse. Paul Weller in his Style Council days dabbled with cycling jerseys. And it appears that Bradley Wiggins' mod haircut is no accident, since his wife reportedly said the Olympic gold medallist "rockstar of cycling" listens to Weller and the Jam while out training. But we have to scrape even deeper down the barrel for other examples.

Little-remembered 80s dance/rock experimentalists Age of Chance briefly took to wearing cycling jerseys and gloves in photo shoots, but there's no evidence they actually got on their bikes. A former colleague claims to remember an edition of the London Cycling Campaign magazine from 1999 featuring Jarvis Cocker giving puncture repair tips, but that could be mere legend. Can you think of anyone else?

COMMENTS

dukiebiddle Have you never heard of David Byrne or Talking Heads.

PeterWalker Good point. It was a particularly silly omission given that we have featured the man himself on the Bike Blog [see page 195].

vorsprung Sheryl Crow used to date Lance Armstrong and her time up Alpe D'Huez was alledgedly around one thirty-ish

masmit I believe Shaun Ryder (no pun intended) lost a few more teeth when knocked off his bike a few years ago.

KidKneestone Lady Gaga has a Chopper.

ColMc100 A couple of years ago I bumped in to Jimmy Sommerville in a bike shop clad head to foot in a purple Lycra one-piece cycling outfit! I tried really hard not to say he looked like a purple sausage!

Beers and bikes: do they really mix?

GWLADYS FOUCHÉ

This evening I will go out for a few drinks and think nothing of cycling home afterwards. Am I wrong to think that way?

I would never consider driving a car after a few sips of wine, but somehow I think it's OK to jump on my bike after four beers. "The police have other things to do than stop drunk cyclists like me," is how I reason it.

And how can I be a danger to other people? I am not driving a tonne of aluminium and steel at 30 miles an hour. If I hit someone, I am not going to injure or kill them. Or will I?

Perhaps the danger is not so much to other people as to myself. Perhaps I should be more careful given that my balance, coordination and judgment will be affected by alcohol.

I once had a colleague who, blind drunk, decided it would be a fabulous idea to cycle down some stairs. He ended up in a hospital with broken limbs – bones sticking out – and was cursing his stupidity when I visited him.

According to the New York Times, some 21% of autopsies for New York City bicyclists who died within three hours of their accidents detected alcohol in the body.

In the UK, the Road Traffic Act 1988 makes it an offence for a cyclist to be "unfit to ride through drink or drugs, that is to say, is under the influence of drink or a drug to such an extent as to be incapable of having proper control of the cycle". Penalties for the offence appear unclear, as you can't be forced to take an alcohol test.

What do you think? Have you ever been stopped while under the influence of alcohol on your bike, or had an accident while drunk?

COMMENTS

vorsprung If I am driving I won't drink any alcohol at all. Not even a half pint, not even one small glass of wine. I went to the pub last Wednesday, had three pints and rode back on my bike.

The main difference is if you are in a car you are using a deadly weapon. Cars kill other people. Bikes do not kill other people. I think there were 3,000 deaths by car last year and about one by bike. If there is a fatal accident then it will be me in the wooden box.

phreakdown This is simple. I do it, all my cycling friends do it, loads of people do it. It feels liberating and fun. But – it's wrong, and we all know it's wrong, and if I ran someone over, as long as they weren't also on the sauce, I'd feel extremely guilty.

Will I stop? No. Because the risk to others is low, the chance of being pulled by the law are slim, the consequences of them doing so are minimal, and because it's hard to carry a kebab on a bike, it keeps me fitter in two ways…

Capt8ball Also the bike is a great sobriety test. If you can't get on the bastard thing, you have your answer.

pinkystan But what if you fall off in front of a car? Surely you're also putting all other road users at risk by cycling drunk? They may have to swerve and potentially harm themselves and their property.

Irresponsible.

KidKneestone There is that, pinkystan but I could cause the same problem walking home from the pub.

JamesHunt Just like foie gras – you know it's wrong, but it's so good.

PhineasPPhagbrake The great advantage of cycling to the pub is that if you do have a few too many you can always push the bike home. Try doing that with a car!

danwoods Drinking on the tube is banned. So I have no choice. If I fancy a drink on the way home, it's beer with the left hand, handlebars with the right hand. I can also smoke and cycle. It's brilliant. Public transport might as well give up and close down tomorrow.

What makes cycling joyful?

BEN THOMAS

Raindrops on roses. Whiskers on kittens. Bright copper kettles and warm woollen mittens.

Every now and again, as commenters often remind us, this blog should be joyful.

There are other threads on the bike blog that debate the bad aspects of cycle lanes, and cycle lanes that are simply bad. Similarly advance-stop lines. But just this once, let's keep it positive. Most of the time, I like both of these inventions. They recognise that my bike exists, and that makes me happy.

Then there's the National Cycle Network – all too easy to overlook on a daily commute, perhaps, but once you've made use of it you keep noticing it everywhere (sustainable transport charity Sustrans say the network now runs within 2 miles of 75% of the UK population).

And, for me, the Outer Circle of Regent's Park in London on a Sunday morning. It may not have been designed to please cyclists, but it sure pleases me – Cumberland Terrace, the London zoo giraffe house, the US ambassador's house, London Central Mosque, 30mph hill. Repeat x2. And the way Victoria Pendleton zips past me every time I ride there (it is you isn't it, Victoria?).

Vending machines selling inner tubes. Well-designed bike stands. Council-funded croissants on the way to work on car-free days. These are a few of my favourite things. What are yours?

COMMENTS

Zoonie I can't wait for the day when I can shed my yellow jacket, the leaves are on the trees and Constitution Hill becomes a green arch with a warm wind blowing in your face as you scoot down it.

Dornier The occasional moments of bonhomie shared with other road users – like when a van driver flashes you to let you out of a side road, or when you let someone out and they thank you for it.

petergilheany The ruddy Ready Brek glow when you get to work on cold winter days, as shivering colleagues arrive off tube and train.

loliummultiflorum Getting to the fork in the road in a rural commute where left goes straight to work and right takes you on a two mile detour through the villages. On a warm spring morning, when it's not raining and your train was on time for once, it's a no brainer as to which way to go.

Drspeedy In spring, riding through a flower-scented patch of air just reminds you how much you notice on a bike compared to a car...

Dublinlayclerk Joy is the commute that takes exactly the same amount of time every day, regardless of weather, school holidays, or public transport disruptions.

lucooper Random chats at the lights with people you don't know and will never see again.

rubylu Riding up a hill where I n e a r l y h a v e t o g e t o f f a n d p u s h b u t then I get over theothersideandsuddenlyI'mflying!